SECURITY

SECURITY

POLICING YOUR HOMELAND, YOUR STATE, YOUR CITY

HOWARD SAFIR

with Ellis Whitman

Thomas Dunne Books
St. Martin's Press ⚏ New York

THOMAS DUNNE BOOKS.
An imprint of St. Martin's Press.

www.stmartins.com

Library of Congress Cataloging-in-Publication Data

Safir, Howard.
    Security : policing your homeland, your state, your city / Howard Safir
with Ellis Whitman.—1st. ed.
       p. cm.
    ISBN 0-312-30194-4
    1. New York (N.Y.). Police Dept.   2. Law enforcement—New York
(State)—New York.   3. Crime prevention—New York (State)—New
York.   4. Criminal investigation—New York (State)—New York.   I. Title.

HV8148.N5S24   2003
363.2'09747'1—dc21
                                                          2002045589

First Edition: July 2003

10 9 8 7 6 5 4 3 2 1

*To my wife, Carol, who always believed what
I set out to do was possible
—with love.*

CONTENTS

ACKNOWLEDGMENTS

I would like to thank all of my friends and colleagues from the NYPD, but especially former Chief of Detectives William Allee, former First Deputy Commissioners Pat Kelleher and Tony Simonetti, former Deputy Commissioner Martin O'Boyle, Deputy Chief Charles Kammerdener, Chief Joseph Reznick, and Captain Joseph Herbert for their invaluable support on this project and during my time as PC.

Thanks to the NYPD's office of the Deputy Commissioner for Public Information, Ninfa Segarra and Michael Cronin at the Police Museum, Dan Rosenblatt and the staff at IACP, Dr. Cecelia Crouse, Dr. Kevin McElfresh, and Tim Schelberg and Lisa Hurst at Smith, Alling and Lane for lending their expertise.

Thank you to my editors, Thomas Dunne and Sean Desmond, at Thomas Dunne Books, my agent, Jim Fitzgerald, and my cowriter, Ellis Whitman. Without them this book would never have happened. And my thanks also to Al McNeill, Tom Belfiore, Russell Crimi, Esta Fischer, Tim Galvin, and Eric Grant at SafirRosetti.

Many thanks to my good friend Rudy Giuliani. But most of all I want to thank my wife, Carol, and my children, Adam and Jennifer, who are always supportive of what I do.

INTRODUCTION

On any given workday the population of New York City grows from 7.5 to 12 million citizens spread over 767 square miles, making it the largest city in the United States and the most challenging to manage. The city is policed by a department of over forty thousand officers in seventy-six patrol precincts, eight borough commands, nine police service areas, and twelve transit districts; and the department employs fourteen thousand civilians, has a fleet of six thousand vehicles, twenty-six boats, and six helicopters. The NYPD has a $3.7 billion operating budget—larger than many Fortune 500 companies.

From 1996 to 2000, the city's five boroughs—Manhattan, the Bronx, Brooklyn, Queens, and Staten Island—experienced a drop in major crimes not seen since themid-1960s. Today New York City is, per capita, the safest city in America that has a population of over 1 million, and during my four years as commissioner the rate of major crimes dropped over 38 percent.

The reversal of the crime rate in the New York was not

a matter of luck, demographics, or a changing economy; it was the result of tough and intelligent policing, based on principles that take into account the complexity of police work. We devised an approach to crime that we called Goal-Oriented Neighborhood Policing. We took a zero-tolerance approach to crime on any level—from panhandling to capital murder—and we identified the patterns of violence and disorder that most affected the city. We set clear objectives to reduce major felony crimes, the number of shootings, youth crimes, domestic violence, enforce quality-of-life crimes, and establish initiatives to achieve them.

With the reduction of crime comes a renewed sense of civic security. If a city is safe, it will flourish; people will want to visit and do business there. I believe that policing should be proactive and preventative, and my crime-fighting strategy is grounded in James Q. Wilson and George Kelling's article "Broken Windows."

"Broken Windows" is based on the concept that if you pay attention to small crimes, you will have a corresponding impact on more serious crime. By addressing quality-of-life crimes you are sending a signal to criminals that the police are not accepting crime on any level. The example chosen by Wilson and Kelling was that of a building with a broken window. If a window remains broken day after day as people pass, that one broken window will indicate to them that the owner of the building does not care. That lack of care will incite others to throw stones at the rest of the windows, and soon enough you will have a building that is full of broken windows.

Letting a building go derelict is akin to what happens when we allow small crimes to take place. Wilson and Kelling identified quality-of-life crimes, like panhandling, vagrancy, and graffiti, as triggers for larger ones. It may seem counterintuitive that arresting petty criminals will bring down the rate of felonies, but this philosophy is backed by statistics that show that those who commit minor crimes, for instance, subway turnstile jumping, are very often the ones who commit or know of major crimes, like murder, rape, and theft.

One of the problems we faced was communication within the NYPD. It was not uncommon for a commander in one precinct to be working on a problem that had already been solved elsewhere. In the traditional chain of command, information went up and down the line, but there was no means of sharing information across the line. To make things worse, there was little or no communication between precincts and specialized divisions, such as Narcotics or Vice Enforcement; and sometimes precinct personnel and beat cops would not even know when a specialized unit was working in the neighborhood.

To make a real difference, the culture of the NYPD needed to change. In the past there was very little interaction between executives—like the police commissioner and the "middle manager," the precinct commander. It was hierarchical; and the sense among officers was that One Police Plaza was a place to avoid, and the only time you went to headquarters was when you were in trouble. We changed that sentiment by rewarding them for merit and holding them accountable for their commands.

To track each precinct and analyze crime conditions objectively, the NYPD developed CompStat, a computer application that allows for the management of information and statistics that allowed us to track criminal activity block by block, precinct by precinct. Each of New York City's precincts has its own demographics, income levels, and crime problems, and executives and precinct commanders need to know what problems are specific to each precinct. Weekly CompStat meetings provided a forum for my team of executives, managers, and commanders to discuss and analyze crime patterns, asset allocation, and quality-of-life violations.

It counts what you count. Before the mid-1990s, success in the NYPD was measured by number of arrests, and precinct commanders and patrol officers were promoted based on this criteria. The numbers told us a different story. No matter how many arrestees the NYPD was bringing in, the crime rate continued to skyrocket. Arrest numbers were not corresponding to the reality of what was happening on the streets. We started to address the core issue when we made the crime rate and not arrest numbers the benchmark. With accurate statistical information from CompStat, an accountability program, the department began to zero in on problems through tactical planning, and the NYPD's focus moved from making arrests to reducing crime complaints.

New York—the capital of the world, and a city that attracts people and goods from all around the globe—was also the hub of drug sales and distribution for the eastern seaboard. In New York City many neighborhoods were tainted by the reputation of being drug supermarkets that drew users and would-be sellers from other parts of the city and even neighboring states. The criminal activity wasn't confined to certain areas of the city; and as dealers and drugs spread throughout the five boroughs, the result was a high rate of violence—one that lasted until the mid-1990s.

There is undoubtedly a nexus between drugs and crime. With drugs comes violence, and where the sale of illegal drugs is allowed to go unchecked, violent crime and neighborhood deterioration follows. Like prostitution, drug sales are part of an alternative economic market, the black market; and the only way to address this is by making the cost of doing business too high.

Drugs, crime, and violence are inextricably linked. To unravel the illegal infrastructure that dealers operate within, drugs need to be treated as a business. If you make the cost of doing business—dealing drugs—too high, dealers will move to a location where it is easier to conduct business. "Driving Drug Traffickers Out of New York" was an NYPD initiative that made circumstances inhospitable for drug dealers, and we were able to drive many traffickers out of the city.

With the data from CompStat, and using the crime rate as a yardstick, we took a fresh look at drug enforcement and developed a new approach that broke ranks with traditional law-enforcement models. What we learned is that there is no magic bullet in crime prevention, but by using a "bottom up and top down" approach to crime, and collating, analyzing, and mapping crime intelligence, we could make critical arrests that have a greater effect.

We need to take a holistic approach to crime and drug trafficking because once narcotics are introduced into the mix, violent crime is sure to follow. In 1996, I brought a philosophical change to our crime-fighting strategies when we moved to Goal-Oriented Neighborhood Policing. This system gives precinct commanders more flexibility and responsibility, and holds middle management accountable for identifying and addressing problems via a coordinated and strategic response to crimes specific to each precinct.

My first NYPD narcotics initiative focused on a particular area—Northern Manhattan, which included Washington Heights and Inwood. The area suffered from a sky-high rate of violent crime stemming from the fact that it was a clearinghouse for illegal drug sales. In the fall of 1996, we drew up plans for a project that took a new and radical approach to crime fighting, and we called it the Northern Manhattan Initiative (NMI).

Undercover agents collected information on high-level dealers and gangs for weeks, sometimes months, until we had enough information on them. Then on a certain date we got warrants and arrested all the drug traffickers on the block. In Washington Heights and other neighborhoods (following the success of NMI we instituted the program citywide), this method was highly successful and netted the arrests of thousands of drug dealers and dismantled over one thousand drug gangs.

Our work did not stop with rounding up drug dealers. We followed up the arrests with an innovative program called the Model Block Program, an attempt at community stabilization. We would put blue barricades up at each end of the block and the NYPD's Community Affairs Unit would have other city departments—including the Departments of Sanitation, Parks, Social Welfare, Housing, and Health, to name a few—come in and help the community clean the streets, repair streetlights, remove graffiti, and plant trees. We were restoring the community so the residents had a stake in their neighborhoods. You want to give neighborhoods a reason to keep drug traffickers out, and once the communities are stabilized it is harder for dealers to come back—and they didn't.

Some people have considered my assertive style of policing harsh, preferring instead to return to the more traditional methods of community policing that was the NYPD's philosophy of the early 1990s. Community policing made the beat cop the central figure in the community's relationship with the police. Street cops were trained to handle the community and conduct meetings, the hope being that this interpersonal relationship between officer and citizens would alleviate fear and disorder.

Although well intentioned, "feel good" cops don't work. Beat cops are not experienced enough, nor do they have the authority to fulfill the expectations set for them in the community policing model. It sounds good—but this kind of community policing doesn't work in urban areas because your average beat cops are twenty-five to thirty-one years old and they don't have the experience or cultural background to solve the community's problems.

In New York City, almost 50 percent of police officers are from the five surrounding counties and not city residents. A kid from Rockland County on his beat in Harlem is happy to complete his tour and go home safely. His experience and cultural base makes him ill equipped to solve the problems of the Harlem community.

Proof of success is in the numbers: When the Giuliani administration came to office in 1994, there were approximately eight thousand outdoor drug markets in New York City. In 1998, a reporter told me that he was writing a story on outdoor drug spots. He said that he was having a hard time with the story because he could not find drugs on the streets anymore. Although he couldn't find a drug spot, I admit I still could have directed him to some that remained. But his comment indicated to me that my drug strategies and initiatives, which systematically eradicated local drug cartels by zeroing in on areas of the city with a high concentration of drug locations, were working.

I left a city in better shape than I found it, and I tried to think of innovative ways to solve long-standing problems. When problems—like narcotics and gun violence—are trenchant, you have to think outside of the box to solve them. I looked to other disciplines for inspiration and got many of my ideas from the business, technology, and science sectors. *Security* gives citizens insight into the workings of the NYPD and a look into how we were able to drastically reduce crime in New York with Goal-Oriented Neighborhood Policing, and how those proven methods of policing will need to be adapted to prevent terrorism.

The challenges that the NYPD faces have escalated with September 11, and the threat of terrorism has forced the department to reprioritize and adapt. With 600,000 police officers in this country ill prepared for the war on terror, the NYPD and other police departments need to become active partners with federal agencies in implementing national security.

September 11 changed the lives of all Americans and significantly altered the role of federal, state, and local law enforcement. With our energies consumed with homeland defense, policing the United States and New York City will never be the same.

There's an old saying, "All politics is local," and to a certain extent I think you can also say, "All crime is local." What I mean is that crime will always come back to the street corner, the house on the block, and its deleterious effects branch out from there. And that's what this book is about. I've learned a lot of lessons in my decades of fighting crime, and one of them is that the methods that clean up a drug-ridden neighborhood can be applied to greater kinds of "terror." That's what *Security* is—it's knowing the methods that keep Americans safe or, as Franklin Roosevelt once said, to enjoy "freedom from fear."

The synergy between Rudy Giuliani and myself was key to successful policing. Although some civil-rights advocates protested our measures and accused the NYPD of infringing on the civil rights of those caught up in our initiatives and new policing models, my response to them was that the number one civil right is the right to be free from crime. In New York we proved how much you could accomplish when the department takes a unified and rational stance against crime. Assertive and enterprising policing is the key to making any municipality a desirable and safe place to live, work, and play. There is an old proverb, "success has many fathers, but failure is an orphan." The success of crime reduction in New York has been claimed by many and each commissioner has had an impact on the falling crime rate, but the real credit goes to the men and women of the NYPD. They are the best police officers in the world, and their commitment, dedication, and skill is unmatched. It is with great pride that I look back on my time as the police commissioner for a city that captured the worldwide attention for reducing crime and for an organization that is truly New York's Finest.

SECURITY

1.

GOAL-ORIENTED
NEIGHBORHOOD POLICING

For many years New York City was considered legendary in the history of crime. Nineteenth-century crime lore encompasses the immigrant ghetto gangs of Five Corners and the corrupt politicians of Tammany Hall; and with the twentieth century came more high-profile crime. Criminal enterprises like Murder Incorporated (Lucky Luciano, Meyer Lansky, and Bugsy Siegel) were set up during the early decades of the century to organize racketeering, bootlegging, narcotics, and prostitution. These criminal ventures evolved into the larger-than-life crime families that New York is known for. These mob families—Gambino, Genovese, Lucchese, Colombo, and Bonanno—and their capos, John Gotti, Vinnie "the Chin" Gigante, the Persicos, have been transformed into modern-day myths by film and television.

Organized crime was and is not the city's only crime problem. From the early 1970s, New York City witnessed an escalating murder rate. The city was known as a dirty and dangerous place, even home to infamous serial killers, like "the Son of Sam," David Berkowitz, whose seven murders during the summer of 1977 led to rampant fear and disorder in the city. An earlier murder, that of Kitty Genovese in 1964 in Kew Gardens, Queens, was particularly infamous. Genovese was murdered at her doorstep as her neighbors stood by and did nothing to help her. The incident has often been held up as a symbol of the beginning of civic apathy and the kickoff of decades of moral and social decay in the city.

Because of these high-profile murders and the homicides of the thousands who never made front-page news, New York City became known as Murder City, and for many years it topped the FBI's index of most dangerous cities. With the increased fear came the exodus of the middle and upper classes to the suburbs, and those who remained in the city were horrified when, in 1989, a woman—who became known as the Central Park Jogger—was brutally beaten in the middle of the park. The vicious, random, and almost fatal attack on an urban professional—a banker jogging after a long day at work—in a place thought to be an oasis and adjacent to the city's most affluent neighborhoods, was a wake-up call to many New Yorkers.

When the city turned its attention to crime, it was not a pretty picture. In the early 1990s, violence and crime were endemic to the city and fueled by the crack cocaine drug epidemic that had started in the early 1980s and was now in full swing. Over the years this volatile and dangerous situation precipitated the flight of the city's tax base to New Jersey, Connecticut, and Long Island, setting off a financial crisis that affected every person and bureaucracy in the city.

The NYPD was not exempt from these negative trends, and thus the enforcement of laws that govern quality-of-life crimes was not a priority. In 1990, panhandlers aggressively solicited money from passersby, drug dealers had taken over entire streets and turned them into open-air drug supermarkets, squeegeemen attacked drivers who refused to pay for unwanted window cleanings at intersections, and muggings were commonplace. Many, including myself, were very concerned with the situation in the city, and within the law-enforcement community new solutions were being formulated to help solve the crime and quality-of-life problems.

Over the years it had become clear that the NYPD's policies of the late '80s and early '90s were ineffective. When I became NYPD commissioner in 1996, I made it my mission to achieve record crime reduction and to improve the quality-of-life for New Yorkers. To achieve this I established Goal-Oriented Neighborhood Policing. The strategies that were implemented in this program were many and involved special units, task forces, and multi-agency partnerships. With these strategies in place, and a total commitment to fighting crime, the NYPD turned the city around.

Much of this progress was made while I was commissioner, during which time the homicide rate dropped 67 percent. To give you an idea of how far we came in less than a decade: In 1990, New York, with a population of 7.5 million, had over 2,200 murders, 700,000 major index felonies, 100,000 robberies, 120,000 burglaries, and 147,000 car thefts. These numbers mean that if crime had been equally distributed across the city's population, 10 percent of all citizens would have fallen victim to a major crime in 1990. In 1998, after I had been in office for two years, there were only 633 murders. This means that in 1998 there were 1,500 people walking around that in 1990 would otherwise have been dead. The same goes for the other serious crimes—in 1998, there were only 44,000 stolen cars, 46,000 burglaries, and 39,000 robberies compared to the figures from 1990. These numbers translated into a city that today is a model for other communities, a destination location for tourists, and a home to New Yorkers, who now feel safe on the streets.

The roots of Goal-Oriented Neighborhood Policing lie in the redisposition of power within the department—precinct-by-precinct—and a reexamination of how the police interact in the communities.

In the past the structure of the NYPD, and many other police departments, had been based on the paramilitary model, which assumes a strict chain of command. Unfortunately, as messages and reports were passed along the chain, key information was getting lost. The top end didn't know what was going on in the field, and the field commanders had no idea what was going on at One Police Plaza. During my administration, the chain of command was reorganized so that the middle manager, the precinct commander (who has access to both ends), was accountable for the crime rate and the behavior of his officers on the streets.

To address the behavior of the police officer when interacting in the community, the NYPD adopted a policy of Courtesy, Professionalism, and Respect (CPR). With CPR we fostered respect for the public, and discipline, integrity, and professionalism among police officers. To monitor officers and make sure they were fulfilling their role as the public faces of the NYPD, I instituted a program of CPR testing—assigning the Internal Affairs Bureau (IAB) and Quality Assurance Division (QAD) officers to test beat cops on their interpersonal skills with the communities they served. CPR testing scenarios included sending undercover officers out onto the streets to ask patrol officers on their beat for assistance and making calls to the precincts to test if the respondents to complaints would act correctly. We cast a broad net in our approach to testing CPR, and although we tested precinct's CPR based on community complaints, we also tested officers, and borough commands randomly.

Testing CPR also included bias testing, and we set up undercover stings with IAB and QAD officers who would employ Hispanic and other ethnic accents to see if the response to their complaints was comparable to the treatment received by nonethnic members of the community.

CPR testing helped us to identify problem officers and pockets of questionable behavior. To educate officers in CPR we set up a Police Advisory Board of community representatives to counsel the NYPD, and the board acted as a complement to the Civilian Complaint Review Board (CCRB) in overseeing the NYPD's interaction with the community. The CCRB examines civilian complaints and allegations against officers and publishes their findings in a semiannual report chaired by a group of community members appointed by the mayor, the NYPD police commissioner, and the New York City Council.

To ensure that officers were responding to the community appropriately, civilian grievances were tracked and assessed. We monitored individual officers who received an excess of three CCRB complaints. Officers who received excessive CCRB complaints were enrolled in monitoring programs, their enrollment based on a formal process point system that track brutality and discrimination. The level of monitoring is determined by the severity of the offense or track record of offenses. Counseling was provided at the command level, and when an officer received complaints, commanders brought them in and questioned them about what was going on. Were there

racial issues? Personal problems? Depending on the outcome of these meetings, different measures—counseling, retraining, reassignment—would be taken.

One of the biggest challenges of an agency that is
40,000 strong and polices a city with 7.5 million residents
and another 4.5 million commuters is coordination and
accountability. To determine the success of Goal-Oriented
Policing, the NYPD's strategies to reduce crime need to be
tracked. To understand what was happening in each community, the NYPD developed CompStat, a computer-
comparison statistics program that allows us to track
crime trends and patterns with pinpoint accuracy.

We need to manage crime, and not be managed by it.
CompStat meetings forced precinct commanders to be familiar with every block, every known criminal, and the
genres of crimes committed within their jurisdictions; and
it made them accountable to monitor these crimes, enforce
the law, and lower the crime rate in their precinct.
Through exchanges with borough and precinct commanders, my team would determine the best route to crime reduction for each borough and precinct.

Beat cops who wander the streets reacting to crime and
hoping that their presence will thwart it, are wasting their
time and our money; whereas officers who know their
neighborhoods intimately and know where, when, and
how crimes are committed can—and always have had—
an impact on crime. "Feel good cops" are very little help
in areas that are overrun with drug dealing.

In New York, to address each precinct individually, I
changed this approach. My department had just one philosophy in regard to who was the responsible community
policing officer, and that was the precinct commander.
Holding the precinct commander accountable retains con-

trol, but it also serves to empower those at the midlevel of the organization.

Having established precinct commanders as the department's chief community-policing officers, my team worked on enforcing specific types of crimes and quality-of-life problems. The Giuliani administration established the strategic components that we would use to fight crime:

- Getting guns off the street
- Curbing youth violence on the streets and in the schools
- Driving drug dealers out of the city
- Breaking the cycle of domestic violence
- Reclaiming public spaces
- Reducing auto-related crime
- Reclaiming the roads of the city
- Courtesy, Professionalism, and Respect
- Bringing fugitives to justice
- Rooting out corruption

The strategies were identified through focus groups conducted with officers, precinct commanders, community members, and an analysis of the root problems the city was facing. We gave officers on the street clear instructions on what they should do, not just what they were *not* to do. By holding officers more responsible for their own behavior with CPR, and giving them clear directions to put the safety and well-being of citizens before their own, we saw NYPD officers making more arrests with less force.

The ability of police officers to have an impact on crime is something that criminologists—who believe that the fluctuations in crime are due to social and economic forces—have often refuted. Many criminologists believe that these problems are beyond the ability of police officers, or law-enforcement agencies, to address. In New York City we demonstrated that this is not the case. Police activities *do* have a significant impact on crime, but success is not just in the numbers of officers on the streets, but in what they are doing while they are there.

The mistake that the NYPD and many other local law-enforcement agencies have made when it comes to drug enforcement is to think globally. The real key is to be more local in your approach. It was my responsibility to ensure the safety of the citizens in my jurisdiction, and I would encourage the mayors of towns around New York, all over the country, and the world to implement the same tough stance toward the illegal drug trade as I did. Until a way is found to successfully reduce demand, cutting off the supply of drugs by reducing trafficking and making the sale of drugs a losing proposition is the only way to moderate the drug trade.

My job was not to chase heroin and cocaine traffickers across continents and across oceans. Getting drugs out of New York City was my goal. I was very pleased when early in the Northern Manhattan Initiative (NMI), a wiretap picked up drug dealers discussing moving their businesses to New Jersey because Manhattan had gotten too hot to operate in. I do not wish my Jersey neighbors ill will, but I believe that each city must adopt a policy to drive out drug dealers. If every community made this effort, the aggregate effect would be a large-scale reduction in crime and narcotics distribution nationally. In some ways this philosophy is akin to the Old West marshal's "not in my town" approach to law enforcement.

NMI was our most ambitious and large-scale model for eliminating drug gangs. Three precincts—the Thirtieth and

Thirty-third in Manhattan North and the Thirty-fourth in Washington Heights—had been drug-distribution centers for many years. In 1990, those precincts accounted for 157 murders; but in 1998, with the NMI in place, that number dropped to 28. The results of the drug-enforcement techniques in Northern Manhattan and, later, in other parts of the city—we used the tactics in the Bronx (in the Fortieth, Forty-first, and Forty-third Precincts) and in Queens (in the 103rd, 105th, and 113th)—reveal how we had so much success in reducing crime.

Taking back streets and parks is one thing, but maintaining them is another challenge. Without diligent follow-up, locations often fall back into the hands of criminals. This is perhaps the most frustrating aspect of crime prevention—spending time and resources to clean up a neighborhood only to give back all of the gains after we move out. The Model Block Program was a collaborative effort between the police department, block residents, community organizations, and other city government agencies to turn the worst blocks into the most vibrant ones in the community.

Tracer Units, uniformed officers trained in the methods of patrolling the streets and drug dealers, were assigned to areas that we had reclaimed to assure that drug locations did not slip back into their original state. Vertical patrols performed a similar function in the city's most dangerous buildings and in the public-housing developments (in New York City 600,000 people live in public housing), treating each unit as a beat. Officers began on the roof and worked their way down the stairwells, looking for illegal drug sales.

In the interest of community stabilization, we also took this method to private apartment buildings where we felt it necessary. The Trespass Affidavit Program was designed with lawyers to have landlords sign agreements that allowed the NYPD to arrest individuals for trespassing who were on the premises without a legitimate explanation. Before this the police would have had to track down the management of the building before making arrests. To further monitor the stairways, elevators, lobbies, and hallways in public housing and on the streets of drug-ravaged neighborhoods, we used Tracer Units to police them and installed closed-circuit TV cameras and had up to a 35 percent decrease in crime in some of the locations.

More often than not, crime does not happen on the streets, and it is not random. Domestic violence—a crime that was once overlooked in law enforcement—came into the forefront of the American consciousness with the brutal murder of Nicole Brown Simpson. In 1999, one-quarter of the city's murders resulted from domestic violence, and the NYPD instituted programs that aggressively enforced laws that help those who are victims of domestic violence.

We established Domestic Violence Units in every precinct, which included household visits, a mandatory arrest policy, and setting up a domestic violence hotline. We were also more proactive in obtaining Orders of Protection and actually served them to offenders to prevent them from committing violence against the victim. In domestic violence cases, the assigned detective was instructed to make every effort to contact the victim within twenty-four hours of receiving the case, and squad supervisors reviewed each case within three days of assignment.

Many domestic abusers are repeat offenders, and often victims of abuse don't leave. To handle these ongoing cases, the NYPD developed a High Propensity Offender Tracking List and identified the ten most violence-prone families in the precincts. Each month an officer and a social worker visit these homes in hopes of preventing further violent behavior by letting the aggressor know he or she is being watched and a social worker is there to counsel the family.

Another way that the NYPD was proactive in its approach to the public safety and fighting crime was with our Fugitive Enforcement Division that worked with the Warrant Division and the Cold Case Squad on cases. Fugitives who failed to appear in court, were wanted for parole violations, or on outstanding warrants were pursued by the warrant squads that we established in each borough. These teams used sting operations to apprehend hundreds of suspects, and made it a priority to incarcerate known fugitives, parole absconders, and violators of Orders of Protection.

Fugitive apprehension tactics were used most notably in 1997 with "Broadway Transfer" when we mailed 2,700 fugitives letters that they were owed money by a fictional agency, the New York State Division of Abandoned and Unclaimed Funds. They were instructed to call and make appointments to collect their money, and NYPD detectives arrested them when they arrived. The sting netted 261 fugitives; some had traveled from as far away as New Mexico.

Integral to the success of apprehending fugitives is the involvement of every officer—from beat cop to commissioner. To this end we put computers in police cars and gave officers cell phones to run warrant checks. We also established a joint task force with my old organization, the United States Marshals Service, to utilize their expertise and resources. There were many times when fugitive apprehension and zero tolerance met with great success. We also motivated our Cold Case Squad and started addressing unsolved violent crimes. The squad has apprehended close to one thousand suspects, some for murder cases as far back as the 1970s.

Goal-Oriented Community Policing requires that the department draw on the experience of those officers and detectives who know their precincts and know how to enact quality-of-life improvements and reduce crime within these precincts. The experience of the NYPD over the past years demonstrates the effectiveness of this innovative method of policing, and the department learned important lessons in implementing it. The most important lessons are that strategies must be applied consistently and aggressively, and that the entire agency must marshal its resources to capitalize on technology and focus proactively on crime and quality-of-life problems. Crime patterns change and evolve over time, and police departments have got to maintain flexibility to deal with the patterns and move away from bureaucratic rigidity and formulaic solutions to complicated problems.

2.

QUALITY OF LIFE

Fortunately only a small percentage of the population is touched by homicide. However, many experience conditions that make life intolerable—public urination, drug paraphernalia littering the sidewalks, homeless people living in the parks, abandoned cars, and property crimes, like auto theft and burglary. To the criminal the inattention to these so-called minor quality-of-life offenses signaled that it was okay to be indifferent to common decency and law. What we found by speaking to community members was that what they were most concerned with were quality-of-life offenses.

In 1993, the average number of people who jumped over subway turnstiles was 214,000 monthly—it was almost an Olympic sport—and the message that we were sending to criminals was that if you jumped a turnstile, you were going to get away with that and more. We started enforcing the fare-evasion laws, and we reduced the numbers to about 15,000. Not only did we increase the revenue of the subways; but also by 2000, crime on subways was down 60 percent. An example of quality-of-life enforcement working well was when we arrested one of these turnstile jumpers and found a submachine gun under his coat. Imagine if he had been allowed to board a crowded subway train.

Fare jumping was commonplace, and one fare jumper in particular—John Royster—exemplifies the success of this quality-of-life philosophy. John Royster was a vicious felon. He was a rapist, an extremely violent aggressor, and ultimately a murderer, who went on an eight-day spree in June 1996.

Royster's reign of terror began in Central Park—within feet of a crowded playground—on the afternoon of June 4 as an unnamed thirty-two-year-old woman, a piano teacher, took a walk. Royster, then twenty-two, assaulted her, slamming her body to the ground, repeatedly bashing her head against a large cobblestone, and left her for dead. She was so badly beaten, we needed to fingerprint her to identify her. She would remain in a coma for weeks following the attack.

Royster had intended to rape her, but the excitement of the attack led him to spontaneously ejaculate onto the woman's skirt and a napkin that he left at the scene. The following night Royster victimized another woman, Shelby Evans Schrader, as she was jogging along the East River at Sixtieth Street. He grabbed her from behind and smashed her face into the tarmac. The assault caught the eye of a passerby, who scared Royster away. The next day Royster violently assaulted a young woman on a footbridge in Yonkers, leaving her comatose.

Royster's final victim was Evalin Alvarez who was beaten to death by Royster while she opened her shop, the Dutch Girl Cleaners, on Park Avenue. Her head was repeatedly slammed against the pavement and the wall. She was so badly disfigured by the assault that when they arrived at the scene, EMS workers thought that she had fallen from a high floor of one of the adjacent buildings.

At first the four crimes had seemed random, and had it not been for cooperation among the detectives and investigators it would have been hard to piece things together. There was a bloody fingerprint left at the Alvarez murder scene. When we ran the print through the New York State fingerprint database and the FBI's Automated Fingerprint Identification Systems (AFIS), it matched that of a fare beater who had been arrested jumping a turnstile at 116th and Lexington months earlier.

Now we had a name and an address in the Bronx. When we arrested Royster on University Avenue, it turned out that we had a one-man crime wave on our hands. He was brought to the Nineteenth Precinct, where after hours of interrogation he confessed to the three assaults and the murder on videotape and in writing.

Because the fingerprint lifted from the window of Evalin Alvarez's dry-cleaning shop matched that of a turnstile jumper, we were able to stop a rampage killer from committing more violent crimes against women, and it indicated to me once again why quality-of-life strategies work. If you pay attention to the minor crimes, you end up solving major crimes.

While New Yorkers were concerned about quality-of-life issues, during the previous administration the department had continued to focus most resources on major crimes, and resources were allocated almost exclusively to units that dealt with murder, burglary, robbery, and other felony offenses. This led to a feeling in the community that City Hall and the police didn't care, and that nothing could really be done about the citizens' basic concerns. Police officers felt the same way, and this is why we took a very different stance in regard to policing.

My department's policy toward quality-of-life issues was zero tolerance, and to enforce these crimes we retrained our officers so that they more clearly understood the nuances of the law—civil and criminal—and gave them the proper tools to make arrests that would stand up in court. For example, noise pollution. To prove excessive noise in court one needs proof, and so we gave cops noise meters. Although they were not absolutely necessary, these meters allowed us to make arrests that would stand up in court and issue tickets that resulted in convictions in criminal court for small fines and in civil court for larger penalties.

Occasionally we reaped even greater benefits when civil courts would give us orders that allowed us to keep the offending vehicle or radio for auction. We also addressed noise pollution with "Operation Sound Trap" that allowed us to target cars that were blaring loud music and "Operation Cycle Check," which addressed loud noise that comes from altered motorcycle exhaust systems. If a car, or motorcycle, was pulled over under these programs, the officers were allowed to confiscate and impound the offending vehicles until satisfactory proof of payment of the summons was given.

In the 1980s, almost every subway car in the New York City Transit system was emblazoned inside and out with graffiti, and these graffiti-covered subway cars and their scratchiti-carved windows became emblematic of New York City. To others they were the representation of a city gone off the rails. What many didn't know was that these were not merely wall decorations; graffiti is one way that gang members communicate, and that at one point the subway system was a message board of territorial markings, threats, and responses.

The problem of graffiti vandalism was most acute in the subway. We merged the antigraffiti units of the Housing and Transit Bureaus with the NYPD unit and they all reported to the chief of department and shared a "tag" database of graffiti markings. The newly formed Anti-Graffiti/Vandalism Unit set up sting operations on trains, with undercover officers videotaping culprits.

Narcotics sales, prostitution, DWI, and underage drinking were among the more serious crimes that affected the quality-of-life in the city. To curb these crimes we began to use innovative programs and enforced the laws already on the books that prevented them. Officers began to aggressively issue summonses to stores who sold alcohol to underage drinkers and those individuals caught with an open alcoholic beverage in public. We regularly conducted sting operations at stores who sold liquor to underage drinkers, enlisting civilian youths as volunteers. If these teens were able to purchase alcohol, the store owner was arrested or given a summons; if multiple sales were made, the store would be shut down.

When in 2000 we noticed rashes of burglaries in the 104th Precinct in Northwestern Queens—which covers the towns of Glendale, Maspeth, and Ridgewood—and that it was the only precinct in the borough that was experiencing an increase in crime, we dispatched teams of officers from the precinct and Crime Prevention Units to blanket the community. For ten days we relentlessly handed out literature, patrolled blocks, and provided residents and business owners with tips on avoiding crime. Soon we saw a dramatic decrease in burglaries. The initiative was called "Total Community Involvement," and although it was technically a quality-of-life initiative it had an impact on overall crime in the area.

In 1999, we instituted an innovative program against first-time drunk drivers. I instructed NYPD officers to begin seizing the cars of those caught driving under the influence of alcohol. The groundbreaking drunk-driving initiative was conducted at traffic checkpoints and on any New York City road. After questioning drivers they found suspicious, officers would have them take Breathalyzer tests. If the suspect was found to be legally intoxicated, the officer would confiscate that person's motor vehicle.

This was called a hard-line approach by many—especially those who had their cars taken away—but we know that deterring drunk driving saves lives. The American Civil Liberties Union (ACLU) took issue with this initiative, calling the NYPD "Nazis." I disagree. Seizing cars from drivers who operate vehicles while intoxicated is akin to taking a three-thousand-pound weapon off the streets. So while I was the enemy of drunk drivers citywide and the ACLU, Mother's Against Drunken Driving (MADD) commended me.

Street prostitution was another problem. For many years the enforcement of prostitution was limited to the Vice Unit, comprised of about two hundred officers citywide; but in 1997, we made it the responsibility of every officer to crack down on prostitution. Precinct commanders utilized a variety of strategies to correct these conditions. Some placed officers in civilian clothing in observation posts with binoculars on lookout duty to identify potential johns who were soliciting prostitutes and then have uniform officers move in and arrest those soliciting. Others would use a program called "Operation Losing Proposition."

"Losing Proposition" was a two-tiered program: Officers would start by going to areas known for street prostitution and arrest or disperse prostitutes. Female officers would also pose as prostitutes, with officers in civilian clothing nearby to protect them. Both the "hooker" and the undercover officer would wear recording devices, and, when possible, clients who approached the "hookers" were recorded.

Once an agreement was made to pay for sex, the backup units moved in and arrested the want-to-be johns. If the would-be client was in a car—which they often were—the car was seized and, through a civil forfeiture process, we often obtained the rights to auction it.

We publicized these arrests to let the public know that if they solicit prostitutes they will be arrested; after which they would have to go home and explain to their wives and friends what happened to their car.

The Multi-Agency Response Program to Address Community Hot Spots, or the MARCH program, focused on the quality-of-life problems that are fostered at bars and clubs. These places stay open late at night, disturb neighbors with loud music, serve liquor to minors, and attract strangers to neighborhoods. In the past, vehicles—often operated by drunk drivers—came and went in residential neighborhoods, stereos and horns blaring, and low-level drug use and sales proliferated in certain locations.

To address these problems creatively, precinct commanders worked with multiple state and city agencies to inspect locations and enforce both penal and civil law. For example, in New York City the city clerk is able to examine licenses to determine if the business has the authorization to operate at the location. Often they don't; so we found that many businesses had never filed a legal document to register their existence. Other agencies we teamed up with included:

- The New York State Department of Taxation and Finance helps by examining tax stamps on official documents—which are sometimes forged. Another way to close down illegal businesses.
- The New York State Liquor Authority enforces laws regarding how many people can be in a location. They also assertain whether dancing is allowed or if hard liquor is being served in beer- and wine-only locales.
- The New York City Department of Consumer Affairs issues their own summonses to businesses that are engaged in deceptive trade practices, which can command up to $3,800 in fines.
- The New York City Department of Health & Mental Hygiene examines food and hygiene conditions.
- The New York City Fire Department (FDNY) and the Department of Buildings can check building construction to ensure that it meets fire and safety codes and crowd limitations.

In the Thirtieth Precinct in Upper Manhattan we used the MARCH program in "Operation Rack-Em Up" as an initiative to combat illegal gambling and narcotics in the neighborhood. In this program precinct personnel worked with the Departments of Taxation, Consumer Affairs, and Buildings to close pool halls that served as off-the-street gathering locations for illicit activities. The MARCH program is not limited to clubs and bars; it can be used to inspect any business that is disrupting the quality-of-life of a community. This includes delicatessens, bodegas, liquor stores, auto parts stores, and car junkyards, which are often used to store stolen car parts.

With the MARCH program we used every available law and every governmental agency to tackle crime. The premise of civil law is that property used in the commission of a crime is an instrumentality of the crime and therefore part of the crime and subject to government seizure. The advantage that we find in using civil law is twofold—first, civil law in the United States relies on a lower standard of proof than criminal law. To prove your case you have to merely present a preponderance of evidence. Second, civil law allows us to attack crimes that have not been amenable to traditional law enforcement.

With crime at some of its lowest levels in thirty years New York is going through a renaissance, but we should not be complacent about crime reduction—if the NYPD is not diligent, the potential for returning to the bad old days is great. Because of the September 11 attack, and the resulting financial problems the city is facing, cutbacks in the NYPD *will* affect the crime rate. Criminals are very alert to the reduction of resources, and the NYPD must maintain constant vigilance.

Success in law enforcement is measured in lives saved, crimes prevented, and the vitality of a city restored. In New York this was achieved by enhancing quality of life and working in partnership with the community. All of our innovative police tactics and problem-solving strategies respected constitutional rights, enforced the law, kept the peace, and provided a safe environment for citizens. The result was a city that is the focus of admiration from police agencies, criminologists, and politicians, and it is emulated in the public sector all over the world.

3.

TECHNOLOGY AND POLICING

The first professional police force was London's Metropolitan Police Force, established in 1829 by Sir Robert Peel. A lot has changed in over the century and a half since Peel's "Metropolitans" patrolled the streets of London in search of criminals. Policing philosophies have been adapted to reflect society's changes, and the way that police do their work has been transformed by technology.

The English were ahead of us in their organization of a formal police department. Early nineteenth-century Manhattan (until the consolidation of the five boroughs in 1898 Manhattan *was* New York City) was still dependent on the volunteer patrolman and night watchman who walked informal beats. These early New York cops—called roundsmen—were armed with a nightsticks, rattles, or whistles. Today NYPD officers use wireless technology and state-of-the-art weaponry.

Later in the nineteenth century, police in the city were responsible for checking door handles, breaking up brawls, and responding to complaints, and they did this armed with a thirty-three-inch club, rudimentary hand-cuffs, and a leather helmet (hence "leatherhead," the vintage New York City term for police officers). Face-to-face communication was supplemented early on with other devices to transmit information. Police used whistles, horns, and couriers to alert citizens and patrolmen. When they entered a residence or business, they would hang a green lantern on the door, and this basic communications technology is memorialized to this day by the green light that hangs outside each NYPD precinct house.

New York's first structured police force was the Metropolitan Police, established in 1845. Even after the establishment of an organized department, the police weapon of choice remained the club, as firearms manufactured early in the century were risky to use, involved a lot of care, and often ended up backfiring or exploding in your hand. However, in the mid-1800s, companies like Colt, Derringer, and Smith & Wesson were able to produce more dependable weapons that were integrated into the police's arsenal.

Police communications also improved in the 1880s when the Gamewell Company invented the multialarm call box—a one-way signaling device that connected the street corner to headquarters. The box allowed for communications between the beat officer and the police precinct, and lights placed atop each box allowed for the policemen to communicate by flashing codes. The multi-alarm box went into use in Chicago and Detroit in 1885, in Indianapolis in 1895, and a variation of this system—call ERS street boxes—remained in extensive use in New York City until 1996 when, as fire commissioner of the FDNY, I had many of them removed. (By that time 93 percent of the calls received from these boxes ended up being false alarms.)

In 1877, the first telephone was adapted for police use in Albany, New York; in 1883, the Detroit Police Department installed one of the seven phones in the entire city; and in 1891, the New York City police began to switch over from telegraph to telephone.

Law-enforcement strategists realized that, not only did the police need to communicate locally, they also needed to be able to share information nationally, and this led to the establishment of the International Association of Chiefs of Police (IACP) as a clearinghouse for information. As a result of IACP's consolidation of information, they realized that indexical systems for tracking criminals needed to be developed and archived so that criminals could be identified more easily. The Bertillon body-typing system of the nineteenth century had fallen by the wayside when in 1904, then police commissioner William McAdoo sent Sgt. Joseph Faurot to London to study fingerprinting at Scotland Yard. He brought it back to the NYPD and within several years they solved their first case based on fingerprint evidence. Fingerprinting and mug shots soon became the standard methods for indexing criminals.

At the end of the first decade of the twentieth century, police departments began to resemble what we see today as a modern force. Around the country, local departments experimented with cars and motorcycles; and in 1912, the Radio Act opened the door to two-way communications between the individual officer on the street and the managers at the precinct or headquarters.

During WWI, radio was fine tuned, and high-power, low-frequency radios were available for commercial use. In 1923, the first police department, the Pennsylvania

State Police, went on the air, and they were also the first to establish a network of TeleType machines to collect information from 110 machines in ninety-five cites. Throughout the 1920s, radio technology was integrated slowly; and by the early 1930s, most big city police departments were using radios to communicate to patrol cars.

Introduced in 1932, by the early 1950s patrol cars with two-way radios were standard in New York City; and their combined potential for catching criminals was thought to be limitless. The hope was that radio would enable police to arrive at the scene of a crime so quickly as to catch the criminal in the act or, better yet, prevent the crime from happening. Unfortunately this dream evaporated with experience, as most victims and witnesses wait an average of an hour to report crimes. From the 1950s through the early 1970s, two-way radios and patrol cars were standard. In the 1980s the department implemented advanced radio technology to allow for better communications.

In New York City we were looking to switch over from patrol radios to mobile digital terminals (MDTs) with computer-aided dispatch (CAD) software. During multiple dispatches, police patrol radio circuits often overload and officers sometime lose communication with the dispatcher. The use of wireless technology, MDTs and CAD, would help alleviate this problem and hasten response time, which in an emergency can make the difference between life and death. We drew up plans to enable NYPD squad cars to receive digital dispatches.

To improve response time, we started an Enhanced 911 system that provides the exact information regarding number and location of a call, status, and dispositions. This information can be generated by the 911 operator via a simple keystroke, and it allows the operator to have automatic number and location identification and connects the operators digitally to the fire department, EMS, and the police. Today when you call 911 to make a complaint, the operator takes your call and enters the pertinent information into a CAD system, which is retrieved by a dispatcher who reads it over a two-way radio that transmits the information out to police cars.

To expedite this system, in the future CAD software will be installed in mobile data terminals or laptops so that instead of being received by the operator and then dispatched by radio, the pertinent information would be typed into the CAD system by the operator and transmitted directly, bypassing the radio dispatch. MDTs and laptops with CAD software would also allow for the patrol officer to have access to vehicle and owner information and run database checks without going through dispatchers, and it would also allow officers in squad cars to communicate with each other through an instant messaging system.

Officers should be able to send queries to the federal NCIC database and get information back within seconds, but because of the limitations of radio this has been difficult to achieve. Police departments must stay on the cutting edge of technology to maintain the upper hand, using twenty-first-century techniques like digital and wireless technologies, Enhanced 911, on-line complaints, global-positioning systems, and CompStat, a computerized mapping system that tracks incidents of civilian complaints, administrative data, and crimes, and crunches those numbers into statistical information.

CompStat was made possible by technological innovations and theories of managerial accountability, but it is rooted in the police tradition of pin mapping crime. These digital pin maps are generated by MapInfo software and the data is coded in a variety of formats, including comparative charts, graphs, and tables.

The CompStat Report is the backbone of the CompStat system and is assembled in several steps. First, an assigned officer from each of the seventy-six precincts, nine police service areas, and twelve transit districts inputs crime complaint data into the CompStat database. Then the data, which includes the specific times and locations at which the crimes and enforcement activities took place, is forwarded to the Chief of Department, CompStat Unit where it is collated and loaded into a citywide database. This information is used to create the CompStat Report, a report that captures crime complaint and arrest activity at the precinct, patrol borough, and city levels.

The CompStat Unit uses the report to produce electronic pin maps of crime locations citywide; analyzes geographical locations of shootings, homicides, and other major crimes; monitors pattern crimes; develops advanced computerized crime-tracking methods; and provides briefing materials for the police commissioner.

While I was at the helm of the NYPD, these patterns were analyzed biweekly in Thursday and Friday morning meetings in the NYPD's Command and Control Center at One Police Plaza. In these early morning sessions we accessed the CompStat database and projected precinct maps depicting virtually any combination of crime-and-arrest locations, crime "hot spots," and other relevant information onto large video screens.

These meetings and the CompStat process were invaluable and with them we could track crime accurately; police executives were able to observe the staff and policies of each precinct and borough command, while the precinct commanders now had a clear idea of the direction that NYPD management wanted them to follow. CompStat's statistical analyses of crime are not the only benefit. With the program we are also able to get management information on overtime expenditures, precinct staffing, numbers of summonses (particularly quality of life), and civilian complaints against officers.

CompStat meetings take place twice a week in the Command Center at NYPD headquarters at One Police Plaza. A horseshoe-shaped table with chairs all around it for police executives to sit dominates the war room. Front and center is the podium where precinct and borough commanders stand to present their case and respond to queries elicited by the CompStat reports and statistics that are flashed on the video screens behind them.

In weekly meetings we would analyze crimes precinct-by-precinct, and during the meetings precinct commanders, borough chiefs, and special unit commanders would be questioned on the performance of their precinct or borough and rated citywide. We had a policy of calling precinct commanders and borough chiefs as many times as it took until we felt that the problems were being addressed. So a commander of a "failing" precinct could expect to be interrogated several times in a row until he or she had resolved the problems of their precinct to my satisfaction. A bad CompStat Report is akin to a failing report card—until your grade gets better, you keep getting held back to do it over.

Former first deputy commissioner Jack Maple, an architect of many of the NYPD's successful strategies, including CompStat, introduced four key elements to productivity and crime reduction: timely and accurate intelligence, rapid deployment, effective tactics, and relentless follow-up and assessment. In the CompStat meetings we looked for trends and patterns that precinct and borough commanders may have missed, and ensured that they were using these key elements to fight crime. In 1994, Jack Maple used CompStat to map murders, robberies, burglaries, and larcenies, and "hot spots" became apparent on the map. Robbery, narcotics, and guns squads were deployed according to the need.

One of these "hot spots" was East New York's Seventy-fifth Precinct. The precinct had 129 homicides in 1993, 3,152 robberies, 1,854 burglaries, 1,474 felonious assaults, and was haven to over 300 fugitives wanted for violent felonies. Maple focussed in on the problem in East New York using data from CompStat to direct resources and manpower to the appropriate locations.

1997, murder in the Seventy-fifth Precinct had dropped 72 percent to 35 homicides and over 42 percent for the seven major felony crimes. By using timely and accurate intelligence from CompStat, rapidly deploying personnel to the locations pinpointed by the system, and using effective tactics we were able to bring crime down. Relentless follow-up and assessment by the NYPD in East New York led to another 13 percent decline in the crime rate. Even though the Seventy-fifth Precinct remains one of the city's more active, today it is far less violent then it was in the mid-1990s.

When you have full comprehension of the crime situation, resources can be used more effectively. When local commanders have a firm grasp of the current crime situation they can more effectively allocate manpower—whether it's a matter of directing extra patrols to problem blocks or closing down locations where there are chronic crime problems. When action is taken, it must be followed up and reassessed to determine whether results have been achieved or the area in question will backslide. Before CompStat we didn't have the big picture or the ability to prevent crimes by analyzing crime patterns.

The system has grown from a statistical and mapping program to an invaluable database of crime and incident data that can track a dizzying array of factors and trends based on sometimes seemingly discrete data. The program was recently expanded to include 734 indicators from quality-of-life crimes to incidents of child abuse, from concentrations of prostitution to administrative issues like overtime and civilian complaints. CompStat has become a blueprint of the New York's underbelly—a map that charts the city's troubles and the NYPD's goals.

We had many corporations, including IBM, come in and look at CompStat to see if it was adaptable to their businesses. Every good business needs a way to hold its managers accountable and the same goes for the NYPD— or any law-enforcement organization. The CompStat system is emulated worldwide, and the NYPD has received multiple requests from law-enforcement agencies and police departments for information and training in the method. Baltimore and Philadelphia have instituted the system, and it is in use in Israel and Germany. Caracas, Venezuela, also has plans to use it.

Although CompStat is a brilliant method of crime reduction, it has failed in places where it is not executed properly. The reason it has failed is that any accountability system requires that the chief executive of the police department be willing to "pull the trigger" and to transfer, demote, or reassign those people who are ineffective. I replaced fifty-four precinct commanders during my tenure and was never hesitant to transfer or replace those who were not doing their job. There are places where CompStat has been put in place where the chief executive has not been willing to do that. If you know where your weaknesses are and don't do anything about them, CompStat won't work.

Another system for mapping and locating crimes or traffic accidents is global positioning. In 2001, the NYPD invested $9 million in a new GPS for its highway patrol. Satellite technology can isolate accidents and transmit the information to a central-dispatching location, which traces the incident from the satellite then transmits that information to the highway patrol officer. The FDNY used global positioning to locate body parts, personal belongings, and lost equipment at the World Trade Center crime scene. The system is very accurate and can plot items, or remains, within an area of from three to six feet.

The NYPD has implemented less experimental uses of technology. Car stops have the potential for danger and often are the riskiest assignment. For the first time I had cameras with audio pickups installed in NYPD Highway Patrol cars to ensure the safety of officers pulling people over and making stops and also to protect the public by having a record of how the officer and the citizen acted.

The NYPD's On-Line Booking System (OBLS) was a way we used technology to expedite the judicial system and save resources. Instead of taking the arrestee down to the district attorney for arraignment, filing of an affidavit, or complaint, and waiting for them to be processed, we used video and telephone on-line booking to send the information from the precinct or correction facility. A suspect would be brought into the facility and arraigned off-site. These technological advances allowed us to process suspects more quickly, and the video feed allowed suspects to interact as they would if they were present in the courtroom, and vice versa, without transporting to them to Central Booking and without infringing on their right to due process. We integrated OLBS information directly into the CompStat System and we were able to track the arrests accurately and the arrest records of both individual suspects and officers.

All of these technologies and others will soon be part of law enforcement's arsenal in the fight against crime— the technology exists; it is just a matter of funding. Computer-aided dispatch (CAD), greater e-mail and Internet accessibility for officers, integrating numerous databases into a central database, and the use of laptop computers, digital cameras, and wireless handheld devices by officers are on the horizon for the NYPD and other law-enforcement agencies and police departments. Soon officers will be able to type in your social security number or your telephone number into a handheld device and be able to retrieve information from the National Crime Information Center (NCIC), get downloads from DNA, forensic, financial and criminal databases, check crime alerts, and compare your face to images of wanted criminals.

Although information access is an asset, the information age has also spawned its own breed of high-tech criminals. Cybercrime is a new challenge to law-enforcement officials to develop advanced methods and tactics. Internet crimes encompass child pornography, pyramid schemes and other financial scams, sexual exploitation and harassment, identity theft, hacking, drug dealing, and copyright issues. To counter these dealers, con artists, and sexual predators, some police departments and the FBI have set up technological crime units that address crimes on the Internet and crimes in which a computer has been used.

And cybertheft pays: While the average bank robber walks with $2,500, the average cybercriminal gets away with $250,000, a major reason why this newest type of crime is flourishing. The NYPD's Detective Bureau has computer-related crime squads that focus on on-line stings, computer forensics, and any crime involving the World Wide Web. The NYPD has found stolen items for sale on eBay, and we have arrested drug dealers who were using the Internet to peddle their goods.

Members of the squads police the Web by posing undercover as minors or as drug purchasers in newsgroups and chatrooms in the hopes that they will be able to intercept criminal activity. In 2000, we made the city's first cyber-drug arrest. Adriano Sanchez was charged with criminal sale of a controlled substance in Las Vegas for distributing Ketamine Hydrochloride, or "Special K," via the Internet. NYPD detectives from one of our computer-related crime squads discovered the alleged cyber-crime while they were in a news group and observed one user give another user, who was interested in purchasing Ketamine, an e-mail address.

The e-mail address given out in the newsgroup led us to a sophisticated Web site—it had a mission statement, a catalogue, and price list—for a company called Biotech International. Detectives went on the Web site and placed an order for twenty grams of the designer drug. When we received the package, with Sanchez's return address, we placed another order for a larger amount of drugs. The original e-mail was from America Online, and we were able to track down an address. Detectives traveled to Las Vegas, arrested Sanchez, seized his computer and records, and charged him with two counts of criminal sale of a controlled substance.

Computer forensics is key to analyzing both computer-related and regular crimes. Electronic crime-scene investigation has become increasingly common, and officers are trained to seize computer equipment and software of suspected criminals. Since electronic evidence is often latent, the confiscated computer, hard drive, peripherals, data discs, CD-ROMS, and other suspicious items are sent to a computer forensic lab for the evidence to be extracted. E-evidence is very fragile, can be easily damaged and altered, and widely disseminated. This means that any investigation involving electronic evidence should ensure that it is properly documented, labeled, and inventoried; examined for latent or trace evidence; and uncorrupted by static or wear and tear.

Electronic evidence can be invaluable, and today many crimes are investigated by electronic evidence collection—from checking the e-mails of a homicide victim to retrieving the computerized financial records of an embezzler. Electronic evidence can also be characterized by crime—with a child abuser or exploiter, the investigators would want to retrieve chat logs, date and time stamps, digital camera software, games, graphic programs, images, Internet activity logs, movie files, and the user's directory and file names. For a death investigation, the police and the District Attorney's Office would want address books, diaries, e-mail/notes/letters, financial records, images, Internet-activity logs, legal documents and wills, medical and telephone records from the computer's hard drive, and the residence of the victim.

Identity theft, perhaps the most prevalent cybercrime, is investigated by confiscating and analyzing hardware and software tools—credit-card generators and equipment to process credit-card transactions, digital cameras, and scanners. Computer forensic specialists search for templates for birth certificates, check-cashing cards, vehicle registrations and driver's licenses, auto insurance documents, scanned signatures, social security cards, and digital photographs, as well as Internet activity related to ID theft (e-mails and newsgroup postings, erased documents, on-line money orders and trading information, system files and activity at forgery sites) on the computer's hard drive. Electronic investigation is already vital to twenty-first century policing, and as more Americans go online and buy computers, this genre of police work will become even more commonplace.

Computers can be used to solve and commit crimes, may be targeted for crime, and can provide evidence that a crime has been committed. The digital age, as with every societal revolution, has a downside and an upside. The Internet is the "Wild West" of our time, and policing it is breaking new ground. Computers have allowed police to cooperate on cases and track criminals, they have allowed for almost instant communications between complainant and officer, and they have provided an invaluable archiving tool. Law-enforcement databases, digital dispatching, CompStat, and the use of wireless technology in policing are the benefits of our time. With these benefits come dangers, and the price that we must pay for greater access to information and to each other is that others may take advantage of it.

4.

CRIME-SCENE EVIDENCE AND FORENSICS

The five bodies were found, shot execution-style through the head, in the basement's walk-in freezer. Their hands were bound and the victim's were gagged with duct tape, their heads wrapped in clear plastic bags. One of them, Jeremy Melc, had also been shot in the chest; another victim was propped up, as if sleeping, next to the door of the freezer; the remaining four bodies were lined side by side on the floor of the freezer. Blood covered the floor and the walls and the boxes of food that lined the freezer; bullet casings from a semiautomatic gun littered the freezer floor.

Patrick Castro, twenty-three, an intended murder victim, had survived a shot in the face by turning his head when the trigger was pulled. As the bag wrapped around his head filled with his own blood, he overheard the two gunmen discussing what to do next. He lay there pretending to be dead as they emptied the gun into two of the bodies. After they left, Castro freed himself and called the police from the fax in the manager's office. Then he

dragged the only other survivor, JaQuione Johnson, eighteen, upstairs to wait for officers to arrive.

Castro gave Queens homicide detectives valuable details. He was able to tell them that two men had arrived
at the Wendy's restaurant at Main Street in Flushing,
Queens, at closing time and asked to speak with Jean Au-
guste Dumel, the fast-food franchise's assistant manager.
Dumel seemed to know one of the men, who asked him
to go downstairs to the basement with them. Minutes later
Dumel came on the restaurant's public announcement system and instructed the employees who remained upstairs
to come down.

Once downstairs, the victims were assaulted, bound
and gagged with duct tape, and plastic bags were tied
around their heads. Then they were shot in the head. The
Queens district attorney, Richard A. Brown, the EMS
workers, and the officers who responded to the call, including Chief of Detectives William Allee, described it as
the most gruesome crime scene they had ever seen. The
next day's tabloids woke the city up with the news of the
"Wendy's Massacre."

Castro's information helped detectives identify the suspects, and renditions of the two were made by a forensic
artist and posted throughout the neighborhood. The apparent motive was robbery—there was $2,000 missing from a
safe, a cell phone, the keys to the restaurant, and the video
and surveillance cameras were taken. But they had not
taken the wallets of the victims, and two safes filled with
money remained untouched. The facts that detectives
culled from Castro and the crime scene—the familiarity of
Dumel with one of the perpetrators, the careful planning of
the crime, the suspect's knowledge of the restaurant's floor-
plan and surveillance system, and the bullets—would lead
us to our suspects and help us to convict them.

Now we knew that we were in pursuit of two men, one in his twenties or thirties, another in his early thirties, and both, perhaps, former employees of Wendy's.

After the victim's bodies had been autopsied, we discovered, by comparing the bullets with digitized ballistics imaging, that the five murders and two deadly assaults had been committed with the same gun, a Bryco .380. Crime-scene investigators also discovered a bloody palm print on a box of food in the freezer.

As our list of suspects grew shorter, our investigation began to focus on John Taylor, thirty-six, who had worked at Wendy's and been fired in October 1999, six months before the May 24 massacre. He had been using the cell phone taken from the scene of the crime, and within hours homicide detectives found him in Brentwood, Long Island, and arrested him. In his fanny pack we found the surveillance video and camera, the cell phone, and, most important to his prosecution, a Bryco .380 semiautomatic pistol.

After doing ballistics testing, and comparing the bullets that we test fired from Taylor's .380 to the bullets found in the victims and at the scene, we confirmed that the Bryco found in Taylor's possession was the gun that had been used to kill all five victims. We also fingerprinted and palm printed Taylor. We found that his palm print matched the one found on the box of food in the Wendy's basement. A driver from the Q58 bus that Taylor and Godineaux used to flee the scene of the crime confirmed the forensic identification. With the overwhelming physical and circumstantial evidence against him, Mr. Taylor confessed and turned in his partner, Craig Godineaux, thirty, who later pleaded guilty to murder.

Without the careful collection and analysis of crime-scene evidence, the cases against Taylor and Godineaux would have been more difficult to solve and more difficult to prove their guilt.

The science of crime-scene evidence is forensics. This is where science and crime solving intersect and determine the evidentiary value of items found during a criminal investigation.

Forensics is primarily based on the theory of transfer—when two objects meet, evidence of their meeting can be established. As children we learn that when we write on a pad of paper our pen impressions mark the remaining sheets on the pad; and an impression of what we have written can be read even after we've removed the original sheet of paper. This is an example of rudimentary forensics. Forensic science is much more sophisticated than a child's game, and today, with DNA, the pieces of evidence found at the crime scene are getting smaller.

Fingerprints, blood, hair, bullets, and bullet casings left behind at the scene of a crime can be the strongest evidence that a prosecutor has, and it is important that the Crime Scene Unit collect all of the evidence available and test it in a standard and accurate way. Immediately after a crime is discovered, crime-scene investigators are dispatched to document the scene and retrieve evidence. They collect, transport, and submit the evidence to a city or state custodian, who sees that the evidence is distributed to the appropriate forensic lab for analysis. The lab's units test the evidence, and the results are submitted to the detectives working on the case, and later to the district attorney. Here in New York, and in most major cities, police departments have their own Crime Scene Unit and their own labs to process material; while departments in smaller communities generally rely on forensic experts at state labs.

The NYPD's Forensics Investigations Division is composed of several squads and units—the Crime Scene Unit, the Bomb Squad, and the Ballistics Unit—and in New York City, all of the evidence is analyzed at the Police Laboratory in Jamaica, Queens.

The forensic laboratory has many different types of testing, and which unit is assigned depends on the evidence submitted. Evidence from a drug sting would go to the Controlled Substance Analysis Unit; an extortion note would go to the Document Unit; whereas a case with blood would be assigned to the Serology Unit; a gas can thought to ignite a fire would go to Arson. Few labs have a Hairs and Fibers Unit, but all laboratories have an Evidence Control Unit. Typical crime-lab evidence may include crime-scene photos, guns, bullets and bullet casings, images of blood splatter and fracture patterns, footprint impressions, hair, blood, and other genetic matter found at the scene.

The basic considerations of crime-scene work are the recognition of physical evidence, the identification of the properties of the evidence, the comparison of that evidence to other evidence, the individuation of the evidence, and then the reconstruction of the crime scene.

There are two kinds of crime scenes—primary, where the crime occurred; and secondary, if the results of the crime (for example, a body) are moved to a subsequent location. And crime scenes can be broken down by crime: burglary, murder, rape, arson, and they can also be labeled by location or type. It is up to the criminal investigator to accurately describe the crime scene as there is no standard for classification.

Once the crime scene has been typed and analyzed, the investigators attempt to establish the motivation or if there is a pattern that the crime conforms to. With the elements of the crime nailed down, the investigators then try to link their suspect, or suspects, to the victim of the crime through eyewitnesses or physical and circumstantial evidence. After the evidence has been collected and the crime scene analyzed, the investigator's next task is to reconstruct the crime. Using the location and disposition of evidence—blood spatters, muddy footprints, or a bloody palm print on a wall—the scene is recreated.

It is not unusual for factual evidence, shell casings, or footprints to contradict an eyewitness's account of the crime. It is important to eliminate suspects and find the true culprit. Once a suspect is identified through their investigations of the evidence and witness testimony, investigators get physical evidence from suspects.

When you are arrested for a crime, your fingerprints are taken, and if consented by the individual, or by court order, blood or saliva samples may be collected and submitted for DNA testing. These samples are then compared to evidence found at the scene of the crime. At the same time the evidence found at the scene, and the samples donated by the suspect, are entered into databases and compared against existing samples to see if there is a match or a "hit." Sometimes the physical evidence will lead you to your suspect, and sometimes it won't. While the physical evidence in a case might not implicate your suspect, small details can give the investigators facts that are valuable in solving the crime.

Types of evidence can be categorized: *Transient evidence,* which is difficult to capture (smell, for example); *conditional evidence,* which may include the disposition and condition of the body, fire, or lighting conditions; *pattern evidence* may be evaluated from broken glass, blood spatters, burn marks; *transfer evidence* such as fiber-and-hair evidence; and *associative evidence,* such as items that belong to the victim in the suspect's possession.

Following a trial, if you are found innocent it takes a

court order to have the fingerprints or DNA profiles expunged from the computerized databases. These databases house millions of profiles or fingerprints. Fingerprints are archived by a software program called Automated Fingerprint Identification Systems (AFIS) and for DNA profiles, the software is the FBI's Combined DNA Index System (CODIS) program.

The importance of good crime-scene work was proven by the O. J. Simpson trial. Dr. Henry Lee, then head of Connecticut's crime lab and later superintendent of the Connecticut State Police, and part of Simpson's "Dream Team," was a key witness at the trial; and with his expertise the defense poked holes in the prosecution's case against Simpson, which was based primarily on crime-scene and circumstantial evidence. After the discovery of the bodies of Nicole Brown Simpson and Ronald Goldman, crime-scene investigators had tainted the scene by traipsing through blood, collecting evidence with their bare hands, and not correctly documenting the crime scene.

I became commissioner shortly after the "not guilty" verdict in the Simpson trial was read, and I was outraged that incompetent crime-scene analysis had led to Simpson's acquittal. Even more worrisome was that the outcome of the Simpson trial was one of many less media-worthy cases, where if the collection and analysis of forensics been more professional the perpetrator would be looking at the walls of a jail cell. The one positive thing that came out of the Simpson trial was the recognition that there were no national standards in crime labs, and as a result of that, in 1995, the American Society of Crime Laboratory Directors (ASCLD) standards were established to perfect the testing of DNA and crime-laboratory procedures.

The National DNA Advisory Board met in 1995 to solidify already existing recommendations and to establish mandatory standards for DNA units. These standards went into effect in October 1998. Crime labs had to fulfill ASCLD standards or were unable to process crime-scene evidence.

The NYPD's Jamaica lab was designed before I became police commissioner, and with ASCLD standards in place it was critical that we fulfill the requirements to be able to continue working with crime-scene evidence. The laboratory, which was originally envisioned to cost $30 million in order to meet the standards, ended up costing $60 million. In 2000, the lab was accredited by ASCLD on schedule, and today the NYPD's lab shares the same standards and requirements as every other accredited crime lab in the country.

The Crime Scene Unit is composed of several different types of investigators. The first responder is usually the detective who calls in the CSI team to document and process the crime scene. The team includes a photographer, the investigative team, the team leader, sketch artists, forensic staff, and the medical examiner.

On certain occasions, forensic specialists such as odontologists and anthropologists are called in. In 2000, a passerby found a skeleton with its hands missing and a skull in a lot alongside the old Jamaica Race Track in Queens and reported it to the police. The remains were retrieved and taken to the police lab, where a forensic anthropologist x-rayed the bones and determined that they were human, female, and those of a teenager. The anthropologist's report concluded that she was 4'8", had been murdered by a blow to the side of the head, and had been dead three to six months, and this data provided forensic artists with information that allowed them to create a post-mortem reconstruction in hopes of identifying the victim.

Specialists can sometimes be the key to getting a conviction. In 1994, seven-year-old Megan Kanka disappeared in Hamilton Township, New Jersey. When her body was found, forensics determined that she had been choked to death and raped, and a key piece of evidence against her neighbor Jesse Timmendequas was a bite mark found on his body.

In Timmendequas's trial, forensic odontologist Haskell Askin matched the alignment of Megan's teeth, which were not straight, and a combination of adult and baby teeth that were "crowded, rotated" and "quite irregular." Then he showed the jury a cast of Megan's lower front teeth and how it matched to a life-size photo of Timmendequas's right palm: It was this evidence that helped to convict Timmendequas for the murder and rape of Megan Kanka.

When a crime scene is first discovered—after the safety of possible victims is secure—the perimeter is cordoned off by police officers to minimize evidence contamination. At the crime scene the primary concern is not to destroy the valuable evidence that permeates the scene, while collecting as much of it as you can. The mere presence of humans in a crime scene introduces the risk that they will inadvertently leave false evidence or take valid evidence with them when they leave. This is especially worrisome when hairs or fibers are transferred from one individual to another.

Where a crime scene is a biohazard, as are all scenes where blood or bodily fluids are wet and considered infectious, great care is taken and crime-scene investigators are outfitted in body suits and boot covers. Latex gloves are always worn when handling blood, fluids, specimens, and evidentiary materials like beer cans, doorknobs, or any type of evidence. All biohazard clothing and gloves are then disposed of immediately after use.

In cases where evidence may be airborne, masks and air filters are used. Investigators use tweezers to collect hair and fibers, and swabs to gather blood. Both still and video cameras document every angle of the scene, and crime-scene artists sketch the scene, usually from above. The investigators may only have one opportunity to correctly gather evidence from a crime scene. Documentation is key to remembering the scene weeks, months, maybe years from the original incident.

Trace evidence, like fiber, blood, semen, dirt, glass, and paint, are photographed and packaged at the scene. The careful collection of blood and semen is important, as often this is the evidence that gives the most probative forensic results. Seminal stains are found either at the scene or in the rape kits of the victims of sexual assault, usually collected at a hospital or Rape Crisis Center. Investigators use infrared, ultraviolet, or alternate light source (ALS) photography to detect evidence—fingerprints, sweat, blood, semen, or saliva—on surfaces not visible to the human eye. Chemicals, like luminol, can also help to locate evidence and can be rubbed onto surfaces to discern whether they had come into contact with blood. Dusting small particle reagents, like aluminum powder enhances fingerprints, or using iodine fuming (which utilizes a wand and iodine vapor to develop the print), and the superglue (cryanoacrylate) fuming process are critical tools. Footprints are located by using an electrified sheet; and blood spatters and the trajectories of bullets are tracked by looping string.

In the case of murder, the body of the victim is left exactly where and how it was found until the medical examiner (ME) arrives and declares the individual deceased. Once approved by the ME, evidence is collected, since moving or placing a sheet over a corpse may destroy valuable clues.

The reason evidence is collected in an organized and documented manner is to ensure that if needed it will be admissible in court. Crime-scene search and seizure of evidence without the legal right to do so is the most common reason that evidence is suppressed in court. In *Mincey v. Arizona,* 1978, a narcotics officer was killed by a suspect. During the next four days, detectives searched the defendant's apartment without a warrant and seized evidence. The U.S. Supreme Court reviewed the case and determined that evidence could be seized only with the consent of the owner or with a warrant authorized by the court. When an officer first enters the crime scene, his or her obligation is to secure the safety of potential victims, and in this capacity they may search the premises. And in their search for victims or perpetrators, the officers may collect clearly visible evidence. This is the plain view doctrine, which allows for officers to seize evidence without a warrant under specific conditions.

Documenting the scene of a crime has been part of police procedure for centuries. In 1879, Alphonse Bertillon began working at the Sûreté, the Paris police headquarters, collecting and filing written descriptions of homicides and suspects and thereby establishing the first organized system of criminal records.

Bertillon's shortcoming was his use of anthropometry, the measurement of the skull and other bones, as a method for identifying criminals. It has since been proven that there is no relationship between skull size or bone measurements and criminal activity.

Fingerprinting, a better way to document large groups of people, was developed by William Herschel, an English civil servant stationed in India. Herschel developed fingerprinting as a way to document Indian veterans (who apparently all looked the same to the colonialists) who wanted to collect their pensions. In 1912, Bertillon was the first scientist to develop the concept of points of comparison, thus making fingerprinting a standard protocol in police investigations. Each print is broken down into specific areas, or "points," that are then compared to the same areas in the print lifted from the crime scene.

With the development of photography in the late nineteenth century, crime-scene photographs and mugshots became policing tools; and in 1900, Paul Uhlenhuth established serology by creating a test to determine whether blood was human or not. In 1909, Karl Landsteiner broke blood down into A, B, and O types.

Fingerprinting is the most well-established method of forensic identification. There are several kinds of prints found at the scene of a crime: latent, patent, and partial. *Latent fingerprints* are invisible to the naked eye and are only discovered after a reagent, and/or fluorescent lighting is used to illuminate them. *Patent fingerprints* are a positive impression and visible, like John Royster's bloody prints on the window of the Dutch Girl Cleaners. *Partial prints* can be latent or patent, but occur when only part of the print is recovered.

Everyone who is arrested is photographed and fingerprinted. The fingerprints are databased in the state and national automatic fingerprint identification system databases (AFIS and NCIC), and when a fingerprint from a crime scene is entered into the state database that automatically transmits it to the FBI's AFIS database.

Until fingerprinting was digitized and the AFIS set up, comparisons were done manually with investigators examining thousands of fingerprint cards trying to make a match. In 1996, I installed live-scan fingerprinting stations in precincts, so that we could expedite the process. Now the computer can give potential matches that the fingerprint examiner can take and compare to the fingerprints found at the crime scene. In recent years the issue of training identification specialists to make sure that the prints stand up in court has arisen; and to mitigate any accusations of "junk science," fingerprinting has to be held to higher standards on what constitutes a match.

AFIS, and other law-enforcement databases, have been made possible by the greater use of computers and the progressive development of computer technologies—search algorithms, image scanning, better and faster computer processors, and storage. Your database network is only as good as the information it contains, so the next step was to create a nexus between AFIS and other print databases: tenprint units, palm print units, and latent and partial units. Integrated Automated Fingerprint Identification System (IAFIS) is a database conceived by the FBI's Laboratory Division's Latent Print Unit and put into operation in June 1999.

IAFIS is particularly good for latent prints and solving cold cases, and it can search up to one thousand latent prints a day. In some cases where fingerprints databased in the AFIS did not register a hit, they did when they were input into IAFIS. Because of this, each new fingerprint found at a crime scene is entered into the system and run against the unsolved murder latent print file.

The NYPD, and other large police forces, has a Ballistics Unit. The NYPD's unit has several divisions: Ballistics Squads, firearms examination, microscopy, computerized ballistics ID (Integrated Ballistic Identification System [IBIS], DrugFire), gun tracing/evidence control, and firearms labs. The NYPD uses the IBIS database, and its subdivisions Brasscatcher and Bulletproof, to track both cartridges and bullets used in crimes. All guns used in crimes, or found at the crime scene, are test fired and the ballistic results are entered into databases. Each gun is tracked in databases by its "ballistic fingerprint": the marks created when a round goes off, and pressure from the barrel that creates grooves unique to that gun. Shell-casing imprint matches can link many crimes to one gun, and discern the unique qualities of bullets and bullet casings, ballistics experts use microscopes and digital imaging to capture the grooves and scrapes on the bullets—called computer ballistics imagining.

Oftentimes hair-and-fiber evidence is found at the scene of a crime—the suspect having unwittingly left traces of his or her presence. Hair evidence can determine race and somatic origin of the hair, and strands of hair can be examined with a microscope and compared. Today, DNA or—if the hair is rootless—mitochondrial DNA (mtDNA) are better methods for determining the source of the hair strand because in past years there have been several cases of erroneous or illegal testimony in the case of forensic experts, especially with regard to hair-comparison analysis.

In January 2001, a forensic expert's report was published in Illinois alleging that a Chicago police crime-lab employee and later supervisor at the Illinois State Police Crime Lab, gave skewed testimony in nine cases. Four Chicago men, Omar Saunders, Larry Ollins, Calvin Ollins, and Marcellius Bradford, were cleared by DNA evidence for the 1986 murder and rape of medical student Lori

Roscetti. In a civil suit they claimed that the police, prosecutors, and the crime lab had used flawed evidence and
techniques to convict them and had conspired to convict
the men because of their inability to solve the high-profile
case. The crime lab employee who was at the center of
the controversy, had testified that the semen taken from the
victim and her clothing matched the semen of Sander, the
two Olline's, and Bradford, as well as identified matching
hair evidence. According to other experts, her notes showed
something else: They showed that the semen samples should
have been discounted because the A, B, O blood-type tests
are fickle and subject to false results. To remedy this, the
protocol of testing a control piece of evidence was put into
place; but instead of stating the results of the control test,
she only testified to the results of the main test.

In February 2002, the two men who police believe are
the real perpetrators were found after a tip was called in
and DNA testing of semen stains on Roscetti's clothing
linked the men, Duane Roach and Eddie "Bo" Harris, to
the murder.

Another state that has had problems with their forensic
experts is Oklahoma. In 2001, Joyce Gilchrist was the
subject of a police report that criticized her for being
sloppy in her testing and mismanaging evidence at the
Oklahoma City Police Crime Lab. The Oklahoma City
Police Department asked the FBI to investigate eight of
the cases that she was involved in: In total, 165 cases
would be flagged for further review.

Jeffrey Todd Pierce was one of the victims of Gilchrist's
misrepresentation. His 1986 rape conviction was one of
the first batch of eight reexamined by the FBI, and in
Pierce's case Gilchrist had testified that hair and pubic hair
found at the scene of the rape were "microscopically con-
sistent" with Pierce's hair. When the FBI did DNA testing

of Pierce's semen, what they found eliminated him as a suspect. In fact, in five of the eight original cases, the FBI found that Gilchrist had erred. Her testimony in twelve death row cases is now being questioned; and three of those cases are being reopened. Gilchrist faces further investigation, and the possibility of civil suits in her future. Gilchrist has filed her own suit against Oklahoma City police and city officials, accusing them of retaliation.

Serology, the science of serums, their reactions and properties, as with hair-comparison analysis, is subject to the testimony of "expert" witnesses. One of these witnesses, Frederick S. Zain, a serology specialist who worked in Florida, West Virginia, and Texas, was tried several times in different states for giving questionable testimony.

Zain's problems started in 1992 when DNA exonerated Glen Woodall, a cemetery worker convicted of kidnapping and sexual assault in 1987. Others who had been indicted based on Zain's testimony came forward and demanded that DNA testing be done. The lawsuits, as well as the complaints of Zain's coworkers that he was falsifying evidence, led to him being tried and acquitted for perjury. Several other trials have followed, including one in West Virginia that ended in a mistrial. The cases mishandled by Zain, Gilchrist, and the Chicago crime lab employee are proof positive that we need to be as accurate as possible in our forensic science.

The American Society of Crime Laboratory Directors (ASCLD) accreditation has made the rules of handling and defending evidence far more stringent, and police labs— including the NYPD's—are subject to inspections by a ten-member accreditation team that monitors how evidence is handled, how quality is assured, and how records are kept. Technicians and scientists are interviewed and tested on their methodologies for handling evidence, and in some cases they are blind tested, where supervisors give them evidence to analyze without telling them that their work is being reviewed by ASCLD inspectors.

Controlled-substance testing, alcohol testing, and toxicology are related branches of forensics. As for illegal substance testing, national standards were put into place and now require that the substance be tested twice—with a color crystal test and a molecular test. The item is sampled, and the sample tested. If it is thought to be a drug, presumptive tests are run—for a white powder we would first test for cocaine, then heroin, and so on. Police officers can field-test a wide variety of drugs, including heroin, cocaine, and marijuana.

Uniformed members are randomly tested and screened for drugs when applying for assignments in specialized units and as a condition of promotion. For drug-testing officers and criminals, we use urine-testing because, although hair testing is more accurate, it is cost prohibitive. Hair is like the rings of a tree, and an individual's history of drug and alcohol abuse, the kind of drug, the quantity, and the duration of use, can be determined by hair testing.

Standard urinalysis can detect different drugs—like cocaine hydrochloride (powder) and crack; heroin and other opiates, marijuana and hashish, and PCP; but if a case warrants it, we also test for other hallucinogens—LSD, hallucinogenic mushrooms; date-rape drugs, Rohypnol and GHB; and designer drugs, like MDMA or ecstasy. Prescription drugs can be illegally distributed so toxicology tests include analyses for Ketamine, a tranquilizer used by veterinarians—called Special K on the street—and for powerful painkillers like OxyContin and Vicodin.

The Document Unit of the NYPD identifies individuals from their handwriting, classifies signatures as forgeries, determines the origin and history of documents, and finds deletions or alterations to documents that are questioned. Document analysis also deals with modern office technologies, like printers and faxes. By the quality of the type and ink, we can often discern not only what type and brand of device was used, we can also identify the specific machine.

To identify forgery handwriting, examples for comparison are taken from the suspect. Handwriting is as unique as fingerprints; there can be similarities, but no one writes exactly the same and no one writes the same every time they write. Document examiners can determine a lot from the handwriting of an individual—the slant of pen can indicate whether someone is left- or right-handed and the formation of the letters can belie some of their personality's characteristics and their sex. As for forgeries, since the forger must choose between accuracy and speed, a signature sample is ineffective. The best method is to take preexisting writing samples from suspects, and if that is not possible have the suspects write a sample. Handwriting examiners then use a triocular microscope to compare the writing letter by letter.

Although DNA is the wave of the future, this is not to say that the other forensic sciences will fall by the wayside. Technology is broadening the field of forensics, and allowing for crime-scene evidence collection and testing to be more accurate than ever before. Forensics is still very important to police work and allows us to track criminals in an innovative and significant way, and forensic science should be used to strengthen the results of DNA testing in many cases.

DNA should be used as often as possible, especially where other methods have failed, and I think that it is important that all cold cases, where appropriate evidence is available, be tested with DNA. Genetic tests should be run on cases in which conviction was based on hair-comparison analysis and, ideally, in all cases whose outcome was dependent on serology. Had the cases of Jeffrey Todd Pierce, Glen Woodall, Omar Saunders, Larry Ollins, Calvin Ollins, and Marcellius Bradford not been retested with DNA they would all still be in jail today. And what's more alarming is that these DNA tests were only run as a response to the fact that the Chicago crime lab techician, Joyce Gilchrist, and Frederick Zain were under suspicion of having misrepresented evidence. DNA is such a crucial tool for defense that the Benjamin N. Cardozo School of Law at Yeshiva University in New York City has launched their "Innocence Project." Lawyer Barry Scheck (of O. J. Simpson fame) spearheaded the project, and its mandate is to examine DNA evidence in cases where prisoners continue to proclaim their innocence. To date the Innocence Project has won the postconviction release of 110 innocent defendants.

5.

DNA PROFILING

On November 22, 1983, the mutilated body of a fifteen-year-old girl was found on an English country lane just outside of the Narborough village of Leicestershire. Her name was Lynda Mann, and she had been raped and murdered. Police found semen at the scene, but after an extensive search the crime remained unsolved. In 1987, another teenage girl, Dawn Ashcroft, was found murdered in the same town. The cases were very similar, and the local police department believed the same person had committed the crimes. Investigators thought they had a lucky break when Rodney Buckland, a seventeen-year-old hospital worker made self-incriminating statements. Although his testimony was contradictory and incoherent, he did admit to the murder of Dawn Ashcroft, but denied any involvement in Lynda Mann's murder.

An officer on the case was dubious about Buckland's testimony and followed up on an article he had read about a new forensic technique perfected by geneticist Dr. Alec

Jeffreys at Leicester University. Most important for forensic science, Jeffreys had discovered that segments of human DNA could be used as "a genetic fingerprint" that was unique to each individual, with the exception of identical twins. Since DNA can be extracted from bodily tissues and fluids including saliva, blood, hair, skin, semen, feces, and urine, and each material has the same DNA sequence, then each can be used to uniquely identify an individual.

In the lab, Jeffreys took the DNA of an individual and put it through a process of enzymatic digestion in order to break it down into fragments; then he separated the strands of DNA out, i.e., placing them in order, largest to smallest, in a gel suspension, using a process called electrophoresis. To illustrate the markers, Jeffreys used a process developed by Edward Southern in England in which he used radioactive labeling and osmotic transfer to visualize the DNA sample into patterns set on X-ray film that resemble bar codes—the pattern or placement of each bar determining that person's DNA profile. These patterns of film were then compared band by band to determine if the two different DNAs were matches.

Intrigued by the new technology, Leicester police submitted semen samples from both crime scenes to Dr. Jeffreys's lab and a sample of Buckland's blood to compare. The DNA tests ascertained that the same individual had committed both crimes; but despite his confession the offender was not Buckland. Realizing that if DNA could prove one man innocent, it could prove another guilty, the Leicester police went into action and collected blood samples from the local male population ages thirteen to thirty. In the end five thousand samples were sent to Jeffreys's lab for DNA testing.

DNA results were much slower in the 1980s, so it took

several months to get results, and disappointingly none of the samples matched the semen found at the crime scenes. The police finally got a break when a young woman who worked at a local bakery overheard a conversation in which a man, Colin Pitchfork, bragged that he had persuaded a friend to take the blood test for him. The police confronted Pitchfork (who had a record for indecent exposure) and accused him of the two murders. In part because he was certain that once samples were taken the DNA evidence would prove him guilty, he confessed to the rapes and murders of Mann and Ashcroft. After his arraignment, a DNA sample was taken from Pitchfork that in fact matched the semen at the crime scenes and proved conclusively that he was the murderer of both girls. Today Pitchfork is serving two consecutive life sentences.

Although the United Kingdom is at the forefront of DNA technology, in the past decade and a half DNA testing has been expanded in the United States solving hundreds of violent crimes, which, left unsolved, would allow felons to further prey on society. In 1987, U.S. law enforcement had its first success with the conviction of Tommy Lee Andrews. Andrews was a serial rapist who lived and preyed in the Orlando, Florida, area. According to an Orange County assistant state attorney, "Without DNA, I don't think we could have gone to trial."

This led to other watershed cases in the U.S. courts in which DNA was used to exonerate or indict a suspect. A seminal case in which DNA was used in court to exonerate a suspect was *State v. Woodall,* a 1989 trial heard in the West Virginia Supreme Court in which the court accepted DNA testing of the defendant at the defendant's request;

but the DNA tests were inconclusive and the court upheld Woodall's rape, kidnapping, and robbery conviction. Later DNA testing proved Woodall innocent, and he was released from jail. In *Spencer v. Commonwealth*, DNA profiling indicted Timothy Wilson Spencer; and Spencer's multiple murder trials in Virginia were the first cases where DNA evidence, semen found in his victims, led to guilty verdicts and the death penalty.

There are many successful accounts of DNA finger-printing criminals, but one of the more ingenious is that of the apprehension in 1998 of a serial rapist in Saint Petersburg, Florida. Police used DNA to nab a robber and rapist, known there as the "Duck Robber" for his waddle. Wanted for two rapes and a series of robberies, the police believed that their "Duck Robber" was Charles Peterson. Peterson attracted suspicion because of his unique gait, but other than that they could not link him to the crimes. The police had collected DNA samples from the rapes and wanted to compare those samples to Peterson's DNA, but he refused to provide them with a sample. After trailing Peterson on his motorcycle in an unmarked car, they saw him spit. The officers pulled up and one of them scooped the spit up in a paper towel. Lab analysis confirmed the police's suspicions, and Peterson's saliva matched the forensic evidence. Saint Petersburg police had the evidence they needed to cook the "Duck Robber's" goose and they charged him with the robberies and rapes.

In some cases DNA identification can correct eyewitness testimony and save innocent people from arrest, incarceration, and indictment. In the mid-1990s, a rape victim was certain that she had seen her rapist on the street. She informed Indiana police, and they arrested the man, Robert Flowers. Flowers proclaimed his innocence, but he wasn't let off the hook until DNA analysis proved him right. The victim, who was so certain of her identification, asked police to inquire as to whether Flowers had any siblings who were similar in appearance. He did; and according to the investigators' profile, DNA fingerprinting showed Flowers's brother to be the attacker.

Had he been imprisoned, Robert Flowers would have had a lot of company. In the United States over one hundred wrongly imprisoned prisoners have been freed because of DNA testing, eight of them from Death Row. All of these individuals had exhausted their appeals, and their postconviction motions had been denied; without DNA analysis they would have rotted in jail. These unjustly accused prisoners, now free because of DNA fingerprinting, are only the tip of the iceberg. Hundreds, perhaps thousands, of other citizens are currently being held for crimes they did not commit.

Since 1989, in about 25 percent of sexual-assault cases referred to the FBI (where results could be obtained) the primary suspect has been excluded by forensic DNA testing. These percentages have remained constant for almost a decade and are not exclusive to the FBI's study—the National Institute of Justice also did an informal survey of private laboratories and turned up similar results (a 26 percent exclusion rate). This means that if DNA profiling is not used, one-in-four sexual-assault convictions is erroneous. At this rate we are wrongly incarcerating thousands yearly and allowing thousands of sexual predators to roam free.

In the interest of freeing those wrongly accused, the U.S. Department of Justice report, *Convicted by Juries, Exonerated by Science,* put forth twenty-eight case studies in which DNA profiling excluded a suspect as the perpetrator of a crime. The study found that in each of these cases conviction was based on a combination of the following: victim and/or witness identification; hair, semen, and/or blood analysis; circumstantial evidence; confession of guilt; and the lack of a viable alibi. Eyewitness identification is not always objective, and witness testimony can be biased; also, innocent people sometimes confess to crimes they did not commit for myriad reasons (usually psychiatric problems), and alibis are not always convenient. When testimony is subjective and science inconclusive (and dependent on the testimony of "experts"), the combination of inaccuracy and bias led to the conviction of these twenty-eight and many others.

The most famous case of someone being exonerated because of DNA is that of Marine corporal Kevin Green. Green was imprisoned for nearly sixteen years for the 1980 murder and assault of his pregnant wife and for the killing of their unborn child. Green denied his guilt, telling investigators that, after going out for a hamburger, he returned home to find his wife beaten, unconscious, and near death.

Green never stopped proclaiming his innocence, and in 1996, DNA testing proved him right by showing that the semen found in his wife's sexual assault was not Green's but that of Gerald Parker, an inmate at California's Avenal State Prison. Faced with this DNA proof, Parker confessed to the murder of Green's wife and admitted to being "the Bedroom Basher." At the time of his confession (taken from him because of overwhelming DNA evidence), Parker was weeks away from release.

DNA helps to exonerate, but often, in cases where there is no suspect, DNA tests are not run on specimens. When I became the NYPD commissioner, I discovered that "rape kits," evidence including body fluids taken from the victim following the attack, were tested only if the victim of the rape could identify the perpetrator. When I started my job in 1996, the NYPD had sixteen thousand rape kits in storage—a treasure trove of DNA evidence with which we could identify serial rapists and prevent future rapes. So convinced was I, and continue to be, that DNA testing is at the crux of contemporary law-enforcement tactics that I changed the department's policy and contracted with private labs to test the kits: The first four hundred kits tested yielded twenty-three hits.

DNA testing could put thousands of rapists behind bars and prevent new rapes, yet rapists remain free to attack because police departments cannot afford the $500 to $1,000 that it costs to analyze the rape kits of sexual-assault victims, even though the victims are led to believe that the invasive process of assembling a rape kit is necessary and that it will result in a DNA sample being taken. This shameful oversight leaves hundreds of thousands of rape kits containing DNA samples warehoused in police evidence rooms and storage lockers. Some remain untested for over a decade, thereby exhausting the statute of limitations on some of the crimes (the statute of limitations for rape varies state-to-state; murder has no time limit).

The National DNA Evidence Bill would allocate $100 million toward creating standardized evidence kits for sexual assaults and ensure that forensic labs would complete the testing of DNA within ten days of receipt. It would also put $150 million toward training more sexual-assault nurses and testing the backlog of DNA samples that are now swamping labs. In New York there is a year backlog of evidence kits and one out of five cases in which DNA is collected is thrown out of court because untrained examiners tested the kits.

Many of the rape kits that are out there have evidence in them, which means that we can identify the rapist. But it goes beyond that. There are a half million convicted offenders who, by law, are supposed to have their DNA samples analyzed, and those samples are sitting out there unanalyzed. The national database kept by the FBI has 1,000,000 samples. If they completed testing the backlog, we would end up with 1.3 million additional samples to bounce these rape kits off.

I found this to be an outrage, and I shared my feelings and my experience at the NYPD with Brian Ross, *ABC News* chief investigative correspondent. I told him about the thousands of rape kits that lie dormant across the country, and we set up an investigative experiment. The news show *20/20* asked the Baltimore police to help us in a unique demonstration project. We offered to pay half the cost of processing DNA evidence kits from some fifty unsolved cases, known as cold cases, to be selected and handled by the Baltimore police with no input at all from *20/20*. The fifty evidence kits from Baltimore were sent to one of the country's leading private DNA labs. The results were then entered into both state and federal criminal databases to see if there was a match. And even the experts were surprised: There were results in five major unsolved rape cases.

Of the fifty kits, thirty-nine had enough evidence, and we entered the results in the national and state databases. We got results in four out of five major cases. One, a Hubert Taylor, was linked to unsolved rapes of two teenage girls in 1998. It took a citywide search and a four-hour stakeout, but when Taylor came home the police were waiting to arrest him. The only reason his DNA was in the system was because of a prior arrest. The Baltimore police matched his DNA and charged him with the two rapes. Until the DNA results in our demonstration project came back, we had nothing to go on in another case, the twelve-year-old rape and murder of Charlene Hardin.

When the DNA results came back, they identified the murderer, thirty-eight-year-old Anthony Mitchell, who was already serving time for robbery and attempted rape. When confronted with the DNA evidence, Mitchell confessed to raping and murdering Charlene Hardin. Mitchell was charged with first-degree murder and pleaded guilty. And the fifth case was a man who had been wrongly identified by a victim and had been in jail; the test showed that he was not the person responsible. DNA profiling cuts both ways: It puts the guilty in jail and it gets the innocent out.

Because of DNA's accuracy and identification power, conclusive evidence can be provided to a jury and a conviction obtained today or even ten years from now. If the environment is ideal, DNA can remain present, and testable, in genetic matter for thousands of years; but it can also degrade quickly under certain conditions. Some of the tissue and bones of the victims of the World Trade Center bombings' DNA had been subjected to violence, extreme heat, toxic and chemical compounds, and decomposition, and this hindered the forensic laboratory's ability to identify victims.

The circumstances of DNA collection at the WTC site were unique, and although it is true that the faster samples are retrieved and tested (like in the case of rape kits) the better, but DNA can be collected from genetic matter for many years. And even if it does decompose, DNA does not break down into different patterns that could look like someone else's DNA; when DNA does degrade, it simply breaks down into fragments of genetic matter that can't be tested. We are able to get genetic profiles and DNA from materials that have been sitting in museums for hundreds of years, and scientists were able to get DNA from a ten-thousand-year-old saber tooth tiger that was found in the La Brea Tar Pits.

In light of the efficacy of DNA evidence, I believe that we should eliminate the statute of limitations for rape in every state. The original reasons for instituting the statute of limitations for rape has been rendered irrelevant. Laws regarding the statute of limitations were set in place when cases were almost exclusively determined by witness identification and circumstantial evidence, and time limits were put into place to ensure that the defendant was able to present an effective courtroom defense, the rationale being that the longer the time that elapses between the crime and the trial, the less accurate the memories of witnesses and defendants.

Because DNA profiling is so precise, this thinking is no longer viable, and today there is no moral or legal reason to have a statute of limitations in rape cases. Not only does the time limit on rape indictments allow violent criminals to roam free, it also says to the victim of rape that the government doesn't care. Others agree with me, and several states have already repealed the time limits on rape because of DNA testing.

Unfortunately the American people were exposed to DNA testing in a case in which the collection of DNA was so sloppy that the results were inconclusive—the O. J. Simpson case. The prosecution's failure to convict Simpson had nothing to do with the failure of DNA science; it had to do with the mishandling of the investigation, which failed to establish a logical sequence of events that would have proven Simpson guilty beyond a reasonable doubt.

After arriving on the scene, investigators moved the bodies of Nicole Simpson and Ron Goldman; detectives used their bare hands to gather evidence at the murder scene; and scientific experts contaminated evidence by mishandling blood evidence at the lab. The incompetence of law enforcement in the Simpson case is not compatible with the painstaking work that DNA testing demands, and the defense team condemned the investigative procedures of the LAPD.

Det. Phillip Van Atter kept a vial of Simpson's blood in his pocket for three hours before submitting it as evidence (and thereby rendering it inadmissible) and Det. Mark Fuhrman's discovery of a bloody glove was questioned. First, there was no proof that the glove belonged to Simpson—a point that Cochran made famous by having Simpson demonstrate in court that the glove did not fit, thereby giving credence to the defense's argument that the glove was not Simpson's. Simpson's attorneys presented a photograph of the glove found at the crime scene that appeared to show a hole on the ring finger of the glove. But the glove booked into evidence had no hole and this indicated to Simpson's team that perhaps the glove had been planted to implicate Simpson. Not withstanding DNA evidence, Dr. Henry Lee's testimony and Johnnie Cochran's brilliant, if carnivalesque, defense cast doubt on whether Simpson had committed the crimes by using the LAPD and their CSI Unit's ineptitude against them. Had the crime-scene evidence been correctly processed in this case, I believe that Simpson would be serving a life sentence.

When first-rate crime-scene investigation techniques are employed, the defense attorney's job is that much more difficult. DNA can be contaminated easily, and therefore crime-scene preservation and evidence collection are critical to avoid situations like the O. J. Simpson case. Crime-scene investigators (CSI) personnel and first responders need to be carefully trained in collection procedures to ensure that evidence is skillfully gathered, stored, and submitted for analysis. First responders to crime scenes are often patrol officers and they, in particular, need to be aware of the careful procedures for collecting evidence and preserving the crime scene.

Temperature and environmental conditions also need to be taken into account during collection and storage. DNA specimens must be kept out of direct sunlight, away from heat sources, and in some cases stored in freezers. The collection and testing of DNA has gotten simpler. Investigators can now retrieve DNA from blood on bullets from through-and-through wounds or from the residue of a criminal's sneeze. At the crime scene, the presence of DNA can be detected by using a laser to see if the stains are fluorescent and therefore DNA evidence may be present. (DNA is present in 60 percent of murders, assaults, and batteries; and hair is found at the scene of 10 percent of robberies and 6 percent of residential burglaries.)

There are two main methods for testing DNA. The original method, restriction fragment length polymorphism (RFLP), is accomplished by Southern blotting (named for the inventor of the process Dr. Edward Southern). RFLP was part of the first wave of biological stain testing, but it has since been supplanted by a second generation of DNA analysis methods using PCR (polymerase chain reaction). The initial PCR-based DNA profiling has been further refined with a marker system called short tandem repeats (STR). (The FBI has established the thirteen STR loci that are used in their National DNA Index System [NDIS] database of convicted offenders.)

RFLP yielded a higher statistical power of discrimination between samples, but it is best used when there is a significant amount of genetic matter present—semen stains, vaginal swabs, and bloodstains (larger than dime size). However, because RFLP required such large sample sizes (STR tests can be accomplished on a bloodstain smaller than the dot on this "i") and takes so long to accomplish (weeks as compared to STR's hours) RFLP is generally no longer used in forensic DNA identification. Because PCR uses a process of amplification (the chain of DNA is copied in the laboratory until enough exists to test from), smaller amounts of DNA are needed for analysis and PCR can be used on items with minute amounts of DNA (cigarette butts, envelopes, fingernails, telephone receivers, fecal matter, vomit, vaginal slides, blood spatters, and old stains). Additionally, the results of PCR testing are more effective on degraded samples.

Once the profile has been created, the markers of the suspect's test are matched to the DNA specimen taken from a crime scene. If the patterns match, then the geneticist uses biostatistics to gauge the possibility of two people having the same profile. The mathematics is the formal version of the following intuitive experiment. If you were asked to go stand on the street corner and predict how long you would stand there until you saw a blue Ford go by, you would predict that you would not stand there very long at all. Conversely, if you were asked to predict how long it would be until you saw a Rolls Royce Silver Cloud, you would argue that it might be years or decades. In DNA profiling numbers, you would have to stand there far longer than the acknowledged age of the earth. In a recent DNA case in Rhode Island, the match statistic was greater than 1 in 1×10^{17}, that's 1 in 100,000,000,000,000,000.

In cases that are unsuitable for RFLP or nuclear DNA PCR testing, mitochondrial (the mitochondria is a part of the cytoplasm of the cell) DNA (mtDNA) testing can be performed on dried bones and teeth, hair shafts, or any sample that has been highly degraded. A limitation of testing mitochondrial DNA is that the genetic information contained within the mitochondria of the cell is only from the mother of the donor.

DNA testing can be problematic under certain circumstances and in multidefendant crimes or, say, when the victim of rape conceals the identity of a consensual sexual partner within forty-eight hours of the attack, or when the perpetrator or perpetrators do not ejaculate. The accuracy of DNA profiling is also compromised in cases where the sample has degraded, the subject has had a blood transfusion, in bodies that have been embalmed (with the exception of bone and plucked hair), in tissue samples that have been submerged for more than a few hours in formaldehyde or formalin, and in urine stains. Also, DNA collected from leather, dirt, or any surface that is dirty— carpets, shoes, car upholstery, and vegetable matter (grass, trees, leaves)—can be difficult to test. However, new and more powerful methods of recovering DNA from biological material are mitigating even these problems.

DNA profiling works better than the older methods for biological analysis, including serology and hair-matching analysis, because it is more discriminating, has greater standards of proof and efficiency, and is therefore more likely to exonerate the innocent and indict the guilty. DNA is also more stable than the polymorphic proteins in blood, and degradation does not lead to erroneous typing results. Serology can only discern A, B, O blood types, sex, and species; and although these facts narrow the field of possibilities, they cannot determine the individual's identity with pinpoint accuracy, as DNA is able to do.

In my view, the lack of funding for DNA forensics in the United States is a national outrage. The United Kingdom is matching five to seven hundred crime scenes a week. In the United States we are probably matching fewer than one hundred per week. In this country, for DNA testing to be truly successful, comprehensive laws allowing for the collection of DNA need to be made federal. DNA collection is currently regulated by state laws, and although many states allow for the DNA testing of all those arrested for felony offenses, every state, including New York, should test suspected offenders. In New York State the legislature has limited DNA sampling and testing to a narrow category of violent crimes, and currently the expansion of the law regarding testing all felony offenses is in the state senate. In New York, we are able to get DNA samples from all inmates convicted after January 1, 1996, for any one of twenty-one violent crimes, including murder, manslaughter, and rape. Additionally, although many states do collect DNA samples, they have only profiled a small percentage of the samples with PCR, the more advanced technique of DNA profiling. The federal government is also remiss in the use of DNA. The federal government, like New York State, have also limited their DNA fingerprinting to convicted criminals and not arrestees.

Currently legislation is divergent in many states and like the United Kingdom, the United States needs to have a uniform law regarding the collection of DNA. Since 1985, the British have gathered DNA profiles on almost a million criminals and suspected criminals, and the number continues to grow with each arrest. Each person arrested, be it for a misdemeanor or a felony, must give a DNA sample; the sample is retrieved at the scene from the suspect by swabbing the inside of the suspect's cheek with a buchal swab. Although DNA is used by Scotland Yard and local police primarily to solve violent crimes, there have been unexpected benefits in combating burglary and robbery. Because violent criminals often commit misdemeanors and nonviolent crimes (in Humberside, England, they identified a murderer from the DNA of a man arrested for drunk driving), it is important that we do DNA testing for every person arrested for a fingerprintable offense.

Since the United Kingdom started requiring mandatory DNA profiling for all recordable offenses, over 100,000 suspects have been matched to crime scenes. With each profile entered into the databank, the possibility of a cold hit grows exponentially. The proof of the efficacy of DNA profiling and data banking is seen in the results of the U.K.'s Forensic Science Service (FSS): Because of the volume of samples in the FSS (over 1 million), a DNA sample taken at the scene of a crime has a 40 percent chance of matching an existing profile.

In an attempt to build a cohesive DNA data-banking system, the FBI has assembled their Combined DNA Index System (CODIS)—renamed the National DNA Index System (NDIS) in 1998—a DNA database similar to the fingerprint system (AFIS) that links state's and the District of Columbia's local data banks. In 1994, the DNA Identification Act authorized the FBI to set up CODIS, under which DNA profiles are tracked using three indexes: convicted offenders, unknown suspects, and population samples (for statistical comparisons only). Unfortunately, the backlog of samples to be processed now exceeds half a million because of the lack of local and federal resources dedicated to the project.

Worse, many samples entered into CODIS are part of NDIS and were analyzed with RFLP so that when the FBI switched over to PCR based testing in 1999, the preexisting samples were rendered obsolete. Additionally new samples need to be taken and tested from around 250,000 convicted felons, while another 250,000 DNA samples already taken from convicted felons are awaiting input into the database. Yet for all of its limitations, even CODIS, and now NDIS, have had some success. Since its inception in October of 1998, NDIS has aided in some way over 4,200 investigations; and in June 2002, the one-millionth DNA sample was entered into NDIS—a major milestone in the mission to create a network for over 130 state, local, and federal laboratories.

Our ability to database DNA is the future in terms of crime reduction. It is clear to me that greater success with DNA profiling and data banking depends on federal government funding for processing the country's unanalyzed DNA samples. To process the entire backlog of DNA samples in the United States would be an expense of about $1 billion—the cost of one less B1 Bomber—but in testing the samples, thousands of future crimes could be prevented. The benefits of instituting a standardized and cohesive system for collecting and testing DNA would far outweigh the costs of testing the backlog and establishing and maintaining a central DNA database. Money would end up being saved in court costs—once a criminal or a defense attorney is told that the police have DNA evidence, they would consent to a plea agreement quickly, saving the tax payer and the government costs in trial expenditures and preventing unnecessary investigations of those who would be excluded by DNA profiling.

Another obstacle to DNA fingerprinting is the opposition of civil libertarians. The ACLU has launched court challenges to DNA data banks in several states, and the constitutionality of DNA data banks has yet to be addressed by the Supreme Court. Claiming that collecting DNA data is Orwellian, the ACLU has tried to block the institution of DNA testing and the process of archiving samples. They argue that DNA collection will lead to genetic discrimination if insurance companies and employers can access the samples collected by law enforcement. What the ACLU has not taken into account is that the short tandem repeat (STR) samples that are so important to police are actually "junk DNA"—or DNA that does not encode information about the individual's genetic markers or predisposition to disease. STR, the faster, less expensive, and more effective method, analyzes only areas of the DNA strand that doesn't indicate a predisposition for disease or genetic markers.

A law that requires that all original DNA samples are destroyed after the bar codes have been extracted could easily remedy this. In New York we wrote a statute that makes it a felony to use DNA information for anything other than for the purpose of identifying criminals. Civil libertarians also contend that taking DNA from unwilling prisoners infringes a citizen's Fourth Amendment rights, which prohibit unreasonable searches and seizures. In a case decided by the Massachusetts's Supreme Court in 2000, the ACLU argued that taking blood from the state's violent convicts to set up a DNA database was invasive. The high court of Massachusetts disagreed and found that "particularly reliable form of identification outweighs the minimal invasion of a pin prick." Today there is not even a pinprick: The buchal swab is gently slid along the inside of the cheek, and collects a person's saliva—as a technique, it is far less intrusive.

DNA samples should be taken from all arrestees, violent or not, along with fingerprints and mugshots. If there is no prosecution of the suspect, then that person's DNA profile would be destroyed. In response to the civil libertarians' position that taking DNA samples from arrestees means that DNA evidence will still be at law-enforcement's disposal (even if the suspect is exonerated) and violates the "innocent until proven guilty" premise upon which our legal system operates, my solution would be much the same as the way in which fingerprint samples are disposed of.

DNA was used to identify many World Trade Center victims, and the fifty thousand bones that were not identified through PCR testing are now being tested for mitochondrial DNA (mtDNA).

Another possible use of DNA profiling is Homeland Security. I would like all immigrants to this country to be required to give a DNA sample that would be coded into their identification cards. This would help the government to track aliens and locate possible threats to national security. Another way DNA can safeguard lives is that it should be taken from infants at birth to identify them. The recent spate of abductions and murders of children have made this even more relevant. In this way the genetic code of the child, which would be kept by the parents in a private storage facility, could be examined and compared to the findings of investigators in these cases.

Scientists are already working on high-tech portable labs that utilize microchip technology and have the capability of analyzing DNA at the scene of the crime. In the future we will have developed a device where you will be able to take a blood sample and extract the DNA from the blood right on the spot and then transmit the code by radio to a central database and get a response within thirty seconds. There is already a company that has developed a chip to analyze DNA but the technology to extract it has yet to be developed.

As we've seen in New York and elsewhere, DNA is the most important tool of twenty-first-century policing, and once DNA testing and collection has been standardized, and a national database successfully instituted, the possibilities of DNA testing in fighting crime are limitless. In the courts juries will start to question prosecutors who offer inconclusive DNA findings if the evidence is available, and over time postconviction DNA testing will subside as testing is performed in all cases where biological evidence is present and relevant. DNA is used to identify perpetrators and exclude the innocent, and DNA profiling will prevent the investigation of many innocent people by immediately excluding them as suspects. If we could eliminate suspects immediately, instead of putting people under surveillance, checking their bank records, and questioning neighbors, the police would be able to focus their time on solving cases and save money and time. Only the guilty should worry about DNA testing.

6.

MURDER

In the early 1990s, New York City was host to approximately two thousand homicides each year. The lawlessness was subsiding in 1996 when I took office, but the number of yearly homicides in the five boroughs still hovered around one thousand. In the four years that I was commissioner, we cut that number almost in half. Criminologists attribute the drop in the murder rate to an improved economy, the end of the crack epidemic, tougher gun laws, and the increased prison population. I think that it had more to do with effective and innovative policing strategies.

NYPD detectives were called on to be aggressive in their pursuit of investigations: they were to solve cold cases, conduct debriefings, apprehend accomplices, conduct sting operations, and investigate suspects; and they were expected to track down and monitor known criminals, recidivists, and parolees. Precincts have a Detective Squad that is assigned to every case, and a detective is assigned at the precinct level. If the case becomes more complex, or part of a pattern that crosses precinct and borough boundary lines, or for a major or a specific crime, more seasoned investigators from the borough's Detective Squad will assist in the investigation and help with coordination and manpower.

Detectives work in various squads, units, divisions, and task forces, and each of the city's eight borough commands has its own Detective Squad that takes care of local homicides, rapes, robberies, and burglaries. Some cases, depending on their nature, will be referred to a squad operating from Police Plaza or from federal buildings in downtown Manhattan, or to citywide joint task forces. Certain borough commands have additional units that specialize in certain types of robberies and burglaries, while others focus on atypical assaults or homicide investigations. For example, a pattern of homicides would be referred by precinct detectives to the Special Investigations Unit or Homicide Unit of the Detective Borough headquarters in which the pattern occurred.

Homicide cases are tough, and you can throw the energies of your detective squads into homicide investigations with varying results. One pattern-killing case that the NYPD solved after years of trying was that of the Zodiac Killer. After Son of Sam, the Zodiac is New York City's most infamous killer, and we dedicated manpower and resources only to have destiny step in and give us a lucky break. On November 17, 1989, the Seventy-fifth Precinct in East New York, Brooklyn, received an anonymous letter on white paper and illustrated with a zodiac wheel. It was signed "the Zodiac" and vowed to kill twelve people, one for each astrological sign. A desk officer received the letter and, thinking it was a crank, did nothing about it.

Four months later, on March 8, 1990, Mario Orozco was walking home from his job as a dishwasher when he was shot. He survived with a bullet lodged in his spinal cord. Three weeks later, German Montenegro was shot in the same area of New York that Orozco had been, near Highland Park, an area that straddles Brooklyn and Queens. Although he also survived, Orozco was left permanently crippled.

A pattern of violence emerged on May 31 when Joseph Proce, a senior citizen suffering from Alzheimer's, was attacked and shot. Proce subsidized his income by collecting food from garbage pails and cans for deposit refunds, and as Proce was walking through the hall of his building on Eighty-seventh Road in East New York, a young man approached him and asked him for a glass of water. Proce rebuffed him and turned to open his door, when the man took out a gun and shot him in the back. At that scene he left a folded note, with three stones on it.

Detectives in Queens had started an investigation into the Proce case when another letter was sent to a writer for the *New York Post*. A copy of the *Post* letter was sent to the squad. The letter had the same zodiacal wheel found on the original letter sent to the precinct, and the same handwriting as the Proce letter. This is when investigators made a connection between the shootings, and on June 1, 1990, formed the Zodiac Task Force, which consisted of sixty-five detectives assigned exclusively to the case.

Now the neighborhoods on the Queens-Brooklyn border had something else besides drug-related violence to worry about; there was a homicidal maniac randomly shooting victims according to their date of birth. The community's fear was stoked by extensive media coverage of the letters and the shootings, which detectives had determined were happening at twenty-one-day intervals.

On June 21, Larry Parham, a homeless man, was shot in Central Park. Detectives on the Zodiac Task Force attributed the location change to the media hype and the increased police presence in East New York. To avoid detection the Zodiac caught a train to Manhattan and had the luxury of the solitude of Central Park in the middle of the night. Next to Parham's body, a note was found with the Zodiac's signature and an upside-down cross. This was the fourth shooting, and it occurred next to the city's most affluent neighborhood, and right under the nose of the NYPD. From the Parham letter, investigators were able to recover a partial print, and the media broadcasted the discovery.

The intense scrutiny and the latent print sent the Zodiac underground for almost two years, and after a period of inactivity on the part of the shooter, the Zodiac Task Force disbanded in November 1990.

Then, on August 21, 1992, Patricia Fonti, a mentally disabled woman, was fatally stabbed exactly one hundred times in Highland Park. Highland Park is a large park with a reservoir, and detectives believe that the Zodiac, who had felt very comfortable shooting Larry Parham in Central Park, had found another place with no people, no traffic, and trees and underbrush to shield his murderous activities.

On June 4, 1993, James Weber was shot in the leg in Highland Park, and on July 21, Joseph Diacone was shot in the neck across the street from the park. Diacone died, making him the Zodiac's third homicide victim. On October 2, 1993, Diane Ballard was shot in Highland Park— she would survive the attack but was permanently disabled. She was the Zodiac's final victim.

In the case of Patricia Fonti, where the Zodiac stabbed her one hundred times, detectives think that he may have been there for hours, and that the switch from shooting to stabbing was an indicator of the additional time provided by this privacy. A jogger found Fonti's body on top of an overgrown bridge that is one of two that stretch across the reservoir. She was stabbed and beaten, but there was no evidence of sexual attack. Fonti, who was in her thirties, like all of the Zodiac's victims had problems: She was emotionally disturbed and on prescribed medication.

The shootings in Highland Park, which is on the border of the Seventy-fifth, the 102nd, and the 104th Precincts, were in different precincts (two shootings were in the Seventy-fifth and two were on the Queens side), and investigators failed to put the crimes together. Of his victims Diane Ballard was the only one who was able to positively identify him. In all of his attacks he had sneaked up behind his victims—in some cases he wore a scarf around his face—so the victims could not give a decent description. We even had a sketch of a large black man circulating. Because Diane Ballard heard someone rushing her from behind, she turned and looked at the Zodiac, and her sketch resembled a Hispanic male.

After this batch of stabbings and shootings, the Zodiac Killer sent a letter to the Seventy-fifth Precinct postmarked August 1, 1994. At this point Lt. Joseph Herbert, the homicide sergeant on the Detective Squad for the Seventy-fifth Precinct, got involved. This letter had maritime flags; and when detectives from the precinct cracked the code it said: "This is the Zodiac speaking, I am in control . . . Who is the master. Be ready for more."

On the left-hand side of the page, the Zodiac wrote: "This is the Zodiac." Under the maritime flags was a diagram with, "NYPD-0" and underneath was the Zodiac's characteristic cross, indicating him and the number nine, next to a smiley face. And, most chillingly, he scrawled at the bottom of the letter: "Sleep my dead how we loathe them."

In the margin of the letter he listed the four incidents that detectives knew of, and also a fifth victim. Investigators turned Highland Park upside down looking for the fifth victim, they even used heat recognition aircraft flying over the park, but they were unable to locate the victim. What they believe is that he probably shot at, and missed, a homeless man who never reported the shooting.

The letter spurred the formation of the second Zodiac Task Force, and Herbert and twenty-five dedicated detectives started hunting again for the Zodiac Killer. There was a lot of detective work that really didn't pan out, but one thing did. The Zodiac Task Force went a mile and a half out from Highland Park each way—North, South, East, West—and got the names of people who'd been arrested. We ran a list of all arrestees.

Because the bullets used by the Zodiac had no grooves, the task force knew it wasn't a standard gun. It was a zip gun, or the Zodiac had filed down the barrel of the gun. When they did the grid of arrestees in the immediate area, they also surveyed for zip gun arrests on the back of each arrest report.

One person who had been on the list of 4,600 suspects was a resident of East New York, a man named Heriberto Seda. In March 1994, NYPD officers arrested Seda for possession of a .22-cal. zip gun outside his home on Pitkin Avenue and held him for eight days; but since the gun was inoperable, the charges against him were dropped and he was released. When the charges were dropped, Seda's fingerprints were sealed, as where those of 1,800 of the 4,600 arrestees. There was nothing specific to Heriberto Seda where we could try to unseal his fingerprints, and the list was too long to legally unseal every file.

Another obstacle to the investigation was that there was no commonality in the Zodiac's killings. As far as we could tell, he didn't know any of the victims; and we knew that they didn't know each other. Many serial killers will stay with one kind of victim, but the Zodiac shot at, and in some cases killed, everyone from a female white, Patricia Fonti; to a male white, Orozco; from male Hispanic, Montenegro; to a male black, Parham; and, finally, a female black, Ballard.

In 1995, the Zodiac Task Force had exhausted all its leads and wrapped up their investigation. Herbert had returned to his squad when, on June 18, 1996, at about noon, he got a phone call from the Detective Borough Brooklyn and the dispatcher told him that there was a hostage negotiator needed in the Seventy-fifth Precinct.

Herbert had recently taken a hostage-negotiation class, and this was his first hostage job. When he arrived, the area was cordoned off and swarming with police officers and Emergency Services personnel. Herbert found out that Heriberto Seda, a resident of Pitkin Avenue, had shot his teenage sister Gladys in an argument over a male visitor. When the police responded to the 911 call, Seda had barricaded himself in the apartment and started firing on them. Gladys had been able to get out, but he was still holding her boyfriend.

Police erected a barricade outside the building for Herbert to stand behind, and he attempted to engage Seda in conversation; but Seda only came to the third-floor window of his apartment occasionally. When he did appear at the window, he had a military helmet on and he was pointing a barrel—it looked like a rifle—right at Herbert, screaming, "Get everyone out of here. Get the cops out of here."

Herbert kept trying to engage him, while an Emergency Service Unit (ESU) evacuated the building. They tried to lower a phone from the roof, but Seda didn't want to communicate and had ripped out his own phone line. At a certain point Seda stopped responding until Herbert, Sgt. Kenny Bowen, and members of ESU climbed through a first-floor window and went upstairs and stood outside his apartment door.

Herbert was still doing most of the talking when, at around 3:30 P.M. Seda started talking. He asked Herbert, "How's my sister?"

Herbert responded, "Your sister's doing well. It's not life threatening."

Then Seda said, "I want to surrender, but what should I do about my bombs?"

Officers immediately started to devise a plan with Emergency Services and the Bomb Squad and Herbert was instructed to tell Seda not to touch the bombs, and that they were going to lower a bucket from the roof and wanted him to put his guns into it; in total they retrieved three buckets of guns, six assembled zip guns, and parts to make another three.

Seda was told to open the door with his hands up, and they arrested him. Once he was handcuffed, the Bomb Squad went into the apartment, where they found two improvised, explosive devices ready to go and smoke grenades.

They brought Seda to the Seventy-fifth Precinct and put him in the interrogation room. That day it was 100 degrees and Herbert went to get a drink of water and pick up his car at the scene, while Det. Dan Powers from the Seventy-fifth Squad, who was assigned to the shooting of Seda's sister, asked that Seda write out a statement.

When Herbert got back, Powers, and another former Zodiac Task Force member, Det. Tommy Maher, brought him Seda's confession to the shooting of his sister and the hostage situation. Herbert, who was the expert on the Zodiac, looked at it, and the *S*s, the *T*s, and the *N*s, were familiar. Then Herbert turned to the second page where there was the upside-down cross with the 7s. He looked at the letter and said to Maher and Powers, "As sure as I am standing here, this is the Zodiac Killer."

The three went back to the command room and developed a plan to make their suspicions probable cause. The first thing they did was fingerprint Seda and run the prints against the partial print from Larry Parham's letter. They also ran the guns through ballistics. By the end of the night it was determined that the fingerprints matched, and that three of the guns matched three of the ballistics on bullets taken out of the victims. Now they had rock-solid evidence. Later that evidence was etched in stone when we matched Seda's DNA to that of the person who licked the envelopes of the letters sent to the NYPD and the *New York Post*. (It would turn out that the DNA evidence indicated that Seda was a 1 in 6 million match in a database of Hispanics.)

Herbert, Det. Lou Savarese, another former member of the Zodiac Task Force, and Det. Danny Powers conducted an eight-hour interrogation of Seda. Whenever they brought up the subject of the Zodiac, he would deflect to another subject. Then they used a little psychology on him and put Zodiac crime-scene photographs on the wall. Seda finally broke and started to talk about Fonti. He said, "Alright, I met her outside the YMCA," and then he started talking. He stated that he had gotten her onto the bridge by offering her a cigarette. She had originally asked him for a cigarette, but he didn't have any, so he found a piece of paper and rolled it up to look like a cigarette and lured her up to the bridge where he killed her.

Seda's justification for his killings was that he was cleansing society of its dregs, the homeless, the drug addicted, the mentally ill, and we found out later that he'd informed on local drug dealers. He himself was looking at a bleak future. As a high school dropout, and army reject, Seda lived with his mother, had never worked a day in his life, and supported himself by stealing quarters out of parking meters.

The people in the East New York neighborhood were thrilled. The Zodiac had terrified them. In 1993, the Seventy-fifth Precinct had 129 homicides, 10 percent of those in the city—and was a notorious crime location. Then you had the Zodiac adding to the fear, writing letters to the press and the police, and randomly shooting people.

A mystery remains as to how he knew the signs of his first four victims. What we did know was that with his first four victims he was into the zodiac signs, and with the last four he got away from that. As far as detectives could tell he had never asked anyone their sign. However, when they found Larry Parham, his bag, his shoes, and his wallet were next to him, and it's possible that Seda had checked his identification then. Montenegro claimed that his passport was stolen, and Proce would talk to strangers, so maybe he had a conversation without them realizing. This is only speculation; we never found out.

In May 1999, Seda went on trial in Queens for the second-degree murders of Diacone, Fonti, and Proce, and the attempted murder of Weber. A month later he was convicted on all counts and for these crimes he was sentenced to 83.3 years to life in jail. He was also tried in Brooklyn for shooting his sister, firing at police, and three attempted murders; and he was sentenced to a consecutive sentence of 152 years, giving him a total sentence of 235.3 years. Thanks to the excellent work of Herbert, Powers, Maher, and Savarese, the case of the Zodiac Killer was solved.

Having a serial killer on the loose is a worst-case scenario, but a police officer's regular fare is one of rape, theft, and murder, as well as robbery, burglary, and assault. With declining murder rates, during the late 1990s came a greater sense of security in communities like East New York that were plagued by crime, but even neighborhoods usually considered safest are touched by violence.

A mansion in Manhattan's Upper East Side was the location of a groundbreaking homicide investigation by the NYPD. In this case we knew who had committed the crime immediately, but with no forensic evidence, no body, and no admission or confession, it seemed impossible to prove. It was the murder of Irene Silverman, a wealthy eighty-two-year-old widow, who was reported missing on July 5, 1998.

It was a Sunday, not a typical weekend day because of the holiday, and the city was very quiet. Silverman's block, Sixty-fifth Street between Madison and Fifth, is always quiet, but that day it was exceptionally so. At around 5:00 P.M. Silverman's friend Jeff Fried put in a call to the Nineteenth Precinct and said, "I believe we have a missing person up here on East Sixty-fifth Street."

The police responded to the call as they typically would—they filed a missing person's report and started a canvass looking for her. Given her age Silverman was deemed as a "special category." She was frail and needed help to get around, so there wasn't very far that she was going to go, and we handled her disappearance differently than that of a forty-five year old who didn't come home last night.

Silverman's disappearance was starting to look to the precinct's detectives like more than a missing person's investigation. Investigators from the Manhattan North Special Investigations Division, led by Dep. Insp. Joseph

Reznick, now commanding officer of the Bronx detectives, were brought in to investigate a potential abduction or homicide. The investigation was commenced and detectives started questioning Silverman's staff. During this phase of the investigation, detectives searched the area around the Silverman town house for the elderly woman with dogs, helicopters, and every conceivable piece of equipment.

Unknown to the investigators on East Sixty-fifth Street, across town on Fifty-fifth Street and Eighth Avenue, the FBI's Joint Fugitive Task Force was locking up a twenty-three-year-old man, Kenny Kimes, and his mother, Sante, sixty-three, outside of the Hilton Hotel for writing a bad check for a car they had purchased in Utah. This arrest was a ruse to question the Kimeses for the murder of David Kazdin. After the discovery of Kazdin's body on March 14, the LAPD had contacted the NYPD and the FBI's Joint Fugitive Task Force when authorities had gotten wind that the Kimeses would be in New York. NYPD detectives and FBI agents from the Joint Fugitive Task Force had located the Kimeses and, using a friend of theirs, Stan Patterson, as bait they had arrested them at the Hilton.

When Fugitive Task Force (FTF) detectives searched the Kimeses, they found in their possession some papers and identification of Irene Silverman. It should have aroused suspicions, but they didn't ask them anything, instead they incarcerated the Kimes, charged them with For Other Agency (FOA), for the Utah charges, and lodged them in our court system.

Back on the Upper East Side detectives were questioning tenants and staff of Silverman's town house, which was subdivided into luxury apartments that she rented out to well-heeled tenants. We found that one tenant, a

Manny Guerin, was also missing. Additionally, Guerin, it was clear from notes and diagrams the woman had made before her disappearance, had made Irene Silverman nervous.

By Monday, July 6, we had a sketch of the missing occupant of apartment 1B. All suspicions were that whoever that man was he had something to do with Irene Silverman's disappearance. Dep. Ins. Reznick went to the media for a press conference with the sketch and the notification that: "We are missing Irene Silverman. And we are also looking for this gentleman, whom she may be in company with."

The press conference paid off, when the next morning, Tuesday, July 7, Det. Edward Murray, who had locked up Kenny Kimes the Sunday evening prior, heard the news on the radio and the name Irene Silverman. Murray called the Nineteenth Precinct and advised them that he had arrested a Kenny Kimes who was in possession of the identification of the missing woman.

Detectives rushed to the courthouses, but to their disappointment Kenny Kimes had already been arraigned. He had gone before a judge and was on Riker's Island, and his counsel advised him not to speak with detectives. His mother, Sante, had not been arraigned, so investigators took her out of the courthouse and walked her across the street to the Federal Building.

At the Federal Building detectives from Special Investigations interrogated her for six hours. She sustained the questioning, denying any association with Silverman or her disappearance. Their impression of Sante Kimes was that she was a hard-core con artist, and detectives realizing that they were dealing with a professional, gave up, and put her into the system. From there on they dealt with her through her attorneys.

We had a missing eighty-two-year-old woman and detectives knew that there was a connection between her and the Kimeses, but we didn't know what it was. We searched the Kimeses' Lincoln Town Car for evidence and found a variety of items: a key from a hotel locker, notebooks, pillows, documents, passports, bank books, a collection of wigs, a GLOCK semiautomatic handgun, and a bag with $30,000 in cash.

The key puzzled detectives. It was from the Plaza Hotel and was inscribed with a number. Detectives canvassed the hotel and other midtown hotels looking for the piece of luggage they believed that the key belonged to. The biggest break in the case came on July 24 when they seized a black bag belonging to the Kimeses at the Plaza Hotel, which contained forged documents signing over Irene Silverman's residence to a fictional corporation, the Atlantis Group. The deed in the black bag at the Plaza was clearly forged. When Kenny Kimes first paid the $6,000 rent, he had asked for a receipt from Irene Silverman and she had signed it. That identical signature was the one that appeared on the forged document. All they did was trace it. We subsequently learned that the Kimeses had a notary public come to Silverman's residence to notarize the deed, while Sante Kimes impersonated Irene Silverman.

Silverman's home is currently on the market for $3.5 million, and for small-time hustlers like Sante and Kenny Kimes this was a big score. They planned to file the notarized deed with the city in the afternoon on a day before a holiday weekend. They got to the City Clerk's Office, but because it was right before the July 4 holiday, and one of the certified checks was in the name of Manny Guerin, the Kimeses were unable to file the deed to Silverman's home.

That is how they ended up at the Hilton. Sante and

Kenny were stuck in the city over the weekend waiting for Monday morning when they would file the deed and skip town. Their arrest on Sunday evening was a huge shock, and had they not been picked up they would have taken possession of the town house. They had recruited a California man, Stan Patterson (the same man that the Joint Fugitive Task Force used to lure them), to act as the super of the building, and he had been instructed by Sante to tell anyone—the police, friends and associates of Silverman—to call the Atlantis Group.

We starting learning that prior to Silverman's July 5 disappearance a lot had taken place. For instance, we learned through various records (phone records and through Irene Silverman and Sante Kimeses' notes) that June 14 was when Sante and Kenny had arrived in New York.

To understand the time line, detectives tracked their movements across the country. The starting point was Los Angeles, where they had allegedly killed a businessman, David Kazdin. Kazdin had been an insurance claims adjuster who had written a 1973 insurance claim on a tapestry belonging to Sante and her deceased husband, Kenneth Kimes Sr. Since the claim Kazdin had become friendly with the senior Kimes and Sante and allowed himself to be listed as a coowner of a Las Vegas property belonging to the Kimes so that they could shield part of their assets.

In March 1998, Kazdin was found dead, shot in the head and wrapped in a plastic bag, in a Dumpster near Los Angeles International Airport. Detectives from the LAPD investigating the case made the connection between Kazdin and the Kimeses, and they were suspects in his murder.

On March 23, the Kimeses headed back to Las Vegas

from where they started their trip across country using Route 10, right into Lake Worth, Florida, and then up to New York City. In Utah they bought a new green Lincoln Town Car and wrote a bad check for it. It was this check that would later get them arrested in New York.

While they were in Texas, they stopped in a trailer camp and asked a resident to use their shower. While they were in the trailer, they stole identification that was used to purchase a cell phone in Florida. In Florida they bought a stun gun and looked at an apartment for rent. While viewing the apartment, they went into the super's wallet and stole an ID, which they used to get a supermarket check-cashing card. The Kimeses random scams and frauds only added to the complexity of the investigation.

At this point they were traveling with a transient man, Shawn Little, and a woman named Roberta Inglis. Inglis got sick somewhere in Louisiana, and they pushed her out on the road; and in Florida, Shawn Little had decided that there was something wrong with the Kimeses and had left.

They made a stop while in Louisiana in a trailer camp and got a price on a new motorhome. They asked the woman who was selling it to deliver it to them in Lake Worth, where they would pay for it in full. When she met them in Florida several weeks later, she became another potential murder victim. During dinner she saw the Kimeses concocting something in her drink that they tried to force her to drink, which she adamantly refused. She was definitely under the impression that they were trying to kill her, and she took her motorhome and escaped. Detectives figured that in this case their scam was to get the motorhome without paying for it.

On June 12, they headed up to New York, but they got there a day early, so on June 13 they stayed in a motel in Jersey City. In Florida, Sante and Kenny had been joined by a Cuban man named Jose Alvarez, whom they had met at a chicken place where he worked. Although he barely spoke English, they asked him to come to New York with them. Alvarez had no involvement with the Kimeses' crimes.

On June 14, they drove into New York from Jersey City. In Manhattan the Puerto Rican Day parade was taking place, there was a massive amount of traffic, and Fifth Avenue was shut down. They parked on Sixty-third Street and walked over to Silverman's town house. Once there Kenny went in and paid the $6,000 rent in cash under the pseudonym Manny Guerin.

Right from the beginning, he asked Silverman, "What's your social security number," and Silverman, who noted this interchange in her notebooks, was taken aback, and responded, "Why would you need that? I am renting to you." They didn't give up, and Sante called Irene several times in an attempt to get Silverman's social security number to steal her identity. In one instance Sante told her that she'd won a prize to a place out in Las Vegas, however, to claim the prize, they were going to need Silverman's social security number.

The apartment that Kenny Kimes rented was 1B, a studio apartment on the ground floor. Originally Silverman had thought she was renting to one person but realized—when Sante arrived and Jose too—that she was renting to three. Around June 20, Alvarez sensed that something was really wrong and left Silverman's building and the Kimeses. He went to Central Park, spent the night, and found out there was a Cuban community in Union City, Jersey. He made his way there—detectives tracked him through a paycheck he got someone to cash from the chicken place—and then down to Florida.

Meanwhile back on Sixty-fifth Street, Irene Silverman

was telling people that she didn't like her new tenant, and that there was something wrong with Manny Guerin. We learned all this through conversations we had with her employees, who also noticed strange things: Guerin wouldn't let anyone into the apartment to clean and every time he came and went from the building he would hug the wall in the lobby to avoid being videotaped by the closed-circuit camera. One of the workers noticed Jose Alvarez, in addition to Sante, and they all wondered what was going on.

Silverman asked her friend Jeff Fried, "What can we do to get him out of here?" She told Fried she was willing to give Guerin back his money. By July 4, Irene Silverman had had it, and for the holiday she had a little party on her roof for her employees and friends. She told them that the next day she was going to confront Guerin and his female companion and throw them out.

Detectives think that the Kimeses overheard that announcement through the courtyard or backyard of the building, and that because of their eavesdropping Sante and Kenny decide to move up the day of Silverman's murder to July 5. If they didn't hear it through the garden, they certainly heard something over the phone lines. Greatly to their advantage, the phone connections ran through apartment 1B, and in our investigation we discovered that they had wiretapped all of the phones and had listened to Irene's conversations.

At this point Special Division detectives had formed a task force dedicated to solving Silverman's disappearance, and Reznick took his seventeen best detectives and dedicated them to the investigation. The task force grouped detectives into specialties; for example, phone records had two investigators working exclusively on them, and the careful organization of the investigation was critical to solving the case and making it stick in court.

Detectives figured out what happened to Irene Silverman that Sunday by plotting phone records. We found out that Irene Silverman's last conversation was with a friend in New Jersey at 11:31, and the phone call lasted ten minutes. This would be the last person to speak with her besides her murderers. This call put her in her office on Sunday, July 5, 1998, at 11:41, when she hung up the phone.

This is what investigators think happened: Kenny went to the office and asked for a *Barron's* or a *Wall Street Journal*. She told him, "I don't have it." She made a note of his appearance and the fact that he was not wearing shoes (detectives think that he was in socks so as not to make any noise) and this notation was the last indication that she was alive. Kenny went back to 1B and gave his mother the green light. The door to 1B was right next to the elevator, and we suspect that as Silverman went to the elevator to go to her apartment, Kenny grabbed her, dragged her into the apartment, and strangled her.

He then hog-tied her 5'2" body, placed it in a shower curtain, and rolled it up. He took the wrapped body and double bagged it with two black plastic bags. We were confident about the plastic bags because we found a box of them with two bags missing and no bags around the apartment. There was some question whether he used a black zipper bag to put her in. Regardless, we think he walked her right out the front door, opened the trunk of the car, and put her body in it.

The Lincoln Town Car provided some evidence, but none of it forensic. We found spiral notebooks with Sante Kimes's notes, and a key that led us to more incriminatory notebooks in the black bag at the Plaza. After her disappearance, we found drops of blood lengthwise on the pavement outside Silverman's mansion, and we sent it out for DNA; it came back negative because UV rays from the sun degrades DNA samples.

We took samples from Silverman's hairbrush and toothbrush and analyzed them, and a small fleck of blood on the Lincoln's seatbelt were tested; the results were disappointing—they did not match Silverman's DNA. We checked for fingerprints on the hundreds of pages of paper that we found in the car, and we tested a saliva stain on a pillow found in the car and the hair found in a duffel bag that was also in the Lincoln Town Car.

All of these tests came back negative and failed to place Silverman in the company of the Kimeses after her disappearance. The circumstantial evidence, the criminal complaints, and the dead and missing bodies that littered the Kimeses' recent past, including two businessmen, David Kazdin, who was found in a Dumpster, and Syed Bilal Ahmed, whose body was never found, made it clear to us that we had the right people. To prove this beyond a reasonable doubt, we went through every item found in the Kimeses' possession and tested each. I received daily, sometimes hourly, reports on the case, and although circumstantial evidence kept piling up, we needed something more concrete to give to the district attorney to ensure that the Kimeses would be indicted and ultimately convicted.

Like crime-scene investigators and police officers, defense attorneys know the importance of physical evidence, especially in a case with no body. Mel Sachs, the Kimeses' lawyer used these facts in his clients' favor and was quick to point out the lack of physical evidence: "There hasn't been any blood. There hasn't been any hairs. There hasn't been any fiber. There hasn't been a single thing to link them to the disappearance of Mrs. Silverman. There is no evidence against our clients." We had circumstantial evidence, but no physical evidence. Had detectives and crime-scene investigators not been so thorough in their collection and testing of the items found in the Lincoln Town Car, the gym bag at the Plaza and Silverman's town house, the Silverman case probably would not even have gone to trial.

Just because there was no body, we did not let the Kimeses get away with murder. Reznick and his team kept going, and their work led to the indictment and conviction of Sante and Kenneth Kimes for the murder of Irene Silverman. It was the first time that a homicide case led to a conviction based on circumstantial evidence, without the discovery of a body or an admission or confession of guilt. By assembling the evidence, creating a time line and a motive, prosecutors in the Manhattan DA's Office were able to convince a jury beyond a reasonable doubt that Sante and Kenny Kimes had murdered Irene Silverman. This case, historical in its lack of forensic evidence, also set a precedent for the future. Since 1998, New York State has indicted and convicted other criminals without a body, forensic evidence, or a confession or admission.

Sante and Kenny were convicted, and each was sentenced to over 120 years in prison. In the end Kenny Kimes, in an attempt to get a more lenient sentence, hinted to detectives that he had disposed of Silverman somewhere in Jersey. In an attempt to locate the body, they videotaped every conceivable path that the Kimeses could have taken that midday in July to dispose of Silverman and returned hoping to get Kenny to view the footage and identify a route. He refused to speak with them again. So the final piece of the puzzle is still missing; and to this day the location of Irene Silverman's grave remains a mystery.

Irene Silverman's case was unique in that we were able to convict the Kimeses without physical evidence *and* after a lengthy investigation. Most murders are solved within seventy-two hours; and the longer the case remains unsolved, the less likely that the perpetrator will be brought to justice. A murder case that the NYPD opened and closed quickly with excellent detective work was the murder of thirty-one-year-old Jonathan Levin, an English teacher at William Taft High School in the Bronx. William Taft is a large city high school that serves a low-income section of the Bronx, and the students enrolled come from lower-income families, many from public-housing developments. By all accounts Levin was a well-liked teacher who took a special interest in his students. He was also the son of Gerald Levin, then-chairman of Time-Warner, something Jonathan had only recently disclosed to his students and fellow teachers.

Levin was single and lived in a modest, even rundown, one-bedroom apartment on the Upper West Side. On Friday, May 30, 1997, Levin got home from work at Taft and walked his dog on Columbus Avenue. The next day, when he failed to appear at a school event, his coworkers were concerned. On Monday, June 2, when Levin failed to arrive for his first-period English class, his coworkers were very worried. That Monday, after school, a friend and fellow teacher from Taft, Georgia Williams, and another teacher went to Levin's apartment, after calling several times. They asked neighbors if they had seen him. No one had seen Jonathan since he had walked his dog the prior Friday evening.

Now frantic, the two teachers and Levin's neighbors called the police. The police arrived and opened Levin's door with a key provided by a neighbor. They found Levin lying facedown in his own blood. He had been shot execution-style in the head, and his hands and feet were tightly bound with duct tape. His dog was locked in his cage in the kitchen, and the apartment was in disarray. Detectives were called, and in their search of the apartment they found a knapsack, a juice box, and a recording on Levin's answering machine from a former student, Corey Arthur.

Levin had gone out of his way to help Arthur, who had been in his English class during the 1993–94 school year. Levin had been a mentor to Arthur and had written a paper on his experience with the student describing the then-sixteen year old as having "a remarkable combination of talent and tragedy." Since '94, when Arthur had left school and been arrested on drug charges, the student and the teacher had grown distant, so Levin was probably surprised to get a message at around 5:00 P.M. that Friday from Arthur: "Mr. Levin, this is Corey, pick up if you're there. It's important."

We learned what transpired later from Montoun Hart, Arthur's alleged accomplice in the crime. Arthur and Hart had bumped into each other on the subway from Brooklyn into Manhattan at midafternoon that Friday. As they sat on the train, Arthur had convinced Hart to join him in a robbery that he was planning later that afternoon. Hart, who had a family to support and had dealt drugs in the past, was eager to make a little extra cash.

Once Hart and Arthur arrived at Levin's corner in the West Seventies on Columbus Avenue, Arthur called Levin from a pay phone to gain access to the building. Shortly thereafter, Levin buzzed Arthur in, and both he and Hart went upstairs. In the apartment Hart helped Arthur over-power Levin, binding and gagging him with duct tape. Now that he was restrained, Arthur began to torture Levin with a knife to extract his ATM code. He cut him multiple times on his chest and head, stabbed him in the side, and dragged the blade across his throat three times. Then, according to Hart's testimony, Arthur had told him to go into the kitchen and watch Levin's dog so that it would not bark.

While in the kitchen Hart drank a guava and orange juice and overheard Levin pleading with Arthur: "What are you going to do? Tell me, what do you want?" Then Arthur said, "I'll kill you." Now alarmed, Hart stated that he made for the door while Arthur pulled out a gun, brandished it, and shot Levin.

They left the apartment with Levin's bankcard and a credit card and at 5:15 P.M. they withdrew $800 from his account and Arthur peeled off five twenties for Hart, keeping the rest for himself. At the end of the day, Hart walked away with $100 for his trouble.

At this point Arthur and Hart split up and moved from location to location for over a week. Hot on their trail, we set up a task force whose sole purpose was to apprehend Hart and Arthur. We got Hart in Brownsville, Brooklyn, and nabbed Arthur when he called a woman whose caller-ID registered the call. We traced the call to an apartment in the Sumner Houses in Bedford Stuyvesant, Brooklyn, and arrested Arthur. We found him with a healing cut on his hand, and in his aunt's house we found bloodstained pants.

The knapsack left behind at the scene linked Arthur to the crime, as did hair and fiber testing. Detectives had found an unused .22 bullet in the knapsack left at the scene of the crime that proved to be same caliber as that used to kill Levin (the gun used in the shooting was never found) and three empty vials of crack. We found Arthur's fingerprints on the roll of duct tape used to bind Levin's hands and feet and the blood-soaked pants belonging to Arthur. DNA tests proved that the blood on the trousers was Levin's, and that the blood found on the knife used to torment the teacher was Arthur's. This evidence, and the message that Arthur had left on Levin's machine, linked Corey Arthur inextricably to the victim.

NYPD detectives working on the case deduced that both Hart and Arthur had been at Levin's apartment. Because Levin knew Arthur, he was the one with the motive to kill him. They were convinced that Arthur had shot Levin to prevent him from identifying him. But when Corey Arthur went to trial, his defense claimed that although he had been at Levin's apartment, he had not gone there to kill or rob him; he had gone there to sell him crack.

Arthur testified at his own trial, and on the stand he said that he had gone to the apartment and sold Levin crack. He claimed that as they were sitting in the living room, Levin had started smoking the crack when suddenly two men had burst in and forced Arthur to restrain Levin with the tape. Arthur testified that he had fought with one of them and fled before Levin was killed, which is how he got a cut on his hand. Because he was on probation for a fare-beating charge, and he had been at Levin's apartment to sell crack, Arthur claimed he was afraid that the police would blame him and that's why he had run away. This still didn't explain why he hadn't tried to make an anonymous call to 911.

Arthur's lawyers sought to bolster the viability of this explanation with the claim that Levin had used drugs and that investigators had found paraphernalia in his apartment. But when the medical examiner autopsied Levin and did a toxicology report, they found none of the basic drugs in his system.

Corey Arthur was convicted of second-degree murder and two counts of armed robbery and sentenced to up to twenty-five years in jail. The reason he did not receive a first-degree murder conviction was that the jury was unsure whether Arthur had fired the fatal shot. Reasonable doubt was introduced by another strain of DNA at the scene, Hart's presence, and the fact that the gun was never retrieved. Regardless, Judge Kahn gave Arthur the maximum sentence because of the depravity of his crime. "As your former friend and mentor pleaded for his life, you did nothing for him." Prosecutor Eugene Hurley echoed her sentiments: "They were acts of barbarity motivated by greed and self-interest." Montoun Hart, who provided damning testimony against Corey Arthur in court, was later acquitted of all charges.

A case becomes "cold" when the primary investigator on it has tapped out his or her resources, regardless of the case's real age. Many of the larger U.S. departments have established squads dedicated to investigating cases whose trail has gone cold. The NYPD's Cold Case Squad started investigating old cases, mostly homicides, in the late 1990s. The decline in homicides in the city and the increased number of police officers allowed for more resources to be committed to unsolved cases. Since its formation, Cold Case has cleared an average of 50 percent of selected cold cases with arrests.

Forensic evidence and the availability of witnesses usually determine the workability of a case, and the Cold Case Squad will sift through information, interview and track down witnesses, and send forensic evidence to be reanalyzed. Resubmitting blood and fluid evidence for DNA testing has been particularly helpful in unsolved cases, and the technology can transform hunches into charges and "probable cause" into "beyond a reasonable doubt." Some departments also retest firearms evidence to learn whether the weapon used in the crime was ever impounded, used in another homicide, entered into a database, or test fired. Tracking down witnesses has become easier in the computer age, and everyone is tagged in some way—by having a driver's license, owning a car, having received medical attention, or using the Internet. Computerized records have been particularly helpful in finding witnesses, suspects, and fugitives, and solving cold cases.

Fugitives from the law are potential repeat offenders, as are parolees. I have been to many crime scenes—including the murders of police officers, children, and rapes—where the person who perpetrated the crime was released from jail on parole for the same type of crime he had just committed.

One man, James Gordon, a repeat offender who had been arrested four times, committed a triple homicide in 1996 while on parole. Gordon, who fled New York after murdering Darlene Johnson, Mary Armstrong Mouzon, and Hadiyah Holliman, was apprehended five weeks after the murders in Memphis. What had started as a robbery turned into a homicide scene so violent that it was hard for investigators to tell if the victims had been beaten to death, stabbed, or shot until the medical examiner's report came back. Gordon's victims had been shot, sexually assaulted, and mutilated. One woman, Zakkiyah Holliman, who survived the attack, and another woman escaped Gordon by jumping naked from a second-story window. Gordon should have been serving time in an upstate prison for selling narcotics. If he had been, three women might be alive today. Gordon was convicted of the rape, torture, and murder of the three women and sentenced to life without parole.

Parole should be abolished. We should have truth in sentencing—if you commit a crime and the sentence is twenty years, you should serve those twenty years. Parole was developed to scale back the jail population and sponsor rehabilitation, but it has been shown that recidivism among parolees is no different than recidivism among those who get out of jail after serving a full sentence. In a survey conducted by the NYPD, we found that twelve thousand felonies had been committed in one year by parolees, that there were twelve thousand victims who wouldn't be such if these criminals had been kept incarcerated. To date, twenty-eight states and the federal government have eliminated parole, and every state, including New York State, should too. There are people who are genuinely a threat to society, and society has the right to protect itself from them.

To track criminals, suspects, and fugitives, we need to use regularized methodologies and monitor violent offenders. But we also need to make sure that the revolving-door justice system doesn't continue. The benefits of proactive policing—reopening cold cases, hunting down fugitives, and working with legislators to eliminate parole—are many. These actions tell the community that the department cares and is moving relentlessly to investigate unsolved crimes, prosecute cases appropriately, and sends a strong message of zero tolerance to criminals.

7.

SPECIAL VICTIMS

In 2002, a fugitive escaped from the Detective Borough Building in the Bronx. After his escape it was concluded based on DNA evidence that he was the perpetrator in a string of rapes in the Bronx of 15 females ages nine to fifty-eight that dated back to 1997. In eight of the rapes, he'd knocked on the victim's door, claiming to be a plumber, raped them, and robbed them of jewelry. The search was made more difficult by the variety of descriptions that victims gave: At the end of the investigation, there were eleven sketches of the same perpetrator. With DNA, we were able to link the rapist to fifteen cases. One suspect, because of his close resemblance to the rapist, was picked up by the police and cleared by DNA within twenty-four hours.

Finally the case broke when, on May 6, 2002, one of the rape victims saw a man fitting the description of her rapist walking along East Mosholu Parkway. Police officers went to the location and brought the man in for questioning. When detectives brought him in, the suspect gave a false name and address, but he agreed to a saliva swab so that his DNA could be analyzed.

A detective left him unhandcuffed and unattended in the interrogation room in the Special Victims Unit. The suspect, who we later learned was named Luis Acosta, pried the cover off the air conditioner's controls and used the metal implement to jimmy the door open and escape. Bronx detectives were unaware of the severity of what had happened until the next day when the man's DNA tests came back that matched DNA found in the rapes.

Immediately after his escape, Bronx detectives launched "Operation Scorpio," and dedicated up to 170 detectives to the case at a time. They disseminated tens of thousands of flyers, offered a $25,000 reward, and a room in the Detective Borough Bronx Building was filled with information about his associates and possible whereabouts. Because Acosta looks like many other male Hispanics, it has been hard to identify him, and his average looks have made it easy for him to fade into a crowd.

Criminals who jump bail, disobey the terms of their parole or probation, ignore summonses and desk-appearance tickets, or escape custody, like Acosta, were the focus of the NYPD's program, "Bringing Fugitives to Justice." When people find that they can easily avoid the consequence of an arrest or a summons without fear of capture, justice is seriously compromised and safety and order is threatened. Many of those who avoid prosecution for one offense go on to commit other crimes, and experience shows that even those who are fleeing minor offenses often will go on to commit major ones.

The statistics on rape are frightening: One in three women is raped or sexually assaulted, and 84 percent of those rapes go unreported. In the United States a woman is raped or sexually assaulted every two minutes, and survivors of sexual assault are nine times more likely to commit suicide. With hundreds of thousands of sexual predators on the streets and the average offender raping between one and sixteen women, the numbers on potential sexual assaults are mind-boggling.

Felony sex offenses, like those apparently committed by Acosta, are handled by the Special Victims Unit in each borough, and detectives specialized in investigating sex crimes are assigned. As in the case of Acosta's victims, tissue and fluid samples are carefully taken and analyzed to match the DNA in rapes that are being scrutinized as part of a pattern. Often it is these "DNA fingerprints" that will link crimes and put a rapist behind bars, and DNA evidence is key to identifying that a rape has occurred and who committed the act.

In New York we had a suspect who had committed seventeen rapes, from 1994 to 1998, on the Upper East Side of Manhattan. We have not yet caught him, and so to stop the statute of limitations, which is five years, on some of the rapes we indicted his DNA code for rape, sodomy, and robbery. The suspect, who we knew to be a light-skinned black or Hispanic male, is now identified as the "East Side Rapist" and by his unique DNA code. When we find him, we'll match his DNA to that in the rape kits of his victims.

One case in particular, that of Aaron Kee, a serial rapist, murderer, and fugitive, illustrates the efficacy of DNA profiling. Kee's crimes included the sexual assault and murders of thirteen-year-old Paola Illera, nineteen-year-old Johalis Castro, and eighteen-year-old Resheda Washington; he was also linked in the rapes of three girls ages thirteen, fourteen, and fifteen. Paola Illera's body was discovered on the roof of her apartment building in January 1991, and after a preliminary investigation the police learned that Kee was perhaps the last person to have seen Illera alive.

Speaking with the girl's parents, investigators found out that they had buzzed her into the building when she had returned from school, but that she had never made it to the front door of their apartment. Kee lived in the same building as Illera, and he told police that he had ridden up in the elevator with her on the afternoon of her disappearance. When we spoke to Kee about seeing the girl in the elevator, he told investigators that a woman in African garb was also in the elevator with them. We never found this woman. In retrospect, it is clear that to cover up the mistake in telling detectives that he had seen Illera, Kee had invented this fictitious woman.

Kee remained on a long lists of suspects. His name surfaced in three of the investigations, but the case was unsolved for years. In 1994, Kee raped a fifteen-year-old Harlem girl in a housing project. The rape fit Kee's modus operandi—he approached his victim from behind, led her to a deserted area, blindfolded her, and then raped and sodomized her. Three years later, it happened again: Kee raped and killed Johalis Castro and burned her body on the roof of an apartment building. She was burned almost beyond recognition, but we did get Kee's DNA from her and matched it to the other cases.

Kee was connected to Castro because she was his girlfriend's friend. He had come over to see his girlfriend; and when she wasn't home, Kee had ended up hanging out with Castro and taking her up to the roof. Phone records showed detectives that Kee and Castro had phoned each other thirteen times on the day prior to her disappearance;

but when confronted by police, Kee denied the murder and his girlfriend told homicide detectives that he was in her company when the crime took place.

Because of Kee and his girlfriend's testimony, police focused their attention on an abusive boyfriend of Castro's, and Kee remained free to commit a string of attacks over the next year that included the rape and sodomy of a thirteen-year-old girl in April of 1998; the rape, sodomy, and murder of Resheda Washington that same June; the rape and sodomy of a fifteen-year-old girl in September; and the rape and sodomy of a fourteen-year-old girl in November, all in the same year.

Kee had met Resheda Washington on upper Fifth Avenue, where he'd raped and murdered her. When we found her, she was on the fifteenth-floor stairwell of the building curled into a fetal position, with her blouse thrown over her. She looked like she had suffered a drug overdose and that's the way officers treated her pending the medical examiner's report. When the report came back, it showed that she had been strangled and raped.

In an effort to close the cases once and for all, the NYPD formed a task force of twelve detectives to solve them. We generated a flyer and distributed it at the projects. We had a suspect in the rapes and murders—Kee, but we didn't have enough evidence to arrest him. We had DNA from the rapes and murders we suspected him of committing, but we needed to get a DNA sample from him to confirm our suspicions. Detective began to trail him, waiting for him to slip up, but no such luck.

In February of 1999, Kee was arrested for petty larceny and taken into custody. Fortunately, homicide detectives found out about the arrest and asked him for a DNA sample. He refused. Investigators then resorted to wilier methods. A detective donned a white smock and pretended to be a doctor conducting a TB study and that he needed cells from the inside of Kee's cheek. Kee refused to comply.

Detectives then offered him a cup of coffee, which he accepted. After drinking the coffee he discarded it in a wastebasket, and they collected DNA from the discarded cup (under case law, the abandonment of property, when a person tosses any object into the garbage, he or she has relinquished the right or expectation of privacy concerning the object).

While the DNA was being processed, Kee was released on bail and fled to a Miami hotel with Angelique Stallings, a sixteen-year-old Brooklyn girl. When it was confirmed that the DNA we had collected from Kee linked him to six of the seven rapes and murders, the NYPD started a manhunt for him. Without DNA analysis, he could have gone on to kill and rape other people. Had DNA samples been allowed to be taken from Kee in 1997 and matched to the samples at the murder scenes of Illera and Castro, one girl would be alive today and three others would have not been sexually brutalized.

Stalling's parents, after seeing Kee's mugshot next to an article about the murders and rapes, filed a missing person's report on their daughter, telling investigators that they had not seen their daughter since her Valentine's Day date with Kee. Eventually a friend of Stallings divulged that the couple was in Miami. Law-enforcement officers from the local Miami Police Department, the FBI, and the United States Marshals Service searched the Miami hotel they were hiding out in and a three-block area around it. They found Kee huddled in Room 601 and arrested him. We feared that Kee had already murdered Stallings, who fit the profile of his other victims, but much to our relief she was still alive.

A jury found Kee guilty on almost two-dozen counts of murder, rape, sodomy, and robbery, and five men previously suspected of Kee's crimes were exonerated through their and Kee's DNA. Another man, who had been identified by an eyewitness and was in jail awaiting trial for a rape committed by Kee, was also freed.

Not all rape cases are as clear cut and obviously criminal as those of Kee, Acosta, and the East Side Rapist. While I was commissioner, a landmark rape case that involved the Internet—the trial of the "so-called Cybersex Stalker" Oliver Jovanovic—would revolutionize the use of e-mail correspondence as admissible evidence and would test the definition of consensual sex. In late 1996, a woman he met in an Internet chatroom accused Jovanovic, a Ph.D. candidate in molecular biology at Columbia University, of torture, rape, and sodomy. After corresponding by e-mail for a month, the alleged victim—a twenty-year-old student at Barnard College—whose identity was shielded during Jovanovic's trial, impressed by Jovanovic's intelligence (and as it would be revealed later in e-mails that suggested a shared interest with him in sadomasochistic sex), agreed to meet him for dinner. They met on November 22, 1996, for Thai food at a restaurant in downtown Manhattan. Having shared confidences by e-mail—many of which were struck from the ensuing court proceedings—she felt enough at ease at dinner that she agreed to return to Jovanovic's studio apartment in Washington Heights afterward.

Once uptown she claimed that Jovanovic gave her a cup of tea, and they started talking. Sometime during the evening, the Barnard student accepted a glass of water from Jovanovic, after which she claimed to feel woozy. Then the alleged victim said that he undressed her, tied her to a futon with strips of fabric, gagged her, and put a pillowcase over her head. Once bound and gagged, he attacked her with various objects, including an eighteen-inch nightstick that he sodomized her with. The victim accused him of biting her, burning her with candle wax, and beating her.

After passing out and coming to at 10:00 P.M. the following night, the woman was able to loosen her bonds and escape Jovanovic's apartment. Unfortunately, she did not report the attack until two weeks later; and by the time she came in to the police, her wounds and bruises had healed and we were unable to collect physical evidence that a crime had been committed against her. When the Manhattan Special Victims Squad arrested Jovanovic at his apartment, investigators seized his computer hardware as well as his printer, diskettes, and CD-ROMs, and books that depicted corpses and hermaphrodites. They found karate belts (the cloth used to bind her), duct tape, a wooden stick, condoms, and K-Y jelly, all items that the victim had said were used in the sexual assault. Accused of aggravated sexual abuse and unlawful imprisonment and assault, Jovanovic stated that the episode in question was consensual and that the woman, like himself, enjoyed rough sex.

In the grand jury trial, the prosecutor on the case described the woman's assault as ". . . a whole new entry in the acquaintance-rape category," and this was the first case of cyberrape that made national, even international, news—a new kind of crime, one that captured the attention of media and the general public. On December 13, Jovanovic posted $350,000 bail and was released. Because of the severity and purposefulness of his crime, investigators felt that this was not the first time he had tortured a woman in this way and investigators got a search warrant to force American Online to download his e-mail correspondences and submit them to the police (his instant messenger communications were unavailable). Once the e-mails were collected, their bizarre sexual content broadened the investigation to other women with whom he had been corresponding.

In the two years prior to the alleged victim's assault, Jovanovic had met face-to-face with half a dozen of the women initially contacted in chatrooms. Some shared stories that were remarkably similar to the victim's. The women he met online described his demeanor as threatening and strange; and one woman who went on a date with him claimed that he showed her violent videos and tied her up. One woman, who had dated him briefly at the University of Chicago, accused him of stealing her credit cards and stalking her after she started dating somebody else. She claimed that he harassed her and even poured toxic chemicals under her dorm room door and that of her new boyfriend. Another woman who met Jovanovic on the Internet moved from Los Angeles to Manhattan to be with him and described their relationship as including sexual acts very similar to those of the other victims.

In April 1997, Columbia University handed over 2,400 pages of e-mails that the alleged victim had written to Jovanovic from September and December 1996, and these made the situation even more complex when detectives discovered that there had been some discussion of sadomasochistic sex in her original correspondences with Jovanovic. In one e-mail she referred to herself as a "pushy bottom." In S and M slang a "pushy bottom" is the submissive party, but likes to retain some control. In another e-mail she wrote, "rough is good," and in another that she was "drawn to the pleasure of hell's pain." Unlike many rape cases, this trail of e-mails provided the defense and the prosecution with a road map of the relationship between the two. What we discovered in this case is that an electronic trail of e-mails is an ambiguous map, and the prosecution and the defense were diametrically opposed in their understanding and presentation of the correspondence between Jovanovic and his alleged victim.

Jack Litman, Jovanovic's lawyer, used these e-mails, and another one that the woman sent after the incident, in which she wrote: "The taste is so overpoweringly delicious and at the same time quite nauseating . . . ," and the fact that there was very little evidence of the assault, to categorize it as consensual kinky sex. He stated that the woman was so repelled by her own perverse desires that because of this she had blamed the violence in their encounter on Jovanovic. Litman characterized the woman's testimony as that of an "embellishing, fantasizing woman . . ." and asserted that Jovanovic had only done what she had expressed she wanted him to do in her e-mails and verbally.

When Jovanovic went on trial in 1998, the woman would claim otherwise. She stated that she begged him to stop and that she struggled to leave. In court she said, "I told him, 'Don't rape me, don't dismember me . . .'" and "Stop! Stop! Stop! Stop!" She begged him not to kill her, and she used S and M code for him to stop—employing a "safe word." Her imploring did nothing to deter Jovanovic, who, she claimed, continued to torture her.

Judge William A. Wetzel, the presiding judge on the case, invoked the rape shield law, and several of these e-mails were removed from the proceedings. Without the electronic evidence, this case was a classic scenario of "he said, she said," and the jury found Jovanovic guilty of sodomy and aggravated sexual assault and sentenced him to up to twenty-five years to life. After the trial, Jack Litman blasted the judge's decision to omit the e-mails as "a travesty of justice . . ." and that "an innocent man faces life imprisonment because the jury has heard only half the evidence."

Sixteen months later, an appeals court agreed. The court found that Judge Wetzel had used the rape shield law incorrectly, and that the e-mail messages needed to be included in a second trial. In December 1999, Jovanovic was released from prison and plans for a second trial were underway when the alleged victim balked against testifying against Jovanovic. The District Attorney's Office offered Jovanovic a plea bargain for time served, but he refused the offer. Apparently he and his lawyers were confident that with the e-mails entered into evidence and a reluctant victim, the trial was leaning in his favor. In November 1999, the new judge on the trial, Rena Uviller, dismissed the case when the prosecution announced that the victim was mentally unstable and would not testify. After five years Oliver Jovanovic walked away from his legal battles a free man.

Clearly Jovanovic had bizarre sexual appetites; the issue was whether his proclivities for rough sex were shared with his victims, or if he had forced them to participate against their wills. In the Jovanovic case, the boundaries between consensual sex and rape were not clear, and what this trial brought to the fore were the complexities and ambiguities that we encounter when we surf the net and meet people online. Electronic mail can be read in a variety of ways—a sender can mean one thing, while the recipient of the e-mail can infer something different. What happened between this young woman and Oliver Jovanovic—was it a sex game gone bad? Was it rape? Or was she an embittered one-night stand? One thing is sure, this case confirmed the value of face-to-face contact when it comes to judging a person's character—their posture, whether they meet your eyes, their body language, all can help us to judge whether someone is a potential threat and computer-mediated encounters mask these attributes.

In rape the single most important tool is DNA testing. After a person is raped, sodomized, or the victim of aggravated sexual abuse, and sexual misconduct, they are taken to a hospital where evidence of the rape is collected. Detectives take affected and stained areas of bedding, clothing, and hairs, and the hospital takes swabs of semen and blood and compile a rape kit, which is analyzed for DNA evidence. The federal government has not stepped up to the plate with regard to rape-evidence testing. We can get justice from a simple scientific test that costs no more than $500 and yet 500,000 kits remain untested in local police departments (I discovered that in New York City 16,000 of these kits lay dormant in police storage facilities) across the United States. A lack of funding, administrative red tape, and simple oversight have led to a critical situation affecting an unknown number of rape victims. I spearheaded the National Rape Evidence Project to expedite the DNA testing of backlogged "rape kits" by directing private funds to local law-enforcement agencies in an effort to raise awareness about this important issue. The National Rape Evidence Project will identify communities in need of funds to test rape kits, to develop policy to guide distribution of funds, and to raise awareness in law-enforcement communities about rape-kit testing.

Awareness about the backlog has continued to grow and the Debbie Smith Act, the National DNA Evidence Bill, was introduced in Congress in September 2001. The bill was proposed by Carolyn Maloney (D-Manhattan/ Queens), and supported by Barry Scheck of the Innocence Project, and Debbie Smith, a victim whose rapist was iden- tified by his DNA six years after the crime. The act would provide $250 million to pay for testing in states that adopt procedures ensuring a ten-day turnaround time between evidence collection and DNA testing. It could also assist in the training of forensic nurses and standardize forensic evidence–collection kits. The bottom line is that law- enforcement agencies seeking to test rape-evidence kits need resources today to incarcerate rapists before they go on to commit future rapes.

8.

SURVEILLANCE

Informants, police surveillance, wiretaps, electronic devices, and now digital surveillance are ways that the police uncover criminals and crime patterns. Surveillance techniques and technologies have proven themselves invaluable in collecting information about organized crime, including terrorist activities and, as a response to September 11 and the need for more effective surveillance, the Patriot Act became law in October 2001.

The act incorporates legislation that was thrown out in the past when it was presented in Congress as part of the Foreign Intelligence Surveillance Act, 1978 (FISA), and finally the Electronic Communications Privacy Act, 1986 (ECPA), then the Communications Assistance for Law Enforcement Act, 1994 (CALEA). It was not until after September 11, that the legislation that modifies over fifty of FISA's statutes (itself a revision of Title III of the Omnibus Crime Control and Safe Streets Act of 1968) that refer to immigration, money laundering, criminal law, and most government surveillance was now palatable enough to both parties to make law.

The Patriot Act expands ECPA, which was put in place to cover beepers and electronic tracking devices, to give law enforcement access to Internet address information, including content, and it gives law enforcement authority to wiretap telephones and monitor and collect undefined Internet activity, such as Web browsing and e-mail, with less review. Service providers are required to turn over both e-mail and voice mail to an investigator with merely a search warrant.

The act amends FISA to make it easier to get warrants and allows for surveillance devices to be placed with trespass and the authority to place "trap and trace" devices (which determine the origin of calls) and pen registers (which record the number dialed, the calling number, and the duration of the call) is expanded to include Internet traffic.

Placing eavesdropping devices has always been subject to the standards set by the Fourth Amendment: "The rights of the people to be secure in their persons, houses, papers, and effects against unreasonable searches and seizures, shall not be violated, and no Warrants shall issue, but on probable cause, supported by the Oath of affirmation, and particularly describing the place to be searched and the persons or things to be seized." Now to seize voice mail, or place a wiretap, or obtain access to e-mail correspondence a federal investigator needs only a search warrant, not a Title III wiretap order.

The Patriot Act allows for investigators to intercept all forms of a suspect's communication including roving wiretaps. In the past a roving tap was used when a suspect would make calls from a public phone in lieu of their own, wiretapped, phone. Suspects began to use cell phones, changing phones frequently to avoid taps; or setting up and closing out e-mail accounts in an effort to dodge interception that roving wiretaps are used to counter.

It also allows for "sneak and peek," or the search of offices and homes without notifying the owner, and permits the FBI to conduct surveillance (wiretaps and secret searches) with lower judicial standards for the purpose of collecting foreign intelligence. The Patriot Act also opens the door to the CIA and FBI sharing grand jury information, and it gives law enforcement the authority to monitor previously confidential attorney-client conversations.

Civil libertarians have been very vocal in their disapproval of the Patriot Act, positing that nothing in the act would have prevented what happened on September 11. They also claim that the act belittles the checks and balances of the government by scaling back on judicial oversight. I don't think that is true. The Patriot Act requires a judicial process, it requires search warrants and court orders, it just lowers the burden of proof.

To understand how the Patriot Act can effectively undermine terrorism, you only have to picture an Al Qaeda operative sitting in front of a computer screen typing messages to a fellow Al Qaeda member sitting in an Internet café in San Francisco. The FBI knows about this man in the café, and they have been watching him since September 11. He has done nothing out of the ordinary. He maintains a job in a restaurant and goes about his own business. He does not attend rallies or burn American flags in protest. At a glance, this man may appear to be an American citizen, but the FBI knows he is originally from Saudi Arabia and he is on a student visa, which expires in one month. This "student" has only been to this Internet café twice, and the first time he never even used a computer, he simply checked the place out. He has also visited the public library and several other cybercafés but has only logged on once at each location.

The FBI, under the old laws, would only be able to observe this man, never knowing the critical information he is picking up each time he logs onto the Internet. This man is a terrorist, and his superior in Algeria is awakening this sleeper cell in San Francisco and ordering it to begin a campaign of suicide bombings this weekend. Under the Patriot Act, the FBI agents tracking this man are able to legally obtain copies of the communications this man has had over the Internet. Under the Patriot Act, this terrorist, and the other members of his cell, are caught while preparing their bombs. Under the Patriot Act, no Americans die due to the fact that vital information is not trapped under a blanket of laws aimed to "protect us."

The Patriot Act and federal programs like the Bush administration's Terrorism Information & Prevention System (TIPS) program have encouraged Americans to keep a watchful eye and report suspicious circumstances. The TIPS program, and the greater flexibility allowed the intelligence community by the Patriot Act, led to the arrest of six Americans of Yemeni descent, some or all of whom had allegedly trained in an Al Qaeda training camp, in September 2002 in Buffalo. Recently a woman in Florida overheard a conversation between several Arab men and reported what she thought were plans for a terrorist attack to law enforcement. This prompted the shutdown of a major interstate, and the apprehension of the men. Americans need to remember that a false alarm is always better than a fatal oversight. When a neighbor down the street receives a large delivery of fertilizer in the middle of the night, or you hear a group of Arab men talk about "taking a building down," it is the time to pick up the phone and call the police.

The number one civil right is to be free from violence and disorder from criminals and terrorists. If we are to win the war against terrorism, our law-enforcement and intelligence agencies need the public to help them gather information and the tools and resources to penetrate and destroy terrorist cells.

The use of surveillance devices is governed by state and federal laws, and they can vary widely. In New York the Handschu Agreement is a stumbling block to the NYPD's monitoring of political activity. Enforced by a three-person panel that oversees surveillance of political groups and activists by the NYPD's Intelligence Division the agreement stops police from attending, photographing, or video taping political gatherings without notification that a crime is likely to take place. It also forbids the NYPD to develop files on political activists or groups, and share the information with federal law enforcement.

Handschu was established in 1986 and arose from a lawsuit filed by radical activists, including members of the Black Panther Party, who were the subject of, they claimed, unwarranted police surveillance. Following September 11 and with the presence of many New York-based suspected terrorists Handschu must be repealed so that the NYPD can effectively monitor potential terrorists and share that information with federal authorities. No other police department is hobbled by such stringent surveillance guidelines and most local, state, and federal laws are far more permissive and favor law enforcement. If we want New York City to remain safe from terror we must roll back the Handschu agreement and allow the NYPD to develop, collect, and analyze intelligence at the same level as other local and federal law enforcement agencies. Handschu restricts the department's ability to conduct investigations, and current state law that governs the affidavit and application for a surveillance device already has to show that you have exhausted all other methods.

The NYPD's Intelligence Division manages surveillance operations, and it collects intelligence from informants, surveillance devices, wiretaps, video, and provides the appropriate information to the operational departments. The Organized Crime Control Bureau, which handles narcotics and vice, and the Detective Bureau, which focuses on homicide, rape, burglary, robbery, and other felony crimes, are the recipients of the bulk of this information. But since September 11 and the establishment of the Counterterrorism Bureau of the NYPD that has changed. Much of the intelligence currently gathered in the city relates to terrorism and terrorist activities.

Timely and accurate intelligence is vital to crime reduction and preventing terrorism. The NYPD's Intelligence Division has been restructured into a state-of-the-art unit that gathers, analyzes, and disseminates criminal intelligence to detective and specialized units, police commanders, and executives. Criminal intelligence is then included in timely reports and the CompStat program for field commanders and operational and investigative units, and is shared with all local, state, and federal law-enforcement agencies.

The Technical Assistance Response Unit (TARU) manages the installation and upkeep of surveillance devices for the NYPD and relays that information to Intelligence or the appropriate unit. TARU is responsible for wiring undercover officers or confidential informants with transmitters and recorders, performing covert surveillance operations, and providing video and audio documentation during stings and special investigations. The unit establishes intercepts and monitors eavesdropping devices, which include pen registers, "trap and trace" devices, wiretaps, bugs, and mobile tracking devices, or "bird dogs," that can be attached to the vehicle of a suspect, and the police can use global positioning (GPS) to keep tabs on a suspect.

Placing an electronic surveillance device, for example, an electronic device, or bug, that picks up audio in a location in the home of a suspected terrorist, is complicated. Strict operational and legal procedures are followed so that the integrity of the operation is maintained. Cassettes of information need to be handled carefully, and originals need to be placed in sealed evidence envelopes and labeled, logs of the intercept must be kept, and photographs and videos may be taken to document any relevant activity.

For a wiretap, TARU works with the local telephone provider to run a wire from a suspect's phone to a nearby surveillance location or to an NYPD facility. The wiretap must be listened to live because of minimization. The law demands that the officer listening in on the conversation must listen for thirty seconds; if the conversation does not relate to the investigation, he or she must turn off the recording device. They can continue to listen, but not record. If they are listening to more than one wire at a time, they may check back a minute later to see if the conversation has turned relevant.

In New York State the process for applying for a wiretap is detailed; there must be probable cause for the wire. In filling out an application, the investigator needs to take several things into consideration:

- What information will result from the wiretap?
- Will the results substantiate criminal activity?

- Will the results, and the warrant, hold up in court?
- Have all other methods of investigation been exhausted?

The application must include information gathered during an investigation; any prior investigations by other law-enforcement agencies are needed. It must also recount all facts gathered from subpoena—the subject's record of previous unlawful behavior, as well as prior search warrants, arrests, and any and all other conversations previously recorded. Once the application has been accepted, the judge hands down a court order authorizing the interception; the order can be amended at a later date to include other suspects, additional criminal activity, change of phone number or location, and the order can be extended.

In hostage and barricade situations, TARU establishes telephone control over the suspect's line, and they provide intelligence, through their use of electronic devices, to assist the Emergency Service Unit (ESU) with their tactical planning. When the Zodiac Killer, Heriberto Seda, barricaded himself in his East New York apartment, TARU established control of his telephone line so that they could monitor his conversations; they do this in every hostage situation.

Should the negotiations be prolonged, they are responsible for deploying Remote Canine Optical Navigator (RECON), a K-9 unit dog wired with a video camera, to investigate what's occurring. The dog and camera give police a tactical advantage and flexibility in situations where only remote-control cameras could be used before. The first time the NYPD used RECON was when Michael Nunno, a Staten Island man, fired on police and then barricaded himself in his apartment. Hostage negotiators were unable to establish contact with him, and surveillance cameras outside did not pick him up. TARU sent in Ace, a RECON, and he was instructed to search the basement and then the first floor of Nunno's house. He searched the kitchen and the living room, and the camera recorded his scouting. When the camera didn't pick up Nunno in the basement or on the first floor, police concluded that Nunno was on the second floor and they were able to enter the house without fear of immediate attack. They found Nunno in the second-floor bathroom. He had committed suicide with a shot to the head.

During major events in the city, TARU provides live video feeds to the Command and Control Center and provide video at demonstrations and civil disturbances. Since September 11, TARU has been called on more frequently to perform special services, like activating panic alarms and emergency-notification systems; conducting security surveys to minimize potential risks by using on-site analysis, aerial photography, and special equipment; and to ensure the integrity of sensitive locations with electronic countermeasures.

Video is the most pervasive form of surveillance in our culture—cameras are installed in hotel lobbies, schools, grocery stores, malls, and banks and the extensive use of video surveillance can serve as a supplement to law enforcement. I am a strong supporter of the city's installing closed-circuit and video cameras in the subway systems, public housing, municipal buildings, and high-crime areas. My strategy for fighting crime has always included provisions for video surveillance. My video-surveillance initiatives drew a lot of complaints from the ACLU, who objected to the proposal that the NYPD install cameras in housing developments. To see what the people in public housing thought of the plan, we had a town hall meeting with the residents of Grant Houses, a crime-infested public-housing development and the first project we had earmarked for CCTV. At the meeting at Grant Houses, a young lawyer from the ACLU stood up and said, "This is Big Brother. This is intruding on people's privacy."

An older woman, a resident of the houses, stood up and said, "Sonny, where do you live?"

He replied, "East Seventy-second Street." She asked him, "Do you have cameras in your building?"

His answer was, "Why, yes."

She said, "Shut up, and sit down."

Why wouldn't a citizen living in a dangerous area want to have all of the security that someone living in an upscale neighborhood has? The mayor and I were confident that we were doing the right thing, so we went forward with the plan to install thirty-nine cameras aimed at public spaces—the courtyards, doorways, and in the elevators— in the project, and within months we had reduced crime by up to 35 percent. Because of the success of CCTV at Grant Houses, we installed cameras in other public-housing developments. With the CCTVs that we installed in public areas, we were also able to catch graffiti vandals, drug deals, and other crimes, including sexual attacks.

One of our most successful uses of video surveillance was in Washington Square Park. The park is in the center of Greenwich Village and is a place where people congregate. Up until 1998, when we installed the cameras, small-time drug dealers used the location to sell a wide variety of illegal drugs. In 1998, to the dismay of many, we installed thirteen cameras on streetlights in the park and assigned officers to a trailer to watch the monitors. In several cases, officers saw "live" crimes taking place and were able to arrest the criminal. In another case, video from the Washington Square cameras provided evidence for a suspect already under arrest.

One of the community's complaints was that the dealers would just move away from the square to the surrounding neighborhood, but we stationed police throughout the area. The numbers proved the success of CCTV in the Washington Square area when drug felonies and misdemeanor arrests declined in 1998, the year the cameras were installed.

In 1991, after seeing a 20 percent drop in crime after cameras were installed in Birmingham, the British government had CCTV put in cities all over England. Today Londoners are caught on film hundreds of times a day. Sometimes the business community will push the installation of video-surveillance cameras, many airports use video-surveillance systems, and the National Park Service has installed them and digital video sensors at the Washington Mall.

As surveillance and national security are increasingly intertwined, new methods and technologies for tracking people are being explored. For security purposes there is no better way to ascertain a person's identity than with biometrics. Biometrics is the science of using unique physiological and biological characteristics to verify identity features—fingerprints, voiceprints, facial recognition, and iris and retinal recognition—that are unique to the individual and cannot be replaced or lost. Each biometric technology has a different code and algorithm—iris scanning has 260 points of comparison, fingerprints seventy points, and facial recognition eighty. This means that iris recognition is the most accurate of the technologies, but it is also the one that will occupy more database space.

One of the most promising technologies for surveillance is facial recognition, a technology that allows for a camera with the right software to scan a crowd for faces that have been databased (mugshots and photographs of known criminals or terrorists are scanned into the database with or without their cooperation or knowledge) and the software encodes each scanned face with four anchor points— both eyes, tip of nose, bridge of nose. The system takes information from the scans and mathematically translates it into a digital string of code called a "faceprint." Facial recognition is the only biometric technology that works for surveillance—the other technologies are more security-oriented—and even facial recognition has been successful only in controlled environments.

Facial recognition also works for access control, but the technology has been most effective commercially, especially in casinos where there are a limited number of clients whom they need to monitor. As the players sit around the playing table, the casino is able to get database images and then use the technology to set off an alert when a face scan of a known cheater matches that of a databased image. There are also some glitches in the current technology—for it to work the lights must be on (currently there are cameras being developed for nighttime) and wearing a beard, glasses, or a hat can trip the system up.

I foresee facial recognition and biometrics most effectively used at airport checkpoints and at borders. Iceland has already installed FR cameras at airports, and Canada has plans for iris-recognition software implementation at eight of the country's international airports. With facial recognition, the controlled area of customs or the check-in area provides a delimited environment where it would be easy to scan people, compare them to databased faceprints, and integrate them into the database. For this technology to work most effectively, we would need to scan the thousands of mugshots on file, but to be able to have a comprehensive database of faceprints of known criminals or terrorists would provide officers invaluable assistance.

Facial-recognition technology was used at the 2001 Super Bowl in Tampa Bay; and in 2002, New York City landmarks were equipped with cameras using facial-recognition software during times of high alert. In Ybor City, the entertainment district of Tampa, Florida, police placed the entire area under surveillance. Tampa police used mugshots to compile a database of felons, and thirty-six cameras search the district for their faces.

The Ybor City experiment was unsuccessful; and after not detecting any suspects and raising the ire of the ACLU, they closed the program down. Mexico uses facial recognition in their voting process, and the United Kingdom has installed cameras equipped with facial-recognition software in many of Britain's major cities. The National Security Agency (NSA), the Defense Department, and the Department of Justice have allocated monies for the research and development of biometric technology systems in federal law-enforcement, and a project called the Human ID system is being developed for use at U.S. embassies and other potential terrorist targets. This system would allow for the identification of known and databased terrorists from five hundred feet away.

The NYPD implemented a biometric technology in every precinct with livescan fingerprinting. The use of digital fingerprinting has made the job of investigators much easier, as it takes very little time to scan a suspect's fingerprint, it is noninvasive, and fingerprinting is accepted, convenient, and reliable. There are several kinds of livescan fingerprinting technologies: the most accurate is the chip-based, silicon scan, which uses the body's electricity to complete a circuit, thereby making it impossible to cheat. While commissioner, I had optical fingerprint scanners installed in every NYPD precinct, and the system uses "points of comparison" much the way that traditional finger-printing did.

In 1997, the NYPD started using livescan fingerprint work stations at all precincts instead of ink-print cards, and the system has made criminal history records more quickly accessible than ever before. The biometric device uses lasers to capture digitized fingerprints and relay them to the State Division of Criminal Justice Services records in Albany, thereby shortening the wait for criminal records. Because the infrastructure and databases for finger-prints are set up already, the cost of integrating biometric fingerprinting is reasonable. Fingerprint capture and veri-fication is more and more common than other biometric technologies, and some companies use it to ascertain em-ployee identification, banks use them to identify check cashers, and fingerprint scans are used for verifying on-line computer transactions. Additionally, capturing finger-prints can also help to stop welfare fraud and other white-collar crimes and identify purchasers of weapons.

The new technologies and enhanced legislation have ex-panded the possibilities for surveillance. In an age of cy-berterrorism, and where even militant radicals use computers, law enforcement has had to develop their cy-bersurveillance skills. Locally, our ability to track crimi-nals is limited, but the FBI has developed a "packet sniffing" software program that is attached to an ISP's network and scans millions of e-mail's subject lines and content per second. The program is called Carnivore and is a "read only tap" that can be adjusted by changing the parameters of the search. For fiscal years 2002, 2003, and 2004, the FBI will receive $200 million each year for their technical support center, which includes Carnivore.

Law enforcement is switching to the use of digital surveillance, which allows for no tape, many cameras, and
audio feeds on a wire, and information sharing. All of
these technologies are dependant on the seamless integra-
tion of the multiple local and federal databases into a network; and with each new technology, a different,
interconnected database—for biometric features, mugshots, video images, and audio—needs to be set up for the
network to be effective.

An example of ineffective databasing is the National
Crime Information Center database of known terrorists.
At least one of the September 11 terrorists, Khalid Almih-
dhar, should have been put on the watch list, and it would
have prevented him from renewing his visa and being on
Flight 77 when it crashed into the Pentagon. We need to
better coordinate our intelligence protocols and systems,
and even this greater care will perhaps not prevent future
attacks. The Foreign Terrorist Tracking Task Force has
expanded their database to include information from the
CIA, FBI, the Department of Defense, and foreign governments, and it includes datalike credit card numbers and
phone records that help in locating and tracking terrorists
already in the country. From January to June 2002, seven
hundred suspected terrorists have had their visa applications rejected because their names appeared on this list.
We have many technological resources to screen and monitor people, and it is imperative that law enforcement—
local, state, and federal—working in cooperation be
timely and accurate in updating intelligence so that we can
prevent future terrorist attacks and crimes.

9.

HOMELAND SECURITY

The first plane hit the World Trade Center's North Tower at 8:45 A.M., ripping apart the building's facade and setting its upper floors ablaze. Almost immediately sirens sounded, the first fire engines began to arrive, and men poured out onto the street in their gear. At 9:06 A.M. another plane flew along Manhattan's Hudson River shoreline and smashed into the second tower. Those who had hoped the first crash had been pilot error, now knew better. In 102 minutes, both towers had collapsed leaving over 2,800 dead—343 of them firefighters and 60 uniformed law-enforcement officers.

The World Trade Center and the simultaneous Pentagon attack were not isolated. Over the past twenty years there has been a pattern of escalating terror against America and its interests. A baseline event occurred in April 1983, when 63 people were killed at the U.S. Embassy in Beirut; and six months later, the U.S. Marine barracks in Beirut were bombed by a suicide truck killing 242 Americans. The Islamic Jihad movement claimed responsibility.

In 1985, TWA Flight 847 was hijacked en route to Rome from Athens and the 8 crew members and 145 passengers were held hostage for seventeen days. Lebanese Shiites murdered one passenger, a U.S. Navy diver, Robert Stethem.

In 1986, a Berlin discotheque was the location of a Libyan bomb attack that killed two U.S. soldiers; and in 1988, Pan Am's Flight 103 was blown up over Lockerbie, Scotland. Libyan government-sponsored terrorists were responsible for both of these attacks. The World Trade Center was first attacked in 1993, leaving six dead and one thousand injured. The men carrying out the attack were followers of Sheikh Omar Abd al-Rahman, an Egyptian cleric who preached in the New York area. The next year Sheikh Rahman and nine other Egyptian extremists were involved in a plot to blow up the Lincoln and Holland Tunnels in New York City. With good police work, these attacks were thwarted, and Rahman and his followers were convicted in 1996.

From 1994 to 1998, most of the terrorist attacks directed at the United States—except for the Oklahoma City Bombing—were planned in other countries. In 1995, Ramzi Yousef, a coconspirator with Sheikh Rahman, plotted to blow up eleven U.S. commercial aircraft in what they hoped would be a day of terror. The bombs were made of liquid explosives designed to go undetected by airport metal detectors, but while mixing the chemicals in his apartment in the Philippines, Yousef started a fire and was forced to flee. He left behind a computer with information that led to his arrest a month later in Pakistan.

That same year in Tokyo, the Aum Shinrikyo cult launched a bioterrorist attack on innocent civilians when they released sarin gas in the subway killing 12 and injuring 5,700.

Timothy McVeigh and Terry Nichols destroyed the Federal Building in Oklahoma City with a truck bomb that killed 168 and injured hundreds of others on April 19, 1995. At the time it was the largest terrorist attack on American soil. And on June 25, 1995, a fuel truck carrying a bomb exploded outside of the U.S. military's Khobar Towers housing facility in Saudi Arabia killing 19 U.S. military personnel and wounding 515 others. Several Islamic groups claimed responsibility for the attack.

At the Hatshepsut Temple in the Valley of the Kings near Luxor, Egypt, an Islamic fundamentalist group (al-Gama'at al-Islamiyya) shot and killed fifty-eight tourists, four Egyptians, and wounded twenty-six others in 1997. On August 7, 1998, the U.S. Embassy bombings in Nairobi, Kenya, and in Dar es Salaam, Tanzania, killed approximately three hundred and injured many others. The USS *Cole* was attacked in 2000 in a Yemeni harbor by a small dinghy containing explosives. This attack killed seventeen sailors and injured thirty-nine others.

Osama bin Laden's Al Qaeda network took credit for the USS *Cole* and embassy bombings. The leadership of Al Qaeda is wealthy and educated, and bin Laden and his circle of advisers come from prominent Arab families and hold professional degrees. They use *hawalas*—a system of brokers that provides a banking network that enables individuals to move large amounts of money from one country to another without a paper trail.

While Osama bin Laden's Al Qaeda is a formidable adversary, there are other terrorist groups that we need to worry about. The Revolutionary Armed Forces of Colombia (FARC) poses a serious threat to U.S. interests, as does the People's Liberation Front of Turkey that protests U.S. operations in Afghanistan. The Islamic fundamentalist groups pose a particularly menacing threat to the well-being of U.S. citizens. Hamas, known as the Islamic Resistance movement, harbors a large and willing population of suicide bombers and maintains an extensive network of financial supporters. Hezbollah, or the party of God, was founded in the early 1980s as a response to the Israeli invasion of Lebanon, and the group takes its ideology from the teachings of Ayatollah Khomeini, the leader of the Iranian Revolution. Hezbollah has been involved in numerous attacks against our country, including truck bombings and hijackings. And Egypt's largest militant group—Egyptian Islamic Jihad—had as its spiritual leader Sheikh Rahman, who was sentenced to life in prison for his role in the 1993 WTC bombing. The members of this group were the perpetrators of the assassinations at Luxor, and a senior group member signed bin Laden's fatwa calling for attacks on the United States. There are many others—Abu Nidal, Abu Sayyaf, and the Armed Islamic Group, to name a few—and their crimes reflect the work of highly organized terrorist operations.

As U.S. intelligence agencies reexamine these groups and their crimes in light of September 11, they recognize that what appeared to be random acts were actually a pattern of coordinated strikes against the United States. By their own admission, the FBI and the CIA underestimated the terrorist threat, specifically the one posed by bin Laden's Al Qaeda network. This fatal oversight calls into question the way in which we approach terror. Twenty-first-century terrorism has redefined the role of police in national security.

The first responders to the 1993 and 2001 World Trade Center attacks were New York City police officers, emergency service workers, and firefighters, and it is virtually

I was sworn in as the NYPD's 39th Police Commissioner on
April 15, 1996. (NYPD)

The mayor and I holding the NYPD Police Commissioner's
shield. Prior to being appointed as commissioner, I was the Fire
Commissioner for two years. (NYPD)

My executive staff. In the front row with me are former First Deputy Commissioner Pat Kelleher (left) and former Chief of Department Joseph Dunne (right). (NYPD)

A weekly CompStat meeting at One Police Plaza. CompStat is the computer application developed by the NYPD that allows police to track criminal activity block by block, precinct by precinct and provides an arena for police executives, managers, and commanders to discuss and analyze crime patterns, quality of life violations, and the NYPD's resource allocation. (NYPD)

The view of the interior of an NYPD cruiser while officers run a warrant check on a mobile digital terminal (MDT). (NYPD)

Irene Silverman's multimillion-dollar townhouse, located on New York's Upper East Side. (AP/Stuart Ramson)

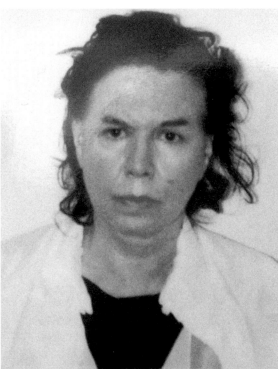

The NYPD mugshots of Kenneth and Sante Kimes. Despite the lack of direct physical evidence linking them to the crime, the Kimeses would both be convicted of Irene Silverman's murder. (AP/NYPD)

Police lead Bible-clutching Heriberto Seda, the Zodiac Killer, from the 75th precinct in Brooklyn's East New York section in June 1996. Lt. Joseph Herbert, the detective who discovered that a man the NYPD had in custody for holding his sister hostage was the Zodiac Killer, is directly behind Seda on the left. (AP/Chris Kasson)

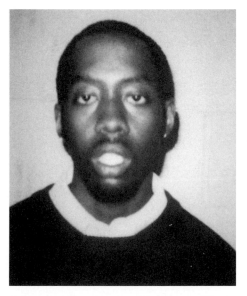

John Royster was sentenced to life in prison without parole for an eight-day rape, robbery, and murder spree in 1996. His capture was made when Royster was arrested and fingerprinted by the NYPD for turnstile jumping as part of our quality of life enforcement. (AP)

A surveillance camera, seen on the top of the light pole at left, scans Washington Square Park in Greenwich Village. Installed in 1998 by the NYPD, the camera proved highly effective in discouraging drug dealing in the park. (AP Photo/Ed Bailey)

Gazi Ibrahim Abu Mezer from the West Bank town of Hebron. Abu Mezer was shot and wounded in a Brooklyn apartment when the NYPD seized five bombs in an early morning raid of the terrorist's apartment. Abu Mezer later admitted the explosives were to be used in terrorist attacks on New York subway system. (APO)

Millennium eve. To prevent a terrorist attack, I assigned over 10,000 police officers to the streets around Times Square and all 37,000 officers were on duty that night. The Times Square area was a frozen zone and the NYPD, with the FBI, was on high alert during the festivities. (NYPD)

Here I'm holding a MAC 10 machine pistol that was bought through a straw buyer in Georgia who was selling such weapons at a hefty profit in Harlem. This particular investigation led to three arrests. (AP/Marty Lederhandler)

Our news conference in 1997 regarding the seizure of more than $45 million worth of heroin and cocaine under the NYPD's anti-drug initiatives. (AP/Rob Schoenbaum)

This photo of Mayor Giuliani and me was taken in 1998. (Eddie Adams)

guaranteed that local authorities will be the first to respond to our next terrorist attack in any city. With successful terrorist attacks in New York City, the Pentagon, in Pennsylvania, and the Oklahoma City bombing, the threat of another domestic or international terrorist attack in the future is very real, and your local police department is on the frontline of the war on terror.

Adequate training and intelligence are key elements to success. After September 11, the NYPD's counterterrorism operation was reprioritized with two new senior positions added. The Joint Terrorist Task Force (JTTF), once part of the Detective Bureau, has now become the core unit of the NYPD's new Counterterrorism Bureau. The JTTF is manned by close to two hundred of the best-of-the-best that the NYPD has to offer, and several hundred federal agents. There is a deputy commissioner for Counterterrorism and another for Intelligence. The Intelligence branch of Counterterrorism, collects, manages, and disseminates intelligence, foreign, federal, and local, and will alert NYPD officers of potential threats in the hopes that they will also be able to collect intelligence or prevent a terrorist attack.

The deputy commissioner of Counterterrorism supervises the NYPD's training in counterterrorist tactics, preparation for another terrorist attack, and the city's security. The establishment of these and other antiterrorism positions at the NYPD reflects that counterterrorism is now a priority of the department.

In early 2002, NYPD officers were sent by Commissioner Kelly to Israel to be trained by municipal and military police in the methods of detection and the investigation of suicide bombers. Kelly's move was appropriate. There *has* been an attempted suicide bombing in New York already. In July 1997, the plot was uncovered when a man waved over Long Island Rail Road police officers John Kowalchuk and Eric Huber in Brooklyn.

They picked up the man, Mohammed Chindluri, who told them that "My friend is going to kill people in the subway," and gave them his Brooklyn address, 248 Fourth Avenue, where he said that a bomb was being assembled to use in the subway the following morning.

The LIRR police officers took Chindluri to the Eighty-eighth Precinct, and there he told detectives that he had come to the United States two weeks prior. He had met a man named Gazi Ibrahim Abu Mezer and through him and other members of the Arab community was directed to the address as a place that he could stay temporarily.

Everything had seemed fine, but over the last week of his stay, Mezer had become increasingly volatile and more and more enraged with U.S. policies in the Middle East and against Jews. Mezer's behavior had intimidated Chindluri, and when he saw that Mezer was constructing a bomb and heard of his plans to bomb a New York City subway line, he left Mezer sleeping and flagged down the first law-enforcement officers he could find.

The NYPD's duty chief that night was Chief Charles Kammerdener. He's a real hero who made all the right decisions and saved a lot of lives. Kammerdener was making his rounds when he got notification about the informant and the bomb threat. When he got to the Eighty-eighth Precinct, detectives were interviewing Chindluri. Kammerdener and the detectives took him seriously, and Intel, Emergency Services, and the Bomb Squad were called in. To make sure that Chindluri's descriptions of the bomb and the location were accurate, Kammerdener had a translator brought in.

There were two problems—they ran Chindluri's name and numbers through databases, but for whatever reason they couldn't confirm when he had arrived in the country or decipher his description of the tenement building where Mezer and the bomb were. He kept saying, "I can see President Street from my window." By then Intel had put the address under surveillance. According to what they observed, it would be impossible to see President Street from any window of the building, and this made them question Chindluri's story. If he was giving them a bad address, the rest of his story was questionable.

Kammerdener authorized checks on the location to determine if anyone who lived there had been arrested and of phone numbers and names of the building's residents. These records indicated that several people with Middle Eastern names lived there.

At this point the Eighty-eighth Precinct had become the mobilization center and a tactical plan to isolate the President Street location and activate the operation was being put together. Emergency Services started to assemble resources and equipment as Bomb Squad detectives questioned Chindluri about the bomb and its explosive potential. FDNY and EMS were contacted in case there was an explosion, and because a train ran under the building we had the Metropolitan Transit Authority (MTA) switch off subway service.

They wanted to keep Mezer contained and get him before he left the building. Evacuating an area within one thousand feet of the building was considered, but the team of NYPD officers put the plan aside after assessing the situation: If Mezer was alerted to a police presence by an evacuation, he might detonate the bomb. This was also the reason the information was kept off the police radio. Everything was kept hard-line, so that the media—who use police scanners—or an acquaintance of Mezer, would not be alerted.

At this point it was 2:00 A.M. and detectives were trying to verify the information that Chindluri was giving them so that they could get a warrant, but parts of his story, his entry into the United States and the location of the bomber's apartment, couldn't be nailed down.

The clock was ticking, and the decision was made to take Chindluri back to Fourth Avenue. Officers put a hood and a bulletproof vest on him and took him to the location. His key fit the lock and he walked down the hallway all the way to the back of the building to a door that led to a courtyard. In the courtyard was a second building. Chindluri pointed at the building and said, "That's it."

At this point time had run out, and there was not time to get a warrant. It was close to five in the morning, and Mezer was going out to detonate the bomb in a rush-hour subway train. Since Mezer was a Muslim, he would be waking up within minutes for his daybreak prayer to Mecca. They decided that Chindluri was credible, and they were going to have to hit the location within the next fifteen minutes.

At 4:45 A.M., the Emergency Services Unit raided the ramshackle Brooklyn tenement and found two young Palestinians, one of them with a backpack bomb full of explosives. ESU opened fire when, after officers yelled, "Police! Don't move!" one of the suspects lunged for a bomb in his backpack. The bomb was built to be detonated by three switches, and the terrorist flipped two of the three switches before they shot him and wounded the other suspect.

As a precaution following the arrest, Kammerdener had the homes adjacent to the bomb factory evacuated, and automobile and subway traffic was stopped in the area for seven hours. It was a good thing, too. At the foot of

Mezer's bed they found ammunition, bomb parts, and pipe bombs; the bombs were packed with gunpowder and nails—in all, we found five explosive devices. The bombs were clearly part of a suicide-bombing plan because none of them had a remote detonator or a timer. Each device, detonated in an enclosed area, would kill people within twenty-five feet—in New York City's crowded subway trains, five detonations had the possibility of killing hundreds. Later we found out they had targeted the Atlantic Avenue subway and the Long Island Rail Road hub station at rush hour because they believed that there were a lot of Jewish people in the area.

The actions taken by the Emergency Services Unit officers prevented an attempt to detonate the bombs. It was a team effort, but they weren't the only heroes that day. A lot of credit goes to Kammerdener, the Long Island Rail Road police, the detectives at the Eighty-eighth, members of the Brooklyn Borough task force, the Bomb Squad, and the Anti-Crime Unit. We also depended on the expertise of the High Intensity Drug Trafficking Area (HIDTA) to get INS and visa information on Chindluri and Mezer. Clear thinking and teamwork on the part of the one hundred or so officers saved the lives of hundreds of New Yorkers and prevented a suicide bombing attack.

Following their arrests Gazi Mezer and Lafi Khalil were hospitalized with gunshot wounds, and the investigation was turned over exclusively to the FBI-NYPD Joint Terrorist Task Force. The task force looked for links to recent bombings in Jerusalem and the 1993 World Trade Center. Mezer had been arrested in Israel and was linked to the Hamas movement. During this period, additional officers were assigned all over the city because we were unsure of how far-reaching the scope of their plan was. Security was tightened for the next weeks at municipal buildings, Jewish institutions, landmarks, and a transportation hubs.

In 1999, Mezer went to trial and was sentenced to life. In his testimony he stated that he had intended the bomb in an attack that would kill a lot of Jewish people, and Lafi Khalil was convicted of having a fake immigration card and deported.

Another incident of terrorist intercept was "the Monument Conspiracy." Terrorists were going to blow up the Lincoln Tunnel, the Holland Tunnel, the Statue of Liberty, and the Empire State Building. When the plot to blow up New York landmarks, including the U.N. Building, was uncovered, with the FBI we pursued and were able, with the help of the FBI, to thwart these attacks. Sheik Omar Rahman and nine other Egyptian extremists were convicted in 1995.

Cities planning millennium celebrations were threatened when on December 14, 1999, border authorities arrested a man named Ahmed Ressam at Port Angeles on the Canadian border with Washington State. After briefly questioning him, they became suspicious and arrested him after a short chase. In his car they found cyclotrimethylenetrinitramine (RDX), an explosive powerful enough to take a building down, and four watches that were to be used as timers.

On Ressam they found a scrap of paper with a name Abdel Ghani (we would later discover his last name was Meskini), a Brooklyn address, and a "718" phone number. Members of the FBI-NYPD Joint Terrorism Task Force tracked down the address and we put the location under surveillance with agents, and officers observing the building for weeks.

We found out later that the plan had been for Meskini, under a pseudonym, to meet Ressam in Seattle in December to act as his guide and translator. He had gone to Seattle to meet Ressam who, because of his arrest, had failed to materialize. Ressam and Meskini were planning to travel to Los Angeles where they had targeted the airport and planned to bomb it right before New Year's Day.

Left high and dry, Meskini had made a call to the man who'd coordinated the plot, Mokhtar Haouari, to figure out his next move, before boarding a plane back to New York on December 17. A bank-surveillance camera at an ATM machine in Seattle confirmed Meskini's presence there.

When we decided to pick Meskini up, the operation was worked out with the FBI, and both agents and officers participated in the arrest armed with assault rifles and bomb-sniffing dogs. We arrested him without incident and took him down to New York's FBI headquarters at 26 Federal Plaza to interrogate him. During an eleven-hour interrogation session he gave a statement that implicated him in a terrorist plot to bomb significant locations in the United States.

Both Meskini and Ressam were members of the Armed Islamic Group, and the plot was extremely complex and covert; but federal authorities arrested operatives in Boston, Seattle, Vermont, New York, and Canada. (After September 11, Ressam was questioned at length about his connections to bin Laden's Al Qaeda terrorist network.) Meskini was tried, convicted, and given a twenty-four year sentence. Ressam was convicted and is awaiting sentencing in 2003.

Although the threat was not direct, on New Year's Eve 1999, we took special precautions to ensure that there would be no terrorist attack. Our greatest concern was that bin Laden's network would choose the millennium celebrations to attack again. Some American cities, most notably Seattle, actually canceled their celebrations. I wasn't going to let the terrorists win by canceling the celebrations in Times Square.

To prevent a terrorist attack, we worked with the FBI and identified and tracked suspected terrorists known to be in the city, we interviewed informants, and we intercepted intelligence. We canceled all leaves, and on New Year's Eve over 10,000 police officers (7,000 uniformed, 700 supervisors, and 3,000 undercover) were assigned to the streets around Times Square and 37,000 officers were on duty citywide. The area all around Times Square was a frozen zone. We towed every parked car in the area to deter a car bomb, and we worked with utility companies to weld every manhole cover to prevent the placement of a bomb under the street. We locked mailboxes and removed garbage cans in preparation for the festivities.

Even though Seattle had called off their celebrations, we refused to give in to terrorism, and during the evening hours of December 31, 1999, we put our antiterrorist operation, called "Archangel," into action. Uniformed officers blanketed the streets, and all six of the department's helicopters hovered over the Times Square area. We were prepared for anything—bioterrorism, a citywide blackout, a large explosion—we had backup power for sensitive locations, like hospitals, we had emergency management equipment available, and we'd stockpiled supplies.

At midnight on New Year's Eve, I stood under the ball in Times Square with my family. Everything ran smoothly, and except for a few misdemeanor arrests it was a night without incident. The party took three years of planning, cost the city $6 million, put the department on high alert, but it was worth it. The arrests of Palestinian suicide bombers, the exposure of the Monument Conspiracy, and the uneventful millennium celebrations reflect that for every successful act of terrorism, there are many that are thwarted.

The focus of local police departments needs to take into account the real threat of terrorism, and cities need to have the funds to purchase the right equipment and stockpile medicines to cope with nuclear, chemical, and biological weapons. Defense secretary Donald Rumsfield warned that ". . . there's never been worldwide terrorism at a time when the weapons have been as powerful as they are today, with chemical, biological, and nuclear weapons spreading to countries that harbor terrorists." A dozen countries have the capability to produce biological weapons so we must remain in a state of preparedness for any eventuality.

The 1995 sarin gas attack in the Tokyo subway by the Aum Shinrikyo cult, an attack that killed twelve and injured over five thousand, is another good example of how vulnerable our urban areas are to chemical weapons. Dirty bombs, poison gas in our subways, our reservoirs poisoned, and suicide bombers in our cities—these are the real threats of today.

In 2001, a New Yorker was the victim of bioterrorism. The mysterious anthrax death of resident Kathy Nguyen (the same anthrax mailed to members of Congress), the deaths of an additional five individuals, and the contamination of seventeen nationwide, frightened many citizens. It has yet to be discovered how Nguyen was contaminated by the anthrax that caused her death. Investigators from the FBI, the Department of Health, and the Centers for Disease Control (CDC), tested her home, the Number 6 line of the subway system, and her place of employment for anthrax, and did not detect it anywhere.

To address bioterrorism, NYPD established a new position to handle the threat. The Hazmat Unit of the fire department is trained to identify biochemical substances and mitigate them; as are the NYPD's Emergency Service Unit and the FDNY and the NYPD also deploy the FEMA-funded Urban Search and Rescue Teams in case of an emergency.

Consequence management is very important, but more important is prevention. Focusing too much energy and too many resources toward consequence management is defeatist. It indicates that you have accepted that there will be another attack, and there is little to do to prevent it.

Homeland Security, and the threat of terrorism, have become the focus of law enforcement since the September 11 attacks. Following that fateful day, President Bush introduced his Homeland Security adviser, former governor Tom Ridge, and requested $38 billion to fund federal, state, and local expenditures. When Congress demanded that the monies be accounted for, Bush sent "The Homeland Security Act of 2002" to Congress. The bill, which passed in late 2002, recommends the creation of a cabinet-level Department of Homeland Security with congressional oversight. This new department will mobilize local, state, and federal resources for domestic security and focus on "the prevention, deterrence, preemption of, and defense against aggression targeted at U.S. territory, sovereignty, population, and infrastructure, as well as the management of consequences of such aggression and other domestic emergencies," and limit the damage and recovery from attacks should they occur.

To provide the new cabinet secretary with needed flexibility and agility, the law waives Civil Service laws that protect federal employees. It will allow the new secretary to hire and fire and move people around based on the security needs of the country. The legislation for Homeland Security reflects key elements to productivity and crime reduction.

It is very important that in a time of crisis we put aside bureaucratic hurdles. I think Homeland Security employees should be exempt from Civil Service laws that dictate their hiring and firing. We are at war with the terrorists, and we have no time to go through burdensome processes to get rid of incompetence. The Homeland Security act will bring into the new department twenty-two existing federal agencies that handle border and transportation security—the Immigration and Naturalization Service (INS), and Customs—emergency preparedness and response—Federal Emergency and Management Agency (FEMA) and the Office of Emergency Preparedness (OEP)—and include a clearinghouse for intelligence gathered by the CIA and FBI in an Information Analysis and Infrastructure Protection Division.

The federal government has a responsibility to cities to protect them, and law-enforcement and emergency-management agencies need access to federal and other intelligence that pertains to them. First responders need to have the correct Hazmat equipment, and emergency personnel need to be trained and must have interoperable communications equipment.

Federal programs are important, but we learned in New York after September 11, that for the first twenty-four hours after an emergency you are on your own. Every large city needs to have a local Office of Emergency Management (OEM) to respond to disasters and provide protection to its citizens. In 1994, when I was fire commissioner, I suggested that we form New York's OEM, in part because of the

first World Trade Center bombing in 1993 and the subsequent lack of federal relief efforts.

Preventing a terrorist attack is ideal, but sometimes this
is not possible and in New York the Office of Emergency
Management works with local, state, federal, and private
entities to facilitate disaster relief, do hazard planning, and
to coordinate responses to natural and man-made disasters. In case of disasters or terrorist attack, OEM coordi-
nates asset placement, disperses life-saving medicine,
shelters displaced people (in New York we can shelter
224,000), databases volunteers and their skills, and sends
out mass notifications on emergencies.

States also need to be proactive about security and
some are also considering legislation, in addition to the
Patriot Act, that will protect their citizens from terrorism.
California is enacting it's own wiretap laws; Florida wants
foreign visitors' drivers' licenses to expire at the same time
as their visas; and Virginia wants to make terrorism, or
plotting an act of terrorism, a capital offense.

I think that our country needs tighter security and
stricter immigration laws as provided for by the Patriot
Act, but I also feel that the act could be improved with
some small changes. The role of local law enforcement in
homeland defense is still less than it should be, and while
the Patriot Act allows for the sharing of intelligence
among federal agencies, it does not allow for the same
sharing with local law enforcement. Today, while 7,000
FBI agents attempt to follow up on half a million tips,
600,000 state and police officers are virtually unused in
the fight against terrorism. The partnership between local
and federal law enforcement is the only way that we are
going to be able to provide the public with the safety they
deserve.

New York Senator Chuck Schumer sponsored Bill S. 1615, the "Federal-Local Information Sharing Partnership Act of 2001" which would provide for "the sharing of certain foreign-intelligence information with local law enforcement personnel, and for other purposes." S. 1615 would give local departments access to grand jury information that pertains to national security; the authority to share wire, oral, and intercept information and foreign intelligence; as well as educational records, electronic surveillance, and information acquired from physical searches; and it gives disclosures to governmental agencies (including local) for counterterrorism purposes. In the war on terror, it is imperative that we clear the obstacles between local and federal law enforcement so that we have a multilateral cooperation in the investigation and prosecution of terrorism.

One way to enforce Homeland Security and be proactive in tracking terrorists and their activity is a national identity card that is electronically linked to government databases and visas with biometric information. In the future, with a national ID card, or a biometric visa, an officer will be able to scan a driver's card on a car stop and learn if there are outstanding warrants, or see if that person is wanted immediately. Identity cards with biometric elements would give us the ability to track aliens and civilians in the United States.

Studies show that Americans are strongly in favor of an identification card, and national identity cards could be integrated in a variety of ways. The most likely scenario is that we will standardize drivers' licenses making them federal. The ACLU claims that this would be a back-door tactic to implement a national identification card without public and legislative debate, but already your driver's license reveals a lot about you—your age, sex, height, eye color, sometimes your social security number and age are registered. Besides, your social security card is a de facto national identity number.

Even civil libertarian and lawyer Alan Dershowitz agrees that the right to anonymity is a luxury that we cannot afford in this age of terrorism. I don't agree with Dershowitz on much, but I did with his October 2001 Op Ed piece in the *New York Times,* where he writes that although a national identity card would not prevent all threats, it would make it more difficult for terrorists to hide among us. I also believe, like Dershowitz, that a national ID card would enhance civil liberties by eliminating the need for stereotyping or racial profiling: "There would be no excuse for hassling someone merely because he belongs to a particular racial or ethnic group if he presented a card that matched his print and permitted his name to be checked instantly against the kind of computerized criminal history retrieval systems that are already in use."

Ideally a national identity card would include a biometric element, probably a digitized fingerprint, and an image of each legal resident, or strands of DNA could be embedded in the card for identification. The biometric, or DNA, feature in the card would ensure that it couldn't be duplicated or stolen.

There are national ID cards in Malaysia (with a biometric fingerprint) called MyKad, which also serve as a person's passport and driver's license. Versions of national ID cards are being used in Brunei and Saudi Arabia, and are being considered in the United Kingdom. In 2003, Hong Kong is planning to introduce an identity card with a biometric chip replicating the cardholder's thumbprint. Hong Kong is especially interested in the national ID card and the biometric technology because of the flow of migrants from China.

September 11 changed the face of crime and local police departments are forced to change with it. We need to work smarter and harder to develop a professional police force that is well trained. New York and many other cities and towns around the world are targets of terror and we need to train officers in counterterrorism tactics and start crosstraining officers, firefighters, and emergency service workers to prepare them for terrorist attacks. Information needs to be consolidated and disseminated to local and federal law enforcement agencies and an accountability program like CompStat should be applied to the problem. Regardless of whether they use CompStat, departments need to start looking toward prevention, greater interagency cooperation, and providing a format for all law enforcement agencies to view the patterns of terror.

GETTING GUNS OFF THE STREETS

Each year 6 out of 10 homicide victims are killed by firearms, and in the United States guns kill over 12,000 and injure in excess of 100,000 others. From 1979 to 1999, firearms were involved in 301,491 homicides, 30,654 unintentional shooting deaths, 301,983 suicides, and another 9,322 fatalities that are not attributed. These statistics show an inextricable link between firearms and violence; and with millions of illegal guns on the streets and in the hands of criminals, police departments must take aggressive measures to enforce gun laws.

While I was in charge, the NYPD used whatever legal means there were to do so, and "Getting Guns off the Streets of New York" was the most crucial law-enforcement initiative designed and launched by the Giuliani administration.

Guns are implements of violence, and being in possession of an illegal firearm, regardless of whether it's been used to commit a crime, should be considered a serious felony offense. Getting arrested in New York City with a loaded gun is a D felony, yet a gun dealer selling dozens of illegal guns gets the same B felony as a drug dealer selling cocaine to an undercover. These are both serious crimes, but the potential damage wrought by a dozen guns in the hands of criminals far outweighs that of ten bags of cocaine.

From 1960 to the early 1990s, homicides committed annually by handguns in New York City increased from seventy-five to fifteen hundred, while the population of New York City declined 6 percent. The problem was that the NYPD had no procedure to follow up arrests for crimes that involved an illegal firearm. They rarely conducted a secondary investigation into the source of the gun. Worse yet, sometimes gun-violence cases were dropped, especially if the shooting victims didn't press charges, or if the victim was a criminal.

Realizing that when guns are not tracked down, they will only be used again in another crime, the NYPD's "Getting Guns off the Street" was a department-wide initiative that directed every member of the force to be aggressive in pursuing gun traffickers and those in possession of an illegal weapon. They accomplished this by identifying and pursuing all accomplices and gun traffickers involved in violent crimes. We started utilizing detectives for questioning and investigating the crime in which the illegal firearm was involved, as well as the provenance of the gun, so that gun arrests held up.

The initiative benefited from the department's aggressive quality-of-life enforcement and our zero tolerance for crime; and with the hostile environment we created for criminals, the carry rate of illegal guns in New York declined, as did shootings. The possibility of arrest was such that many criminals stashed their illegal guns at home. With fewer guns, target-of-opportunity shootings—where people get into a dispute, they have guns, and they shoot each other—plummeted, along with the carry rate and the murder rate.

We instructed patrol officers to make arrests for crimes where an illegal firearm was involved, and have the Detective Bureau investigate if the suspect had a prior illegal-gun conviction. Detectives would run the gun's serial numbers through the NCIC database, and where serial numbers were obliterated, every effort was made to discern them. Where guns and drugs were involved, the Narcotics Division was instructed to check the Narcotics Investigative Tracking of Recidivist Offenders (NITRO) database to see if the suspects have previous firearms-related charges. Where this was confirmed, a member of the NITRO Division would respond to the case and question witnesses and the suspect about the seller of the firearm.

Seized illegal firearms are sent to the firing range and test fired, and the bullets are analyzed by experts who use microscopes and digital imaging to capture the surface of the bullets. The ballistic information—"ballistic fingerprints"—is then tracked through national ballistics databases.

For many years two databases, DrugFire, managed by the FBI, and IBIS, which was overseen by the Bureau of Alcohol, Tobacco and Firearms (ATF), operated separately and with incompatible platforms. The FBI and the ATF are consolidating their databases, and have established the National Integrated Ballistics Information Network (NIBIN). Under this plan, DrugFire will be discontinued and the ATF will assume responsibility for the system's sites, while the FBI will administrate the communications network that links the NIBIN database to police departments and law-enforcement agencies. NIBIN is fairly new, with only 1 million images stored, and a limited number of police departments have access, yet they already have had around six thousand hits.

My tactic was to get illegal guns out of the hands of criminals before they are used in crimes. Everyone in the department was on alert for illegal gun possession, but what really had an impact on getting guns off the street, and reducing pockets of crime in all five boroughs, was the NYPD's elite Street Crime Unit (SCU).

Founded in 1971, Street Crime was a small unit operating from the unit's headquarters on Randall's Island in the East River, whose members were selected for their street-smarts and competence.

Street Crime was the NYPD's equivalent to a Special Forces Unit, and the officers in it were some of the most experienced and motivated that the department had to offer. They patrolled the streets in plainclothes modules of three and four in unmarked vehicles. They were expert in spotting weapons, and used assertive tactics like stops and frisks. The unit used decoy officers to catch criminals who repeatedly preyed on cab drivers, tourists, prostitutes, and citizens. When a pattern of rapes in Manhattan terrorized residents, the unit responded with undercover patrols and female decoy officers. Although no arrests were made, within a week the attacks stopped.

In 1996, the unit of about 120 officers was responsible for 20 percent of all arrests of people carrying illegal guns in the city, and their skill in detecting weapons before a suspect could use them, stealth, and rapid deployment characterized the unit. Street Crime was so successful in detecting criminal activity and making arrests that in 1997 I added officers to the unit expanding it from 120 to 400 members. The results of this expansion were impressive: In 1997 and 1998, SCU cops stopped and searched 45,000, seized 2,072 guns, and confiscated $2.4 million in cash and 231 kilos of cocaine. Representing less than 2 percent of the force, SCU was recovering 40 percent of the guns citywide; and since taking guns off the streets saves lives, these arrests had a beneficent ripple effect on violent crime in the neighborhoods where the units operated.

With the enlargement of the Street Crime Unit we were able to cast a wider net and place a team in every borough. In each borough we established bases and identified targets of enforcement activity for SCU beyond guns, to include all forms of street-level crime, including drugs, homicides, shootings, as well as gun arrests. If there was a chronic and violent crime problem anywhere in the city, we would send Street Crime to address it.

Then Amadou Diallo was mistakenly shot and killed by four Street Crime officers in February 1999. After the shooting, the unit was scaled back, members put in uniform, and its tactics changed. The press vilified them, even using one of their mottos "We own the night" against them. They didn't mean they owned the night from the citizens; they meant they owned it from the criminals. I visited a rape-crisis unit that had the motto, "We own the night from rapists," and no one accused them of being bullies.

The members of Street Crime were totally demoralized by the reaction, and the combined effect—the lack of anonymity, the low morale, and the less aggressive tactics—was that the number of guns seized after the Diallo shooting fell dramatically and the productivity of the unit dropped precipitously.

Statistics showed that from February 4 (the day of the Diallo shooting) to March 24, 1999, officers from the Street Crime Unit made 291 arrests, down from 705 arrests during the same period in 1998 and 775 in 1997.

Meanwhile statistics show the number of shooting incidents and shooting victims were creeping up in neighborhoods usually policed by the Street Crime Unit. There were marked increases in the Forty-seventh and Forty-sixth Precincts in the Bronx, the 113th and the 110th Precincts in Queens. In the Eighty-third Precinct, which encompasses Bushwick, Brooklyn, there were six shooting incidents in that four-week period, up from two during the same period last year and there were seven shooting victims, up from two.

Following the Diallo shooting, the Street Crime Unit's tactics were scrutinized by the federal and state governments, and other critics, who accused the unit of infringing on the civil rights of mostly black and Hispanic individuals by searching them without probable cause.

In the twenty precincts where the Street Crime Unit was active, statistics showed that 63 percent of all people the police reported to have been frisked were black; yet 71 percent of all crime suspects were described by victims as black, and 68 percent of all arrests in those precincts were of blacks. What these numbers don't indicate is that the racial and ethnic distribution of the subjects of stop-and-frisk reports reflects the demographics of known violent-crime suspects as reported by crime victims. Similarly, the demographics of many locations that host violent crime reflect the ethnicity of SCU's stop and frisks, and arrestees in violent crimes who also correspond with the demographics of known violent-crime suspects. What's more important was that Street Crime officers received a low number of complaints from the Civilian Complaint Review Board (CCRB), just 84 in 1997 and 41 in 1998. That is less than 2 percent of the 4,769 complaints against the police department in 1997 and less than 1 percent of the 4,976 complaints in 1998.

In 2002, Commissioner Ray Kelly disbanded the Street Crime Unit. It cannot be a coincidence that in the first four months of 2002 there was a 22 percent surge in shootings, and without SCU policing the streets we have seen more guns on the streets being used in target-of-opportunity shootings and innocent bystanders, even children are once again being caught in the cross fire. There had been a call for the reformation of the Street Crime Unit. Others attribute the jump in shootings to cuts in Operation Condor, the overtime program I developed for extra street patrols. Regardless of the reason, the escalating gun violence in New York is something to be concerned about and needs to be addressed with increased resources and manpower.

NYPD officers are required to be armed at all times with an authorized on- or off-duty handgun. Up until 1996, the standard NYPD firearm was the .38-cal. service revolver. This remained the case until criminals started using more sophisticated weaponry—like 9-mm semiautomatic guns—and often outgunned police officers. The NYPD authorized officers to have the choice of carrying a 16-round Glock 9-mm semiautomatic pistol or the .38-cal. service revolver.

The kind of ammunition used can also make a difference in firepower. In 1990, before they merged with the NYPD, New York City's Transit Bureau and Housing Authority Police switched from full-metal-jacketed bullets to hollow-point bullets, a step taken by most big-city departments and many federal agencies. Hollow-point bullets are now the law-enforcement standard.

In 1996, the NYPD released a study that examined shootings in New York City by Transit, Housing, and

NYPD officers over the prior two years, and what we found was that seven bystanders shot by the police had been struck by bullets that passed through other people or objects. These types of shootings would not have occurred had officers been using hollow points.

When a hollow-point bullet is fired, the perpetrator is brought down with fewer shots—sometimes even stopping criminals before they fire their gun—reducing the possibility of harm to the police officer and innocent bystanders. The empty tip of the bullets flatten on impact and rarely ricochet off their target, whereas full-metal-jacketed bullets often ricochet off objects and pierce their targets, putting civilians and officers at risk.

In 1998, we began to implement the switchover to hollow points, and in 1999, I approved $500,000 to purchase hollow-point bullets for each of the department's forty thousand officers who took a twice-yearly marksmanship test at the NYPD's firing range in the Bronx. By 2000, all NYPD officers had hollow-point ammunition.

Fortunately for the NYPD, New York State's gun laws are stricter than most, but we are victims of states whose gun laws are lax; 90 percent of all illegal guns in New York flow into the city from other states. Despite new laws that regulate the purchase and use of firearms, Congress has failed to pass legislation to limit the resale of guns to secondary buyers. The first sale at the licensed gun dealer is recorded; but guns are also sold at gun shows, through classified ads, and by "straw buyers."

New York Times writers Jayson Blair and Sarah Weissman's article "The Biography of a Gun" traced the history of a 12-shot, 9-mm Jennings semiautomatic from a California assembly line in 1995 to the Property Clerk's Office in the New York State Supreme Court Building in Brooklyn. On the way the gun was used in thirteen crimes, including the murders of a sixteen-year-old boy and a father of four.

According to the *Times* article, it didn't take long for the gun to be bought by a straw purchaser on behalf of Charles Chapman who, as a convicted felon, was prohibited by law from purchasing firearms. Mr. Chapman then drove the firearm to New York, where it was sold to a member of the Bloods gang. Through a series of transactions, the gun ended up in the possession of Demeris Tolbert (a suspect in the killing of a pawnbroker), who was arrested on the roof of the Howard Houses after shooting a New York police officer, Tanagiot Benekos.

This is a classic story—most of the guns used in crimes are originally purchased legitimately and then resold to gun traffickers like Charles Chapman. Following an investigation, the ATF was able to trace thirty guns back to Chapman, and he was charged with gun trafficking and conspiracy to illegally purchase firearms and transport them for sale to criminals in New York.

It's a simple issue of supply and demand. States like New York that have strict gun laws become targets for gunrunners, since the demand by criminals for weapons is high. Gun traffickers go to states like Georgia (where Chapman made many of his illegal gun purchases), Florida, South Carolina, and Texas that have liberal gun laws and hire an individual with a clean criminal record to go into a licensed gun shop and buy dozens of guns. The state and federal checks will clear that person, they are able to buy a gun, and then they turn around and sell the guns to the criminals who resell them to other criminals for use in crimes.

This is what a ring of gunrunners that operated out of Harlem were doing. We targeted the group in a two-month investigation, and during this period the gun traffickers were able to purchase forty-eight guns for the undercover officer in Georgia—including a semiautomatic weapon with infrared laser sight. It is inconceivable that this type of weapon, a high-powered pistol with laser sight, which is clearly not for any sporting purchase, can be purchased so easily in some states.

This particular crew took advantage of Georgia's InstaCheck system, which gives licensed gun dealers immediate approval for the sale of firearms to those who have not been indicted for felony offenses. The system was set up in 1998 to regulate the purchase of firearms, but it has not inhibited the flow of guns to criminals who purchase their weapons via straw buyers or unregulated sources. These arrests were a clear signal to this group, and others, that weapons smugglers would be arrested and prosecuted through the efforts of city, state, and federal agencies. We got three gunrunners in this sting, but they are only a microcosm of the many gangs that move guns from the legal market to the black market.

We live in a gun culture—a sad fact that probably is not going to change anytime soon—but there are ways that we can control the flow of illegal weapons onto the streets. The 1994 Brady Law of background checks helped to do this by preventing fugitives, felons, and other unauthorized people from buying guns. In the years that it has been extant, it has saved thousands of lives, but unfortunately not all gun purchases are subject to background checks. There are 4,500 gun shows in this country annually, and many dealers at these shows are private and therefore not obliged to do Brady checks on potential gun buyers. This fact was brought into national focus in 1999, when two students, Eric Harris and Dylan Klebold, killed themselves and thirteen others at Colombine High School in Colorado.

Three of the guns used at Colombine had been purchased at gun shows without a gun license. A statement from Robyn Anderson, a friend of the two gunmen who purchased the weapons for them, indicates how easy it was to buy guns at a gun show:

> Eric and Dylan had gone to the Tanner gun show on Saturday and they took me back with them on Sunday. They bought guns from three sellers. They were all private. They paid cash. There was no receipt. I was not asked any questions at all. There was no background check. All I had to do was show my driver's license to prove that I was 18. Dylan got a shotgun. Eric got a shotgun and black rifle that he bought clips for. He was able to buy clips and ammunition without me having to show any I.D. The sellers didn't write down any information.
>
> I would not have bought a gun for Eric and Dylan if I had had to give any personal information or submit to any kind of check at all. I think it was clear to the sellers that the guns were for Eric and Dylan. I had no idea what they were eventually going to do with the guns. . . . I wish a law requiring background checks had been in effect at the time. I don't know if Eric and Dylan would have been able to get guns from another source but I would not have helped them. It was too easy. I wish it had been more difficult. I wouldn't have helped them buy the guns if I had faced a background check.

Anderson was not charged criminally in the Columbine incident, but has been named in a civil suit.

At that time anyone in Colorado could buy a weapon. But in 2000, gun-control measures were passed there and in Oregon requiring that buyers at guns shows undergo background checks, using the same procedure as buying from a licensed dealer. Until the Brady Check is instituted at gun shows nationwide and we close the "gunshow loophole," we will continue to have 40 percent of U.S. gun sales go without a background check being conducted.

The use of lethal weapons should be limited whenever possible, even by law enforcement. Officers should use their guns only when absolutely necessary, and to facilitate this they need to be given alternatives to firearms to subdue suspects and criminals. Devices used in lieu of lethal weapons include irritants like pepper spray, which contains oleoresin capsiscum and CN/CS gas (CN gas is a component in pepper spray, and CS is a stronger irritant but wears off in ten minutes or less); and nonlethal projectiles like shot bags, and rubber bullets, which are used primarily for crowd control. To incapacitate a suspect, an officer can use a stun gun that delivers a high-voltage electric shock; or a baton-launched net that can be used to debilitate suspects from a range of up to thirty feet. Disorienting devices, like Tasers, which jam the nervous system of an individual for a few minutes, or a laser that uses random, flashing green light to disorient a subject, can be effective.

Nondeadly technologies that have been developed but are not yet widely available are electric stun projectiles— a wireless self-contained projectile that uses stun-gun technology and "smart guns" that use computer chips to block access to weapons for anyone not authorized to use it.

Acoustic systems that alert officers from a distance that a weapon is present are in the works, as is "see through the wall" technology that can locate an individual and their weapons through brick or concrete. This technology that would enable officers to see suspects before they can see them are in development. It is good to have devices that prevent gun violence, but to truly have an impact, there is a simple formula for success: With fewer guns on the streets, cities are safer and citizens are less likely to get shot or murdered.

To stem the flow of illegal weapons, the NYPD supported legislative proposals that limited access to firearms and increased the penalties. We found ways to use New York's Penal Law to close loopholes that allowed for criminal possession of a firearm and sale of defaced firearms; and the NYPD supported legislation that outlawed the production and importation of Saturday Night Specials (cheaply made, small-caliber handguns). Still, today the bans on these weapons need to be more specific in defining what these guns are and prohibit the domestic production of this kind of weapon.

I also reluctantly supported legislation to have a "one gun a month" law, which would allow an individual to purchase no more than one gun per month. Weapons would be diverted from illegal use—but it is insane that we should have to rely on the policy, which in essence tells people that twelve guns a year is OK.

Proactive policing and the relentless pursuit of illegal firearms and their sources are part of the way that we cut back the crime rate in New York. What we need is increased federal support for the enforcement of gun laws and for the prosecution of gun-related crimes. The Bush administration has committed over $550 million over two years to implement Project Safe Neighborhoods (PSN), a gun-violence reduction strategy based on partnerships with federal, state, and local law-enforcement agencies to coordinate community programs and review gun cases for prosecution. Money will also go to the prosecution of violent gun offenders and heightened federal gun-law enforcement using state-of-the-art technology and intelligence-gathering techniques, such as crime mapping, and the tracing of seized guns and ballistic technology to help connect bullets, casings, and guns. Officers and agents will be trained under this program in current trends, effective gun-violence reduction efforts, and firearms laws and outreach programs with local communities.

My philosophy with regard to gun control is that we need tighter, uniform, national licensing regulations, and the annual registration of firearms to hold owners accountable for the legal weapons they purchase. A yearly safety check would make a huge difference and prevent guns from being purchased legitimately and then diverted to illegal use through straw purchasers or theft. The only way to stop this diversion is to have a yearly safety check and have people account for their weapons. It wouldn't impinge on people's right to own firearms; it would require them to be responsible for them. It is a way to make sure that people are accountable by requiring them to bring their firearm in once a year for inspection. We can call it a safety check, but the main purpose would be to make sure that they have their guns. If they don't have their gun, then they would have to explain why. The only good answers being it was stolen and they have a police report, or that they've sold it in compliance with federal regulations.

Another way to keep track of guns is through insurance. We insist that people insure their cars because they could end up being a three-thousand-pound weapon. Why not have the same standard for guns? As a nation we have what I believe is an obsession with firearms and we need laws that allow citizens to possess firearms but also hold them accountable for their use, and ensure that they are not diverted to the illegal market.

11.

ORGANIZED CRIME

There are many kinds of gangs—the Mafia, street gangs, or international terrorists—and the definition of "gang" can be expanded to include any group that has been organized with the purpose of engaging in criminal activity, including terrorism.

Traditionally organized crime has been investigated by units of the NYPD's Organized Crime Control Bureau (OCCB), established in 1971 as a result of the Knapp Commission hearings on police corruption, which found that to combat corruption the NYPD's battle against organized crime had to be centralized under one umbrella, for supervisory purposes, and decentralized operationally into self-contained modules to promote quality investigations, safety, and to ensure accountability. The system has suppressed corruption and enhanced the effectiveness of enforcement efforts for three decades in New York City.

The OCCB has five divisions—Investigative Support, Vice Enforcement, Narcotics, Auto Crime, and Organized Crime Investigation—and two units, Asset Forfeiture and

Intelligence and Analysis. OCCB investigations are administrated by the Investigative Support Division, which provides technical and financial support. Vice Enforcement handles the enforcement of laws against prostitution, gambling, underage drinking, unlicensed sale of alcohol, ticket scalping, and illegal fireworks; and the Narcotics Division is responsible for suppression of narcotics crimes and seizing assets. Auto Crime was established to deal with and attack organized vehicle theft rings, and the Organized Crime Investigation Task Force was formed with the FBI to work on family, gang, or ethnic-based organized crime.

The Asset Forfeiture Unit works with the operational divisions of the OCCB—Vice, Narcotics, Auto Crime, and OC Investigation—to develop cases where they find that the individuals possess valuable items that are used as instruments of their crimes. The unit works with the Justice Department on seizing the assets, according to the NYPD's involvement in the case that the assets were seized from, and then sharing the proceeds after forfeiture. Intelligence and Analysis is the OCCB's in-house intelligence unit and administrates the multiple databases and interfaces with federal, state, and other local entities that also track criminals.

When assets are seized, state and local agencies share the property and money with the federal government. Once the property is sold off, the amount of money that we receive is formulated according to the extent of our participation in the case. For example, if the NYPD initiated a case, we would get a significant portion of assets seized. On the other hand, if we were just asked by the federal government to help with surveillance in a case, we would get a lesser share of the assets. It was a great addition to the NYPD's budget, and we would use these funds for vehicles, equipment, overhead costs, and narcotics initiatives. In 1998, the department seized $95 million through enforcement activities—$21 million of which we were able to keep and put back into enforcement efforts.

An interesting OC case that the OCCB worked on during my tenure was a sting operation that netted John Gotti's son-in-law Carmine Agnello. Agnello, who was married to Gotti's daughter Victoria, was invested in a variety of businesses—junkyards, salvage businesses, and auto repair shops—and almost all of them were involved in illegal activity. He was a man of enormous wealth; his largest operation was New York Shredding Corporation in the Bronx, which alone was estimated to be worth $50 million.

In March 1997, to counter auto-related crimes, the NYPD had worked with federal and state agencies to close more than 150 chop shops in Queens in a program called "Operation Spring Clean Up." This sweep was part of a larger operation to reduce auto crimes by targeting illegal auto-part resellers and salvage yards associated with organized crime. The focus was primarily chop shops, and during the investigation we closed three of Agnello's and found that he was threatening and robbing other auto-part resellers and was dominating the business citywide through intimidation.

Since no one was willing to sign a complaint against him, we decided to go after him ourselves. To further our investigation we set up our own scrap yard, "Stadium Scrap," in Willets Point, Queens, manned by undercover agents, and waited to see whether Agnello would attempt to threaten our "business."

The intention was to catch Agnello on audio or video extorting or threatening the undercover detectives, so we wired Stadium's trailer with video and audio. Within days

Agnello made a personal appearance and made us an offer he thought we couldn't refuse: He told the undercover officers that they were to sell him auto parts at less than the market price, and he would generously allow Stadium to stay in business.

NYPD detectives told him that they would think about it, which was not what Agnello wanted to hear. So in June 1999, Agnello dispatched a henchman, John Roberts, to torch the scrap yard we had set up. When Roberts cut the locks on the yard NYPD's junkyard, detectives arrested him and, realizing that he was in serious trouble, he became a confidential informant.

Detectives instructed Roberts to return to Agnello and claim that the firebombing had gone awry. Agnello directed Roberts, who was wearing a wire, to commit further acts of arson: "I want it burned . . . Listen to me, all you gotta do is buy glass bottles, fill them up . . . throw them over the fence . . ." We had Agnello on tape instructing someone to commit arson, and I felt that we had a solid case against him.

In January 2000, Agnello was arrested with six others, and the state charged him with using violence, intimidation, and arson to dominate the scrap business. He posted bail and was released. We knew that federal agents were working on a parallel case against Agnello all along—we had the undercover operation at the yard, while they were working with an informant. The NYPD and the state had to clear the first arrest and prosecution with the U.S. attorney and federal agents prior to taking Agnello in, so that we did not undermine their case against him.

Several weeks after Agnello posted bail in the state case, FBI agents dragged Agnello out of bed and into federal court. The second time in court, Agnello was charged with racketeering, extortion, arson, and tax-fraud charges, this time with no bail. He pled guilty to arson and extortion, was given a nine-year sentence, and fined $11 million.

Not as well entrenched as the traditional mostly Italian organized crime families, Russian gangs operating out of Brighton Beach, Brooklyn, were starting to flourish in the early 1990s. These Russian-born criminals brought with them extreme violence—including murder and assault—and the extortion of Russian-owned businesses. Russian gangs also ran brothels, illegal gambling houses, and were expert in frauds, including a gasoline tax-evasion scheme and a cellular phone–cloning network that the NYPD dismantled with the help of the Secret Service.

Federal and local authorities shared a problem in investigating these mobsters—there were few officers and agents who were fluent in Russian. An example of how this language barrier hindered investigations was our attempt to infiltrate Russian-run brothels, which do not cater to non-Russian clients. We used undercover officers who spoke Russian to pose as "johns." But in addition to speaking the language, they required an introduction, which was always difficult to get. Another problem in the Russian community was the fear of retribution, and we investigated numerous cases involving the extortion of Russian-owned businesses where complainants would cooperate until the arrest was made and then refuse to follow through on the prosecution.

These people were being strong-armed by Russian criminal organizations who have been suspects in dozens of murders in New York City, and in many of these murders both the victim and the perpetrators had served time in prison or had been known criminals in the former Soviet Union.

Witnesses in these murder cases were often the least forthcoming. The 1994 murder in Brooklyn of a former Soviet heavyweight boxing champion, Oleg Korataev, who was extorting and trafficking narcotics, is a good example of this reluctance to talk.

Korataev was shot and killed in front of Café Arbat, a popular Russian nightclub on Brighton Beach Avenue. At the time of his murder, he had been among two hundred guests at a Russian New Year's party that the NYPD investigators believed his killer, Alex Taim, had also attended.

We talked to everyone present and the stories were the same, interview after interview. No one saw or heard anything. No one could identify the victim or his killer. This was because Taim, a gang leader, was a "thief in law" of Vyacheslav Ivankov, the most powerful figure in Russian organized crime. This association with Ivankov (who is currently in jail on 1996 federal extortion charges) terrified these witnesses.

Taim avoided prosecution by fleeing to Western Europe after the murder, but despite these obstacles—the language barriers, fear of retribution, and the flight of some of the Russian gangsters abroad—we were able to clear many Russian mob-related homicides and prosecute those responsible by cooperating in Racketeering Influenced and Corrupt Organizations (RICO) investigations with state and federal law-enforcement agencies.

By the late 1990s, street gangs like the Netas, the Latin Kings, the Bloods, the Crips, and all of their subsets, were dealing drugs, selling illegal guns, robbing cars, defacing property with graffiti, and extorting money for protection.

To counter this "disorganized crime" in New York City, we developed a strategy that we used as the standard to dismantle gangs. My gang initiative was designed to counter all criminal enterprises—from traditional organized crime to more loosely associated groups—and it was extremely successful; from 1994 to 1999, we identified 13,045 drug gangs of all sizes in New York City and dismantled 1,100 of them.

We formed major drug initiatives in thirty-nine precincts and developed a strategic plan to identify and discourage both violent street gangs and narcotics trafficking. To oversee the initiative, I named a Citywide Gang Coordinator (CGC), and this program involved the CGC working with borough, precinct, Police Service Area (PSA), and Transit District commanders to designate high-priority targets in their areas. We relied on the eight borough commanders (Brooklyn North and South, the Bronx, Manhattan North and South, Queens North and South, and Staten Island) to identify significant drug, gun, and shooting locations. Once the locations had been identified, the coordinator, with the department's Intelligence Division's Gang Intelligence Unit (GIU) reviewed and analyzed the information and shared it with investigators from the Narcotics Division, Auto Crime, Patrol, the Citywide Anti-Gang Enforcement Unit (CAGE), and other appropriate NYPD divisions and units.

The initiative was staffed with gang-suppression units and investigation squads (the OCCB placed units made up of a detective squad, a narcotics module, and a Street Crime Unit in each borough). As undercover agents executed "buy and busts," street-crime officers investigated locations that had seen gang-related activity, and the detectives, working with precinct-based detectives, followed up on drug- and gang-motivated crimes.

We also instituted methods to collect, maintain, analyze, and process gang intelligence by using Gang/Group Incident Reports and the On-Line Booking System

(OLBS), and typing crimes as gang-motivated (when the gang is directly involved in the activity) or gang-related (when an individual gang member is involved). We placed Gang Intelligence Units citywide, who worked with informants collecting intelligence on the streets, and with the Department of Correction and their "Gang Intel" unit to collect jailhouse information from gang-member prisoners.

Gang Intelligence also interviewed victims and witnesses of gang-related crimes and gathered information from confidential informants to identify key members of the gang and their associates and keep them under surveillance. In some cases we would supplement the intelligence with undercover buy and busts, but these operations also relied heavily on informants who would give us information that would allow the undercover to fit in better. The OCCB's policy was that nobody knows the criminal business better than those involved; and in 1996, right around the time I took over, the bureau used fewer than two hundred informants. In 2000, when I left, we had more than two thousand informants.

To make sure that we had the most comprehensive and up-to-date information, investigators entered gang intelligence into the Gang Investigative Unit's central and secure data-management system, which is linked to other law-enforcement databases and maintained by the Intelligence Division. The information allowed us to provide local commanders of the department with systematic guidelines to accomplish their objectives of identifying, targeting, and dismantling gangs, determine gang membership, their chain of command, and method of operation.

The blueprint for the NYPD's gang initiative's strategy was demonstrated by the sweep of the Diego-Beekman complex and the tenements along Beekman Avenue in the

Bronx, where for years gang members had converged, selling drugs and committing crimes. In the early 1990s, the NYPD had broken up the largest gang—the Wild Cowboys—who were responsible for a dozen murders, only to see their territory taken over by smaller gangs. In 1995 several members of the Wild Cowboys were tried, convicted, and sentenced to long prison terms.

By 1996, the situation had become intolerable again, and we set up an operation to dismantle these gangs. We sent in undercover officers and federal agents to work their way up the chain of command by purchasing larger and larger quantities of drugs from the gang members.

We carefully developed the case, and once we had obtained enough evidence, we got search warrants and planned our sweep on a date certain. NYPD officers, FBI, ATF, Secret Service, the National Guard, and United States Marshals—six hundred investigators in all—searched abandoned buildings for drugs and guns, and we arrested the thirty-five known criminals we had targeted.

Other areas, also having a large number of gang-related homicides and other violent crime, were included in this pilot program. Public-housing complexes were the location of much gang activity. Under the gang initiative, we arrested 402 members of three separate gangs in Brooklyn's Marcy Houses on drug charges, as well as suspects in 5 murders and 18 attempted murders. Until we cleaned up the complex, the Marcy Houses were plagued with nightly gun battles, gang members hanging out selling drugs in front of buildings, along with random violence in the hallways.

Once we had made our arrests, we kept our foothold in the projects by coordinating and unifying police protection with officers policing the projects by foot and bicycle. We executed vertical patrols in Housing Authority buildings by uniformed officers who inspected mailboxes, elevators, lobbies, stairwells, roof landings, and each floor staircase and hallway within the building from top-to-bottom. CCTV in public housing also helped us police the projects, and in some places reduced crime by over a third. CCTV provided us with documentation if crimes were committed; but most important, the cameras were a deterrent to crime, and many crimes that would have taken place never did.

Another operation "Red Bandana" was executed by our citywide Anti-Gang Enforcement (CAGE) unit in 1997, and it swept up 160 gangbangers, mostly members of the Bloods, who identify themselves with red bandanas, and the Crips, who wear blue beads to indicate their allegiance. The Bloods and the Crips are street gangs that originated in Los Angeles; in the late 1990s, they were establishing outposts and taking over drug enterprises in urban areas nationwide.

The Bloods were an active and violent gang, and we began seeing a violent trend of gang-related incidents: random slashings and stabbings, mostly on subways, with box cutters and knives, that we associated with initiations. The gang lived by their code of "Blood in. Blood out." To be initiated you had to spill someone's blood; and to get out of the gang your own blood was spilled. Because of the NYPD's enforcement of low-level crimes, many of the gang members had stopped carrying guns, and so slashings and stabbings with box cutters fulfilled most initiation rites and solved some of the disputes that in the past would have involved shootings.

We heard through intelligence sources that gang members were planning to expand their operations, and we were determined to prevent the estimated five hundred gang members in some sixteen subsets (a large percentage of those who claim to be members of the Bloods or Crips are often wannabes) from making New York an outpost for this type of criminal activity.

"Red Bandana" was a response to this threat. It was a four-month, multiagency drug-and-gang initiative that we set up to dismantle street and other violent drug gangs in targeted areas of the city. The operation was focused in precincts in Upper Manhattan, Southern Queens, Northern Brooklyn, and on Riker's Island. Criminals arrested during this operation were accused of selling drugs, committing robberies, weapons' possession, and murder. With strategic arrests under "Red Bandana," we dismantled seven sets of Bloods and one set of Crips and achieved the purpose of the sweep, which was to stop the gangbangers from expanding their activity.

Another gang, the Latin Kings, was founded by Hispanic inmates in Chicago during the 1940s to protect themselves against other prison gangs. The New York branch of the Kings was established in 1986 by Luis Felipe, or "King Blood," who is currently serving a life term in solitary confinement for ordering hits on several Latin King members in the early 1990s.

To take down the Latin Kings, the NYPD worked with the FBI on "Operation Crown," a nineteen-month undercover investigation that ended with simultaneous citywide raids. The 1998 sweep by one thousand federal, state, and local law officers began before sunrise and netted close to one hundred gang members, including Antonio Fernandez, a Brooklyn man known as "King Tone," who was the gang's leader.

Until then the Latin Kings had been approximately three thousand strong, and Antonio "King Tone" Fernandez was their guru. Fortunately, we already had an outstanding warrant for his arrest from his participation in

the 1997 sale of sixty-two grams of heroin to an undercover officer. We found Fernandez sleeping in his apartment and arrested him on that outstanding warrant. He
pleaded guilty and was sentenced to twelve and a half
years in prison.

The Latin Kings are a dangerous group of criminals,
but now they are less so because of these 1998 multi-
agency raids and the resulting arrests. Latin King members
were charged with a series of crimes, including felony drug
sales, murder, and conspiracy. In the raids, we seized
$229,288 worth of drugs (4.5 pounds of heroin, 4.5
pounds of crack, and 41 grams of marijuana), 39 guns,
and 3 bulletproof vests.

The arrests destroyed the command structure of the
Kings by removing their "King," who supervised operations in New York State, and their borough leaders, or
"Crowns." In "Operation Crown" we dismantled one of
the most well-organized and violent gangs in New York
City, one that was responsible for more than one hundred
crimes—assault, attempted murder, robbery, rape, and
drug dealing.

In "Red Bandana," "Operation Crown," and all our
anti-gang operations we were always careful to coordinate
our investigations with other law-enforcement agencies,
bureaus, and district attorneys' offices, and whenever possible we used tactics that helped to build RICO, Continuing
Criminal Enterprise (CCE), or conspiracy prosecutions.

In 1991, the department, noting an alarming increase in
home-invasion robberies committed by crews of thugs
against the Dominican community, set up the Joint Robbery Apprehension Task Force with the FBI. A New

Yorker is 180 times more likely to be the victim of a property crime than of murder or assault. Crimes against property, which include burglary, larceny, and auto theft, account for around two-thirds of the crime in the seven major categories. Even if they are not injured—and often, they aren't—victims of these kinds of crimes feel violated and vulnerable, and many criminals start with property crimes and graduate up to more violent crimes.

Because violent crime had been a priority for years in the city, often these "smaller" cases would get overlooked. Crimes against property are lesser crimes, but often a simple burglary can turn violent, so I adopted departmentwide strategies to respond to burglaries and recover stolen vehicles. The NYPD increased the number of sting operations targeting specific crimes—like computer crimes, or stolen auto parts fencing—and to direct resources by developing specialized operations like the Robbery Apprehension Modules (RAMs), and I made sure that preventing property crimes was a priority. We targeted groups who profited from these robberies, chop shops, and the exportation of stolen auto parts, and shut down the fencing operations that moved the stolen objects and made theft profitable.

Burglary and robbery, unlike homicide, have very low clearance rates and this means that these criminals, who often work as part of crews, on gangs, are repeat offenders. We directed commanders in precincts with a high number of residential and commercial burglaries to look for patterns that would indicate that a known individual was the perpetrator of the heist and ran the results through CompStat to discern the pattern. Teams were instructed to canvas witnesses at the scene and collect evidence, especially fingerprints and DNA. Property crimes have lower clearance rates, and DNA testing is one way we can close that gap. Burglary and robbery have only a 14 percent chance of being solved. To increase the clearance rate on these crimes, I think we should take DNA at every burglary or robbery scene and car theft.

We have seen countless times that when individuals form a gang, they organize themselves and tend to be more violent and more dangerous to the community and commit a disproportionately high number of gun, drug, and violent street crimes. Terrorists are also part of a "gang," and we can use similar tactics and laws to regulate them that we have been using to indict and convict gang members and organized criminals. To address all kinds of gangs effectively, we need laws that make it illegal to recruit new members, make gang profits subject to asset forfeiture, and impose harsher punishments on those involved in gang-related crimes.

12.

DRUG ENFORCEMENT

Drugs aren't new to New York City—for much of its history the city has been host to the drug trade. From the late 1960s, heroin, cocaine, marijuana, and many other drugs were freely available for purchase, but the drug problem was steady and moderate enough to remain under the radar.

That situation remained until the early 1980s, when the drug industry "invented" crack cocaine and it became the catalyst that ignited the drug epidemic. By the mid-'80s, crack had set off a domino effect that resulted in brazen drug dealing, gang wars, rampant drug abuse, an exploding black market, and the decay of urban communities. The city's open-air drug markets, like farmer's markets, were part of the cityscape, and walking down the street in some neighborhoods you would be bombarded by dealers soliciting you with: "Smoke?" "China White?" "Smack?" "Down?" "Up?" "C?" On certain blocks in the East Village and uptown in Washington Heights, drugs were available twenty-four hours a day.

On any given day in New York City about half of the male arrestees held for arraignment test positive for cocaine, and 80 percent of male and female arrestees test positive for drugs—cocaine hydrochloride (powder) and crack, heroin and other opiates, marijuana and hashish, and PCP.

The drug trade, which services at least 14 million current illicit drug users in the United States, is the engine that drives crime. Illegal drugs, their sale and use, are the biggest crime and quality-of-life issues facing New York City and other urban areas, and CompStat reports show that the precincts in New York City with high drug activity are the same precincts that experience more violent crime.

The symbiotic relationship between drug abuse, narcotics sales, and crime has created a population of criminals and inmates who have serious drug dependencies: Drug abusers steal to make money, and dealers commit violent crimes to continue to sell narcotics. Narcotics crimes spur other types of crime and I believe that most crime is drug-related.

Perpetrators are often not the only intoxicated party in a crime. Many victims of murder and nonnegligent homicide test positive for drugs, and every year 30 percent of all homicides in New York City are drug-related. In addition, five hundred users overdose and die every year in New York City from cocaine intoxication and about the same overdose on heroin; overall approximately two thousand deaths have drugs mentioned in the medical examiner's report.

For all of these reasons and more, "Driving Drug Dealers out of New York City" was a priority initiative. To implement my war on drugs I had zero tolerance for drug dealing and we changed the way that the NYPD handled narcotics crimes. In the past NYPD policy restricted a patrol officer's ability to make drug arrests because the brass was afraid that drugs and money would corrupt the officers, and drugs were the exclusive purview of the department's relatively small narcotics unit. This meant that for decades only a fraction—some 10 percent—of NYPD officers addressed narcotics, while the remaining tens of thousands of cops were not even allowed on the battlefield in the war against drugs.

By 1998, the Narcotics Division had four thousand officers, not including precinct-based street narcotics units, with another one thousand officers in Tracer Units. Tracer Units are uniformed officers trained in policing drug-ravaged neighborhoods and are comprised of one lieutenant, four sergeants, and thirty-two police officers. They respond to all narcotics-related radio runs, provide mobile-and-foot patrol in designated areas, and uniformed support during the execution of search warrants. They also provide follow-up at locations that have been subject to Narcotics Division investigations.

The problem during the 1980s and early 1990s wasn't just the lack of manpower dedicated to drug crimes; the Narcotics Division of the NYPD was entrenched in antidrug programs that did not work.

The flaw in earlier methods was that they'd clean out a neighborhood, and then they'd leave. In New York during the Dinkins administration, the Narcotics Division used Tactical Narcotics Teams (TNT) to go into neighborhoods for a short period of time (no more than ninety days) and execute "buy and busts." The tactical approach was to attack certain parts of the city and then move on with no community-based follow-up.

Once TNT left the area, the Patrol Services Bureau (PSB) would put "Operation Pressure Point" into effect.

"Pressure Point" placed uniformed police officers on foot patrol to maintain the areas that TNT had just cleaned up. This two-step approach was largely ineffective because of the department's dependency on patrol officers and not officers trained in narcotics work to police drug-prone areas. TNT netted low-level drug dealers, but the big fish would relocate; then once the coast was clear, they would return and the "cleansed" area would go back to lawlessness.

Narcotics falls under the Organized Crime Control Bureau (OCCB) and enforces narcotics crimes in New York City. OCCB's Narcotics Division has several task forces, including the Drug Enforcement Task Force, a multiagency task force that targets middle- and upper-level traffickers and works extensively with other law-enforcement agencies (FBI, ATF, Customs, DEA, and the INS) to track and apprehend fugitives and drug traffickers. Until 2001, the Kennedy Airport Narcotics Smuggling Unit (KANSU) was a joint effort between the Queens Narcotics Unit and the U.S. Customs Service designed to interdict illegal narcotics being smuggled into the United States via Kennedy International Airport. Another division of narcotics is the Narcotics Control Unit (NCU), a partnership with the Department of Housing Preservation and Development that polices drug-related crimes in New York City–owned buildings.

The Narcotics Investigation and Tracking of Recidivist Offenders (NITRO) are intelligence-gathering units that work out of police narcotics boroughs (Narcotics Borough Brooklyn, Bronx, Manhattan, Queens, and Staten Island) and coordinate narcotics intelligence with other law-enforcement agencies with a focus on career felony drug offenders and firearms violators.

Each borough has a Narcotics Borough Command and Street Narcotics Enforcement Units (SNEU) and other specialized squads, like the Special Narcotics and Gun Units (SNAG) and the Street Crime Unit (SCU), that operate out of unmarked buildings. These specialized units work in modules of investigators and undercovers that are led by a sergeant who reports to a lieutenant.

Tactically their approaches are similar: The undercovers go out on the streets and make the buys from drug dealers, while investigators make and process the arrests so that undercover officers can retain their anonymity and are able to continue to work undetected.

SNAG, SNEU, and sometimes SCU modules work with precinct-based drug units conducting "buy and busts" and making arrests. The squads work in teams as purchasers and ghosts; as an undercover officer making a drug deal, your "ghost" is the narcotics officers assigned to watch over you in buy situations. Both the undercover and his or her ghost practice distress signals and buy codes. Precinct-based field teams also provide backup and observe the transactions and surveillance teams. They audiotape, and sometimes videotape, the deals and, if the investigation calls for it, remain on-site to monitor the criminal organization. Undercover officers carry nonregulation firearms, and if the case demands it, are given "flash" cars and fictitious identifications and registrations.

The old wives' tale among drug users and dealers that if you ask an undercover officer if he is a cop, he must reply truthfully is not true. An officer can use deception to retain his or her cover, and it stands up in court. Sometimes, to prove that they are not police officers, dealers will force undercovers to ingest drugs. To ensure the safety of undercover officers who engage in buy and busts, we train them in simulating using drugs as a last resort.

Narcotics cases are not simple. They often involve the surveillance of suspects and the purchase of larger and larger quantities of drugs by officers in hopes of getting bigger fish and longer sentences. The key to combating drug traffic is to take a comprehensive approach, not just going after drug traffickers, but also the infrastructure that supports them.

We started using informants or arrestees to purchase drugs and apprehend the sellers in controlled buys, and we collected gang intelligence. Another technique that the NYPD used with success was reverse stings, or "sell and bust," to discourage buyers from purchasing marijuana. With this tactic we put undercover cops on the street posing as drug dealers with marijuana that we had previously seized and arrested those who attempted to buy drugs. Federal agents had employed the tactic for years, but this was the first time the NYPD had used it.

Reverse sting operations were set up mostly in parks. We started with Central Park, then targeted six parks in the outer boroughs, and then expanded it to drug-prone locations throughout the city.

We used the reverse stings in Washington Square as part of our crackdown on low-level drug deals involving mostly middle-class clientele. We knew that marijuana sellers kept going through the system and getting out— one dealer in Washington Square Park had been arrested eighty-two times for marijuana distribution—so we needed to attack the demand side of the business by letting drug customers know there is a probability that they will be buying drugs from a cop. Washington Square is a tourist center and home to a bustling marijuana trade, and we had to deal with drug customers, and let them know that if they bought drugs there, in all probability they would be arrested.

Attacking misdemeanor crimes, like marijuana use, sends the right signal and is a cornerstone of quality-of-life crime fighting. There is no doubt in my mind that marijuana is a gateway drug, and the overt distribution of it in a central location encourages others to commit crimes in their purchase of drugs, and lures other dealers to a seemingly wide-open location that has got brisk business.

Drug crimes are broken down by offense: manufacturing, sale and possession, and type of drug. Possession laws in New York State are: If you are found selling two ounces or more of an illegal narcotic drug (heroin and cocaine fall in this category) or possess in excess of four ounces you are charged with a Class A felony (in New York the Rockefeller Drug Laws set a mandatory penalty of fifteen years to life in state prison if you are convicted of a Class A felony). If you sell more than a half ounce of heroin or cocaine or are in possession of two ounces or more this is a Class B felony. Sale and possession of less than these amounts are misdemeanor offenses. Those caught in possession of marijuana are sentenced less harshly. In New York if you sell more than two ounces of marijuana it is a Class A misdemeanor and twenty-five grams gets you a Class B misdemeanor. Depending on the severity of the misdemeanor the court will determine fines and/or jail time.

The Rockefeller Drug Laws, which govern the prosecution of drugs in New York State, have been the subject of heated debate. The laws were created because judges were giving drug traffickers light sentences. But they impose harsh sentencing on nonviolent drug offenders, sometimes in excess of the penalties imposed on those who have committed violent crimes.

We need to continue to punish traffickers but not those arrested the first time for possession. In New York City we set up drug courts in Manhattan and Brooklyn to process nonviolent first-time drug offenders. These courts required that the offender enter a treatment program and successfully complete the program. If they did this, and were not arrested for another crime, their record was expunged.

In 2002, the Rockefeller Drug Laws were debated in the state senate, but because of political infighting the hope that the laws can be revised has dissipated. Both sides of the debate agreed that the laws should be revised so that low-level, nonviolent drug offenders have the option of treatment rather than jail time, but they were unable to agree on the criteria to decide which offenders were eligible for treatment.

Another tool for cutting back on drug crimes is the Nuisance Abatement Program, which allows the NYPD to close a commercial location for one year by court order if, on three separate occasions, illegal activity is documented on the premises.

In the past cops would buy drugs at a storefront location, arrest the seller, only to find that a new person had replaced them the next day. If officers are able to buy marijuana in a store three times, we shut it down and padlock the door, and in rare instances we've been able to padlock residential buildings that are being used almost exclusively for the drug trade. Nuisance Abatement can also be used for locations that sell alcohol to minors or deal in gambling, fencing, and prostitution; and if a property is closed down, an owner has to wait a year to reopen or sell the location. From 1994 to 1999, the NYPD closed down 3,200 locations through this program, and collected over $5 million in fines and fees.

Using nuisance abatement laws in 1998 we got a search warrant and ended up arresting 102 gang members for selling crack to white-collar workers. It was one of the largest drug operations in the city, and twenty-seven of the dealers identified themselves as members of the Bloods. All together seven gangs ran three drug operations out of the Mammoth Pool Hall in midtown Manhattan and over several years sold millions of dollars' worth of crack to the suit-and-tie crowd.

Until we crashed their party, these gangs had a booming business. The white-collar workers they sold to were willing to pay a premium—for an item that would cost $5 in another location, this clientele was willing to pay $10, $15, even $20. For years the dealers worked together and cooperated, sharing space and time; the gangs would work shifts and dealers from different gangs shared customers and worked as lookouts for each other. That was until renovations in the pool hall displaced one of the gangs, causing a territorial dispute that resulted in a shooting that alerted the NYPD.

We placed the Mammoth under surveillance and observed men and women in suits and carrying briefcases purchasing drugs at all times of the day. Some smoked crack there, but most left with the drugs. When we got our warrant and raided the pool hall we discovered a lot of drugs and very few guns; further testimony to the success of our initiatives to get guns off the streets.

I organized strategic teams to aggressively identify felons, execute arrest warrants, and seize drugs and money. We started to focus intensive uniformed resources in drug-plagued areas of the city—starting with Washington Heights in Northern Manhattan—to shut down drug deal-

ing from top to bottom. The most ambitious antidrug initiative we undertook was the Northern Manhattan
Initiative (NMI).

Certain key blocks in Northern Manhattan had been
taken over by gangs, who had converted abandoned
apartment buildings into drug supermarkets, each apartment hosting one or more narcotics businesses. The residents who remained in the neighborhood were terrified to
even leave their homes, and, worse yet, the effects of what
was happening in the largely Dominican community had
a negative impact far beyond the streets of Washington
Heights. Drugs sold on the streets of the Thirtieth, Thirty-
third and Thirty-fourth Precincts flowed to other parts of
the city, and up and down the East Coast, and it became
clear that efforts to contain the trade and control the volatile situation in Washington Heights were necessary.

NMI was the first multiagency drug task force to use
state, federal, and local police. We invited other law-
enforcement agencies active in Northern Manhattan to
help us. With so many big-time dealers in the neighborhood, other agencies, the DEA, the FBI, and the New York
State Police, were also conducting investigations. Instead
of having each agency work on separate cases, many of
which overlapped, we asked them to take part in a multiagency task force that we housed at the NMI Intelligence
Center in East Harlem where analysts from the NYPD and
the federal agencies targeted drug gangs for elimination.

The event that gave me the impetus to start NMI occurred right after I became commissioner when I was
holding a town meeting in Washington Heights. As I was
reading off the crime statistics, a woman stood up and
said, "Commissioner, have you walked our streets? I challenge you to walk our streets; they're covered with drug
dealers."

So that evening I went out to 163rd Street and Broad-way—the hub of the Manhattan North drug trade—and as my three black cars pulled up, about twenty kids, all of them wearing beepers, fled down the block to Broad-way.

They congregated in the islands that run down the avenue's median strip. I walked over and sat down on a bench and started talking to a couple of them, when one of them came up and said, "Where are the cameras?"

I replied, "What do you mean, where are the cameras?"

"Nobody like you comes up here without cameras."

I said, "I came up here to see what's going on."

It was clear to me that they were all selling drugs, and in a community where 25 percent of its almost 200,000 inhabitants are under eighteen, this was a serious problem. The trade had completely overcome the neighborhood, and a new generation of drug dealers was alive and well on 163rd Street.

Primarily Manhattan North is Washington Heights and Inwood, residential neighborhoods populated by immigrants from South and Central America. Because of the Heights's location—easily accessible to the Bronx and New Jersey via bridges and highways—the neighborhood was a magnet for the distribution of narcotics and firearms. In 1995, drug arrests in North Manhattan accounted for 35 percent of all area arrests (citywide this number is closer to 25 percent); and by the early 1990s, some blocks in North Manhattan had become full-service drug supermarkets with dozens of young men dealing on the street twenty-four hours a day.

These were professional and well-funded operations. Drug gangs would have lookouts stand out on the corner and lead the customers into unoccupied apartment buildings that lined the street where the actual drug deals would take place. The transactions would occur in the lobby or upstairs in an apartment, or "office," where dealers converted the remaining vacant apartments into marijuana farms and strong rooms for money and drugs. To protect themselves, gangs employed sophisticated security systems—some used pinhole cameras and motion detectors, and one drug business was so blatant that a dealer's enforcer used a stick to keep the junkies waiting in line to buy drugs to stand in a row.

To focus on the whole trade, address the power structure of these illicit organizations, and to make the most effective arrests, we developed the "bottom up and top down" approach to pursuing drug dealers. Instead of moving in and arresting the street dealers, we would monitor their activity to identify the couriers, enforcers, lookouts, and the drug organization's managers. Undercover officers would then approach the drug gang's lower level and work their way up the chain of command by buying a couple of hits from a street dealer and then buying more and more.

Once this was established, the undercover would indicate that they were interested in buying significant amounts of drugs, hoping that they would be referred to the gang's executives, and perhaps the top tier of the organization. We waited until we had the drug organization's hierarchy identified and then, when we had enough information, we applied for warrants and moved in to arrest the whole organization from the street up on drug charges.

These communities were vulnerable because of demographics, their location, and poverty, and for these reasons drug dealers targeted them. We weren't just targeting drug gangs and going on to the next one, we were staying in the neighborhood. I made every effort to stabilize these communities so that the dealers would not come back, and on the day of the arrests I would visit the community for a meeting to explain to residents that they had been given their block back and we needed their help to keep the drug traffickers from returning.

We started our Model Block Program to facilitate a drug-ravaged block's transition into a vital neighborhood and involved other city agencies—Sanitation, Welfare, Housing, Parks—to help the community reclaim their neighborhood.

Communities wanted us to help them. In returning a clean, drug-free block to them, the hope was that community pride would help to stop the block from sliding back into actual and moral decay. Beyond enforcement, the Model Block Program worked to improve the lives of the citizens of New York City, and we worked with other city agencies to remove graffiti, clean up empty lots, remove abandoned cars, and repave streets; and officers worked to stabilize the community with the neighborhood to organize block associations and tenant patrols.

Community outreach and stabilization are vital preventative measures. If diverse communities in the city understand and trust what the police are doing, they will be more cooperative in helping them to keep drug dealers from coming back. On Model Blocks where the drug trade was particularly pervasive, I would authorize precinct commanders to put up blue barricades and set up vehicle checkpoints leading to the blocks that were known for drug sales. The officer would stop each vehicle, check driver's identification to ensure proper licensing, and inquire as to why they were in the area. This might seem unduly invasive, and they had no legal requirement to comply, but it is legal to stop them. The idea was to have a chilling effect on drug trafficking, and having officers questioning people inhibited many dealers from returning. This method was extremely successful, and from time to time those individuals pulled over were arrested for an outstanding warrant and/or a crime.

In the first two weeks of 1999, there was a slight spike in the crime rate for the first time in seven years, and as a precaution I launched "Operation Condor," an overtime program using officers on their days off to execute drug sweeps and quality-of-life patrols.

Condor was an effort to expand the philosophy of Wilson and Kelling's "Broken Windows," to address street-level drug trafficking, and it placed an additional one thousand to fifteen hundred officers, some in plain clothes, others in uniform, from all the divisions and bureaus of the NYPD, on the street. Mayor Giuliani understood crime and that you have to be constantly vigilant to maintain crime reduction. Condor was an innovative program that cost some money but was worth the investment. In the first two months, Condor decreased crime dramatically (up to 19 percent in some places), and had a significant impact on the homicide rate.

We told court officials to be prepared to handle an additional three hundred to four hundred arraignments daily, mostly for misdemeanor drug violations, and since it was put into place "Operation Condor" has netted tens of thousands of arrests by eliminating the signs of lawlessness—drug dealers hawking their drugs on street corners all over the city. With these arrests, crime decreased dramatically. And as a result of Condor, crime never went up again during my tenure.

To capture drug traffickers, local police departments should work both alone and in concert with federal agencies like the DEA, the United States Marshals, the FBI, the CIA. Partly because of my background as a federal agent,

I have always been a proponent of using whatever programs, federal, state, or local, are available to help out.

Federal programs that address drug-related money-laundering operations like the Treasury Department's Geographic Targeting Order (GTO), provide financial disincentives for drug dealers and hit them where it hurts—in their wallets—by inhibiting their ability to launder their profits through the use of licensed money remitters, banks, and offshore accounts.

Beginning around the late 1980s, New York City began to experience a tremendous surge in the number of licensed money remitters, or check-cashing locations, and their agents. Working with the federal government, we had a GTO placed to regulate specific, geographically based cash transactions: Normal reporting requirements regarding cash transactions over $10,000 were imposed on all transactions over $750 to and from Colombia via money remittance from the New York metropolitan area. Almost overnight the flow of dollars through this system back and forth from Colombia stopped.

Another joint antimoney laundering program is the El Dorado Task Force. Begun in 1992, this federal, state, and local initiative includes agents, police officers, and support personnel from thirteen agencies—including U.S. Customs, IRS criminal and examination divisions, U.S. Secret Service, the NYPD, and the New York State Banking Department.

El Dorado targets financial services that facilitate money laundering, and has resources that focus on non-bank financial institutions, banks, brokerage houses, and bulk transportation and smuggling of cash.

One of the better examples of federal, state, and local cooperation against drug trafficking and money laundering is the High Intensity Drug Trafficking Area (HIDTA) program that operates out of the Organized Crime Investigation Division of the OCCB.

Because of the volume of drug traffic and the area's transportation hubs—three airports, three train and bus stations, and the extensive waterfront—HIDTA initiatives are aggressive in the city. The New York metropolitan area is an international gateway for drugs, and the NY-NJ HIDTA is the country's busiest (since it is a federal program run by the White House's Office of National Drug Control Policy [ONDCP], there are HIDTAs nationwide).

HIDTA is dedicated to disrupting drug traffic and dismantling gangs and money-laundering operations; and the task force has proven to be effective in drug interdiction, investigation, intelligence, and prosecution. When I became commissioner I visited the HIDTA Intelligence Center only to discover that it was open five days a week, nine to five, with almost no staff.

Realizing we had a federal program that addresses problems that plagued the city—drugs, guns, and fugitives—I assigned forty officers to the programs, and today the NY-NJ HIDTA Intelligence Center is manned by a multiagency task force twenty-four hours a day, seven days a week.

Currently the information stored at HIDTA is being used in the war on terror by the NYPD's new Counterterrorism Bureau. The detailed investigative and INS data warehoused there has proved invaluable in tracking known terrorists and running backgrounds on suspected terrorists.

HIDTA programs include the Drug Trafficking Organization Task Force and the Joint Fugitive Task Force. Drug Trafficking is a DEA, FBI, and NYPD Task Force that works on narcotics investigations, and the Fugitive Task Force is led by the United States Marshals Service with help from the INS, and the NYPD. A Department of Defense Task Force is also a part of HIDTA and its members target the most dangerous drug fugitives in the New York metro area.

In New York we saw what we can achieve by combining the talents and resources of federal, state, and local agencies in the fight against drugs. When you send drug dealers the message that you will arrest and prosecute them, destroy their distribution network, and seize their assets, they are less inclined to ply their trade in your jurisdiction.

The illicit narcotics trade drives the crime rate. People talk about the legalization of drugs that may have some medicinal use, rather than just mind-altering use. I am totally opposed to drug legalization, drugs should not be legalized by plebiscite if they have some legitimate medical benefit.

They should be legalized the same way that pharmaceutical drugs are legalized. They should fulfill the Food and Drug Administration's (FDA) requirements, and the National Institutes of Health (NIH) should do testing and patient studies. If people think that there is a medical use for marijuana, submit it and run it through the system. That way the pharmacological reason to have it legalized is shown and defended by studies.

We need to prevent our youth from becoming drug dealers' future customers. Youth programs need to educate and guide young people who are vulnerable to pressure to stray. Whether it is the DARE program, a school-based antidrug program, or the ASPIRE program, which combines lessons in avoiding drugs with after-school activities for kids who live in public housing, we must work to reach our children before criminals do.

One injection of antidrug education in the fifth or sixth grade is not enough—they need to get kids a lot earlier and give them more information. The NYPD runs youth academies in the summer for six weeks and bring kids from the inner city into youth academies and teaches them exactly what the police do. This helps to make them our allies, and it has worked very effectively. We also run citizens academies and create block associations to make the community part of what we do.

One of the things that we want to make clear to all of our inner-city communities is that we're not an occupying army—that we're their police force.

When it comes to drugs I believe in education and rehabilitation, but this is not law-enforcement's job. Demand reduction is a lofty and long-term goal. With regard to the drug problem, demand reduction is the only way to get rid of the drugs. Until then we are in a holding pattern while we figure out a long-term solution without aggressive and effective drug enforcement, we will lose thousands of young people to a tragic life of substance abuse.

13.

MANAGING THE POLICE

With over 40,000 members of the force—1 officer for every 198 citizens—the NYPD is one of the largest police departments in the world. Being at the helm of a formidable force responsible for the civil defense of over 10 million takes the management skills of a business executive and the strategy of a four-star general. That, and the support of your principal, in my case Mayor Giuliani, and the mutual commitment of all the officers on the force, were key to the success we saw in New York.

The department retains a strict chain of command. The police commissioner appoints the deputy commissioners and the chief of department. The chief of department oversees the department's operational bureaus; and below him or her in rank are the bureau assistant and deputy chiefs; inspectors and deputy inspectors; then captains; then lieutenants and sergeants, detectives, and patrol officers.

All NYPD officers begin by patrolling. After several years some will transfer into a Plainclothes Division, like

Anti-Crime, and many then typically go to Narcotics for eighteen months until they earn their detective's shield.

Detectives are the key players in the investigative functions of the department, and they are graded third, second, and first grade, first being the highest. While some police officers pursue a gold detective's shield, others choose to remain on patrol, and yet other officers go into the administrative branches of the NYPD. The uniform titles start with police officer, sergeant, lieutenant, and then captain, and for these positions you need to take a Civil Service exam to qualify. After that it is at the police commissioner's discretion to appoint higher ranks such as deputy inspector, inspector, and deputy or assistant chief.

Since everyone should be held accountable for the job that they have taken—especially police officers, who have sworn an oath to protect and serve—we established a new system to evaluate officers. Before, very little attention had been paid to management and to the evaluation of employees, and when I first looked over the records I found that virtually every officer whose personnel files crossed my desk had been rated as satisfactory or above.

We reviewed the entire department, each person, unit, squad, precinct, borough command, division, office, and bureau; and I looked to business models to guide me in my assessments.

We put the whole force on a bell curve—with 25/50/25 parameters—to determine their effectiveness. The top 25 percent were our best, the 50 percent in the middle were doing an acceptable job, and the lowest 25 percent needed to improve. Officers were rewarded for positive evaluations with public recognition and certificates of merit, transfers to desired assignments, and career-advancement points; on the other hand the department acted against those who failed to maintain a professional standard after training and counseling.

Unfortunately, the NYPD's collective-bargaining structure is very rigid; and when I suggested financial incentives (merit pay) for exceptional NYPD officers, the Patrolman's Benevolent Association (PBA), the police union, rejected the deal on two occasions. I attempted to give exceptional officers incentives by creating new positions—with raises—for them and introduced a new title, Police Officer Special Assignment, to the department. We had assigned police officers the title and had given a $1,400 raise to those deemed by their precinct commanders as exceptional. We were trying to encourage police officers to be outstanding and to reward those who were better than their peers, and we gave raises to one-third of those eligible.

The PBA sued us—they said that if you don't give them to everybody, you can't give them to anyone. Merit pay is very important, and the truth is that everyone is not the same. If we pay everyone equally, no matter what the quality of the work is, what we are doing is operating on the lowest common denominator. Unfortunately the union won their case in arbitration and we had to rescind the pay raises of their members.

Law enforcement is a service profession, and the members of the community are clients. If members of the community are reluctant to approach the police for fear of a negative experience, then we have truly not met our obligations. An officer's job is to give the community the best possible service so that they will rely on and trust their police department.

Outreach is very important. The cooperation and input

of the public is crucial to our ability to fight crime, and valuable information is lost if the community is reluctant to discourse with police officers.

I spoke to community leaders, clergy members, and residents in every borough, in neighborhoods from Harlem to Bushwick, from Jamaica to the South Bronx, and the responses were the same. The majority of the public—regardless of age or ethnicity—was supportive of the police and appreciated the job we did. This is not to say that I didn't hear criticism. The complaints, however, were generally not of officers being brutal, but of officers being brusque or rude.

I met with a group of three hundred high school students in the South Bronx. I could tell from their body language when I spoke to them that they were not very receptive, and even a little hostile.

The purpose of the meeting was to ask them about their relationship with the police. I asked them how many of them had been stopped by a police officer. About half of them raised their hands. Then I asked how many of them had had a pleasant experience, and none of them raised their hands. I asked them why it was an unpleasant experience. None of them said they were brutalized; none of them said that racial epithets had been thrown at them. They said it was the attitude of the police, as if they had the right to stop them, and they had to comply. There were no reasons given, and in fact, if it was a mistaken identification which it was in most of the cases—there was no explanation or apology.

I asked the group, "What if you get stopped by a police officer, which is of course never a pleasant experience, and they say to you, 'I am sorry that I stopped you, but you fit the description of someone who is wanted for a robbery around the corner. It's not you, and I am sorry.' " I asked them if that would change their attitude, and they all raised their hands. I found that with adults as well as students the issue was not brutality but police attitude, and that was something that I worked very hard to change.

By moving from reactive, complaint-driven policing, to a more proactive form of enforcement, the city saw a remarkable drop in the crime rate.

The gains we had experienced in New York with assertive policing needed to be tempered with benevolence and tolerance. The NYPD achieved dramatic success in reducing crime, fear, and disorder through a variety of avenues; but the initiative that I feel had a great deal of impact in gaining the community's trust was Courtesy, Professionalism, and Respect (CPR).

To increase the level of cooperation from the public we worked toward making every NYPD contact with citizens a positive one; and instead of telling officers what not to do, we trained them on how to be more polite and respectful, and defined what the behavior we expected from them. The guidelines for CPR are these:

- Address and introduce themselves to members of the public during the course of duties, as appropriate. Use terms such as Mr., Ms., sir, or ma'am, Hello and Thank you, and refer to teenagers as young lady or young man.
- Respect each individual, his or her cultural identity, customs, and beliefs.
- Evaluate carefully every contact with the public, and conduct themselves in a professional manner.
- Explain to the public, in a courteous and professional manner, the reason for your interaction with them and apologize for any inconvenience.
- Think safety tactics in every encounter.

The job of the NYPD is to make New York the largest safe city in America and to encourage understanding between the police and the citizens.

This means a tough balancing act between swift enforcement and the need to take the time to explain our actions and treat the public with civility. Some critics derided this initiative; but the fact is, for those New Yorkers who felt they have had negative interactions with the police, the issue was civility not brutality.

The plan for CPR was released in June 1996, and its components set professional standards, revised recruitment criteria, incorporated CPR into police training, implemented comprehensive performance monitoring, adjusted our reward and discipline system to support CPR, and expanded public involvement in policing.

Because our officers were trained to enforce the law with restraint, they did. The department's record of restraint exceeded its performance in crime reduction. Around 70 percent of the complaints filed against NYPD officers while I was commissioner were unsubstantiated; and in 2000, because of CPR, excessive force allegations dropped 13 percent and offensive language allegations fell 26 percent. All complaints went down each year I was commissioner—force and abuse significantly. We were the most restrained large-city police department in the United States, and in bringing crime down 38 percent we used our weapons less, we fired fewer shots, and we harmed fewer people.

Police officers are human beings, and as with any segment of the population, some will commit unethical or criminal acts, but most officers are dedicated and hardworking. Of 6 million documented contacts with the public a year, the NYPD had only 5,000 civilian complaints, and under 400 are actually substantiated by the Civilian Complaint Review Board (CCRB).

If you look at that in terms of contacts, the NYPD is a very restrained force. Each time an officer interacts with a civilian there is a possibility of a civilian complaint; and most of the complaints don't come from arrest situations, the majority come from rude contacts.

Being respectful is important, but an officer's primary duty is to preserve human life and to use only the amount of force necessary to overcome resistance. Members of the service at the scene of an incident are instructed to exert minimum necessary force and use nonlethal alternatives whenever possible. Deadly physical force is only to be used as a last resort and in compliance with the department's policies and the law. The excessive use of force is not and was not tolerated at the NYPD, and officers are held strictly accountable for their use of it.

From time to time you may have some officers who are brutal or abusive; and some police officers, like all of us, make mistakes. There were two cases that emerged during my time as commissioner that would make headline news nationwide: The violent beating and assault of Abner Louima in the bathroom of the Seventieth Precinct in Brooklyn, and the accidental shooting of Amadou Diallo in the Bronx.

The differences between the Diallo case and the Louima case were significant. The Louima case was an act of commission; it was a deranged act committed by criminal officers, and I took very quick disciplinary action against them, not only the people who were involved, but anybody who could possibly be involved. I wanted to send a clear signal to the community that we took this very seriously.

On August 9, 1997, Justin Volpe, an NYPD officer, brutalized Abner Louima in the bathroom of the Seventieth Precinct. Louima, a Haitian immigrant, had been at Club Rendezvous in Brooklyn when a scuffle broke out and the police were called. The police arrested Louima and several others and transported them back to the precinct house.

Stories differ as to exactly what happened, but it is certain that Louima was tortured and sodomized with a stick by Volpe while another officer held him down. Louima ended up being hospitalized with a ruptured intestine, a punctured bladder, and broken teeth.

When I got a call from Charles Campisi, the chief of Internal Affairs, who relayed the allegations, I told him that I found it hard to believe that it was true. His response was, "I hope you're right." I told him to follow it where it led him—the facts are what the facts are.

He called me back the next day and said, "This looks like it happened. We have a victim, the medical evidence is clear, he's credible . . . and we have a witness." One officer, Sgt. Eric Turetsky, had come forward, and he would later be a key witness in the trials against the other officers.

I was horrified and wanted to tell the mayor without anyone overhearing our conversation. I had a secure phone, as did the mayor in his vehicle. He was at one of his son's soccer games, and he had the same reaction I did.

We called a community meeting with the Haitian community and explained to them how horrified we were, and that we were going to take very prompt action. The next day we visited Louima in the hospital, and I promised him, and his family, that justice would be swift; that all officers who had been party to his torture would be punished.

Because of the heinousness of the crime, I reorganized the Seventieth Precinct, reassigned the two top supervisors, suspended the desk sergeant, and placed nine officers present that night on modified assignment. None of the officers present that day, or their supervisors, could be put back on the streets until it was clear what had happened. Mayor Giuliani and I also demanded that any officer on the premises that night set aside allegiances and come forward with their story.

I committed the entire staff of the Internal Affairs Bureau—some seven hundred officers—to the case to find out what had taken place that night. Even after the thirty-day suspension allowed by New York State's Civil Service law expired, I refused to let the officers return to work in any capacity, modified or not, unless they were cleared of charges.

Ten days after the Louima attack, Mayor Giuliani created a task force, the Police Community Relations Task Force, that met for eight months to examine ways in which we could improve our policing and community relations. Many of the suggestions that came out of the meetings, and a later report published by the group, were implemented. We expanded CPR training, and field training for officers was extended from three to six months; and we created a Board of Visitors comprised of civilians at the Police Academy who acted as an advisory committee. And because the attack was so brutal, and Justin Volpe's actions so perverse, I launched a comprehensive review of the department's psychological testing.

I helped the Brooklyn DA get an indictment against Volpe the week after the attack on Louima, and I pushed for the case to be passed on to the federal courts because of the civil rights infractions against Louima. The federal indictment charged that officers Volpe, Schwarz, Wiese, and Bruder had engaged in a conspiracy to violate the civil rights of Abner Louima through the use of unreasonable force against him while he was in police custody. Volpe and Schwarz were charged with sexually assaulting Louima; and Sergeant Bellomo, the patrol supervisor that night, was charged with covering up the beating and lying to federal prosecutors. Volpe was also charged with obstruction of justice resulting from the threats he made to Louima to prevent him from revealing the assault.

In May 1999, all five officers went to trial at the Brooklyn Federal Courthouse. Eric Turetsky testified that he saw Mr. Louima with his pants "down below his knees" as Officer Volpe, his uniform in disarray and holding a stick three feet long, escorted Mr. Louima from a restroom at the Seventieth Precinct. With an overwhelming amount of evidence against him, Justin Volpe admitted to sodomizing Abner Louima and was sentenced to thirty years; and Charles Schwarz was found guilty of being Volpe's accomplice. Officers Bruder and Wiese, as well as Sergeant Bellomo, were acquitted.

In the investigation and trial, Abner Louima had been unable to positively identify Schwarz as the man who had held him down while Volpe sodomized him, only that the man who had restrained him had driven the car the night of his arrest and assault. Schwarz was the driver of the car, and the physical similarity between Wiese and Schwarz further confused the case when, days after his admission of guilt, Justin Volpe released a statement through his lawyer that Schwarz was never in the bathroom and that the second officer present was Wiese.

In 2000, there was a second trial for obstruction of justice, and Schwarz, Bruder, and Wiese were charged with lying to the authorities to falsely exonerate Schwarz of the crime he was convicted of in the first trial, and all three were convicted: Schwarz to fifteen years and eight months (for the attack and the cover-up); and Bruder and Wiese to five years each for obstructing justice.

Early in 2002, the Second Circuit Court of Appeals overturned Schwarz's conviction on taking part in the assault, returning the case to a lower federal court, and threw out the obstruction convictions of Schwarz, Wiese, and Bruder and ordered a new trial for Schwarz. In July 2002, a jury found Schwarz guilty of perjury, but was deadlocked on the civil rights charges. On the eve of his fourth trial, Charles Schwarz's lawyers came to a last-minute agreement with federal prosecutors, and he was sentenced to serve five years in jail for perjury.

There is no predictive tool, no probability test for such a heinous crime—all big-city forces have some bad cops; it's not reflective of the vast majority of the department. But unfortunately, after Justin Volpe's attack on Abner Louima, the media painted the NYPD with a broad brush. This event was tragic, and there is no doubt in anyone's mind that the torture of Louima was undoubtedly one of the worst examples of police brutality; but the shooting of Amadou Diallo was another matter, a tragedy affecting New Yorkers in every community—civilians and police officers alike.

Amadou Diallo was shot nineteen times on February 4, 1999, in the vestibule of his apartment building on Wheeler Avenue in the Bronx. Four Street Crime Unit officers were involved: Kenneth Boss, Sean Caroll, Edward McMellon, and Richard McMurphy.

I was in California at a major city Police Chiefs' meeting when Diallo was shot. I remember speaking with the first deputy commissioner, Pat Kelleher, and asking him, "Tell me about this?"

He said, "It was a stop of someone who looked like a

rapist. We stopped him, we asked him to comply, and he did not. He reached for his wallet. They thought it was a gun, and they fired forty-one shots and hit him nineteen times."

"No gun?" I asked.

"No," he said.

"Criminal record?"

"No."

"Assault?"

"No," he said.

"Pat, this one has legs," I said.

I found out in the course of my many conversations with Kelleher that the Street Crime Unit officers involved in the shooting were driving unmarked police cars when they saw Diallo, who they believed resembled the sketch of a Bronx serial rapist, later identified as Isaac Jones. Jones, in fact, looked very much like Diallo; and when he was finally arrested several months later, it was in the Soundview section of the Bronx where Diallo had been shot.

In Jones's sentencing, Justice Joseph Fisch of the state supreme court in the Bronx brought up Diallo in his sentencing and asked Jones and the court the question: "Would Amadou Diallo be alive today were it not for your activities here in the Bronx?"

On that evening in early February 1999, Officers Caroll and McMellon got out of the car and approached Diallo, who was standing in the doorway of his building. As they approached Diallo, one of the officers said, "Police. Can I have a word?" and repeated the question. Diallo, Officer Boss testified in court, "turned abruptly and darted back into the vestibule." In the vestibule he held up his wallet that Caroll and McMellon mistook for a gun.

Officers Murphy and Boss, who were still on the street,

testified that there were loud voices and then, Boss testified, Officer McMellon, fired a shot, stumbled, and came flying down the stairs of the building onto his back, all the while firing into the vestibule. The other three officers, thinking they had an officer down, opened fire on Diallo and shot him nineteen times.

Mr. Diallo did nothing wrong, but what he did engendered in the minds of these officers that they were in danger. They were mistaken, but they were honestly mistaken. There arc no rookies in street Crime Units—these were good cops in a bad situation; and unless you've been in that terrible situation, you can't imagine how fast you have to react to what, to the best of your knowledge, is a crisis.

When you hear that Diallo had been shot at forty-one times, and struck nineteen, the average person thinks that minutes must have gone by, but the truth is the gunfire took place almost instantly. We had four people shooting semi-automatic weapons, and Diallo was killed in a tragic accident that took only eight seconds.

These were four young men with good records who thought they were in a firefight. Diallo didn't fall down and he was pinned upright to a wall with reflective red paint that showed the muzzle flashes coming back at the officers. A number of the bullets ricocheted over the officers' heads, making them believe they were under fire. All of these elements contributed to the officers' mistaken impression that they were being fired on. As a police officer you are in combat—these officers believed that they were, in fact, in danger of losing their lives.

I have great sympathy for the Diallo family—no one should lose a child, and no innocent man should lose his life. But I think you have to put it into the context that these are police officers who mistakenly believed Diallo had a gun, and they reacted as they were trained. As a law enforcer in a contained situation and confronted with somebody who you believe has a weapon, all the training in the world is not going to change how you react.

Louima was a clear case of brutality; I condemned it and took action against the officers. In the Diallo case it was not clear to me that there was misconduct.

It appeared to me to be a tragic series of errors. The first police officer made a mistake and fired his gun and fell backward as he fired it. His partners thought he had been shot at. Anybody who has been in a shooting—which I have—knows it is very easy to make a mistake. I can tell you that any police officer in a similar situation could end up doing exactly what happened in the Diallo case.

The jury came to the conclusion that the cops involved in the Diallo shooting were innocent of criminal conduct. It was an act of misjudgment not of intent. All four were indicted on second-degree murder charges in the state court after a change of venue to Albany and were acquitted of all charges. The jury in Albany came to this conclusion. The federal civil rights investigation also came to the conclusion that there was insufficient evidence to establish that the officers had a criminal intent to use more force than was necessary under the circumstances.

I took a tremendous amount of criticism, both professionally and personally, during the period after Diallo's death. There were large demonstrations outside of One Police Plaza almost every day. Both the media and many activist groups called on me to denounce the four officers. I refused, and asked everyone to withhold judgment until the facts were determined.

It would have been easy for me to denounce the four cops, and I would have had a much easier time. That is not what leadership is about. I know what a tragedy this was for the Diallo family and it distresses me to this day. I also know that these four officers made a terrible mistake. But they did not go out that night to kill Mr. Diallo, or anyone else. They believed that a fellow officer had been shot at and that they were in danger of their lives. To attack them for this would be something I could never in good conscience do and look in the mirror each day.

I mourn for the death of Amadou Diallo, and for his family. I also mourn for the lives of the four accused officers whose lives will never be the same. It was a tragedy that hurt us all.

The Internal Affairs Bureau and Civilian Complaint Review Board (CCRB) provide the NYPD with oversight internally and externally. And they are commissioned to investigate incidents like that of the attack on Abner Louima and Amadou Diallo's death. The NYPD is perhaps the most scrutinized police department in the country. Not only does it have the largest Internal Affairs Bureau of any police department, it has five independent district attorneys who have oversight over police misconduct and corruption and we have two U.S. attorneys—the Southern and Eastern districts of New York—who examine the actions of the NYPD.

The CCRB is composed of civilian representatives who review citizen complaints of police brutality and abuse of power. The mayor has the majority of appointees, the city council has some appointees, and the police commissioner also appoints members to the CCRB. The problems with the CCRB, which is a good concept in theory, is that it has become politicized and CCRB investigators are inexperienced, with no background in law enforcement and no idea how to investigate civilian complaints against officers. The NYPD ends up reinvestigating most of the cases, and this is a waste of time, effort, and police power.

CCRB investigators often substantiated ridiculous cases; and charges can hang over cops' heads for months and very often with nonsubstantiated accusations. I advocated that the CCRB be the prosecutors, rather than the NYPD in these complaint trials, so that they had the responsibility to prosecute based on their own evidence. In 2001, the NYPD removed itself from prosecuting substantiated cases against officers, and now the CCRB is mandated with substantiating and prosecuting their own cases. Hopefully this will dispel the sense that the NYPD and the commissioner control the outcome of these internal trials and will instill a sense of accountability into the process.

Even with accountability to the CCRB, the NYPD had fewer civilian complaints, and shootings by police officers declined. In fact, in 1998, citizens of the District of Columbia were six times as likely to be shot by a cop than those in New York City. To make sure we knew what was happening in the community, I added CCRB information to the CompStat program, and we set up several CCRB monitoring programs—in addition to the already existing ones—to comply with the results of their surveys. I closed cases and imposed penalties on cops I felt had made errors in judgment and fired officers whose behavior in the community was unacceptable.

The Civilian Complaint Reduction Program was designed to identify members of the department with extensive CCRB complaints and was expanded to include every officer who received in excess of three civilian complaints within five years, not just members of the Patrol Services Bureau. After the third complaint, we brought them in, profiled and interviewed him or her, and decided whether or not to keep the officer in his or her assignment.

The NYPD performance-monitoring program also include CPR Compliance Training and integrity testing. Members of the Quality Assurance Division (QAD) would pose as civilians and ask on-duty officers randomly for service. In order to see how the officer responded to a compromising situation, QAD and IAB members use scripted scenarios that are designed to test officer's compliance with CPR and integrity. The test subjects for the CPR program were rated on initial contact, appearance and verbal introduction, demeanor, and accuracy of information.

Those who were integrity tested were placed by an undercover officer in a situation that was ripe for corruption or brutality to see how they reacted. The most extreme examples of integrity testing was when undercover officers set up a situation that invited corruption: They rented an apartment and posed as drug dealers in possession of money and drugs. Internal Affairs Bureau (IAB) officers would call 911 and direct the suspect officers to the location and monitor their behavior, whether they vouchered the money and drugs or pocketed it. Integrity testing monitors vehicle stops—which provide an opportunity for theft and brutality—with hidden cameras and places undercover agents on the street posing as someone who found valuable property. The undercover approaches a cop on the beat, gives them the item, and then monitors whether the officer in question vouchers it or pockets it.

Commanding officers were notified when a subordinate was included in a monitoring program, and they were held accountable for tracking officers with complaints. The Central Personnel Index (CPI) is a snapshot of sick days, disciplinary records, the results of monitoring programs, and a roster of how often an officer has discharged their weapon. Each time an officer fires his or her weapon, the

Shooting Review Board scrutinizes the incident; and when an officer is in a shooting, a Shooting Team lead by at least a captain, investigates, in tandem with precinct detectives, to see whether the shooting was in compliance with policy. Every officer involved in a shooting must go through the monitoring system, and depending on the outcome of their investigations, we determined whether they need reassignment, retraining, or disciplinary action.

With these monitoring programs, and others, the NYPD aggressively polices itself. As an officer you are sworn to protect the people; if you fall short you must suffer the consequences, and as a commander, you are held accountable for the actions of those in your service. While I was commissioner, I replaced fifty-four precinct commanders; some were promoted, others transferred to noncommand positions for "failure to supervise," and a few were dismissed.

In 1998, an Internal Affairs investigation revealed that twenty officers from our Midtown South, a precinct that includes Times Square and the Garment District, had been protecting a brothel in exchange for sex. We identified over two dozen officers who were alleged to be trading favors—immunity from arrest and protection—for sex, cash, jewelry, and other valuables. This decade-long disgrace was put to an end, but I was outraged; and because of the misconduct I pulled nineteen officers from duty and transferred Midtown South's three precinct supervisors, including the precinct commander. Although they were not engaging in illegal acts, they were not overseeing their officers in a responsible manner.

The Internal Affairs Bureau had been investigating the precinct and the brothel since 1996, and the case developed suddenly when the Vice Squad had raided the multifloored establishment around the corner from Midtown

South. The establishment housed over sixty prostitutes working out of small cubicles, and the madam informed the Vice Squad that they had police clientele. Officers—in uniform and out—had been visiting the brothel for sex and crashing at an apartment across the street. Later, when she turned state's evidence, the madam testified that she was paying the $15 to $25 fee for officers to have sex out of her own pocket.

Corruption in the NYPD has a long history. It reaches back to 1896 when Judge Clarence Lexow heard testimony that police officers took bribes from gambling houses and brothel owners. In 1930, Judge Samuel Seabury heard testimony that twenty-eight Vice Squad policemen had extorted prostitutes; and in 1954, Harry Gross, a Brooklyn bookmaker, testified that he had been paying $1 million a year to the NYPD for the protection of his gambling business. Gross's accusation would set off a five-year investigation into police corruption by the Brooklyn District Attorney's Office that led to three hundred resignations (including the mayor, William O'Dwyer, and the police commissioner, William O'Brien), twenty-two indictments, and ten convictions.

The Manhattan District Attorney's Office investigated police payoffs in 1968, an inquiry that resulted in the dismissal of nineteen officers. In 1972, the Knapp Commission, a federal investigation of payoffs to the Special Investigations Unit (SIU), called corruption in the NYPD "an extensive department-wide phenomenon, indulged to some degree by a sizable majority of the force." The Knapp Commission's investigation led to a series of indictments and several suicides. In 1981 and 1983, officers from the Tenth Precinct were charged with accepting bribes—five were sent to jail.

In 1994, a NYPD officer from the Seventy-seventh Precinct, Michael Dowd, was convicted and sentenced to eleven years in jail for shaking down drug dealers, selling cocaine himself, protecting drug dealers who had paid him off, and plotting to kidnap a Queens woman. So egregious were Dowd's crimes that an outside committee, the Mollen Commission, was established to investigate him and corruption in the NYPD. The commission discovered another group of corrupt officers in the Thirtieth Precinct in Washington Heights, who were taking payoffs, tipping off drug dealers to the presence of Narcotics units, conducting illegal searches, and perjuring themselves. They refined the process with "key jobs," where they would go to a building where there were known drug dealers. They would grab them, go through their keys; and when they found Medeco keys for heavy-duty locks, they would drag the dealer back to their apartment building. The corrupt officers would then try all the doors until they found the apartment that matched the key and steal their drugs and money.

This group of thirty-five officers, called the "Dirty Thirty," also ended up being part of the Mollen Commission's investigation. The commission found that there was a continuum of corruption in several precincts, and their final report indicted the department's recruitment, training, and screening policies and criticized the NYPD for maintaining a culture of negligence that encouraged officers and supervisors to look the other way in cases of brutality and corruption.

In response to the Mollen Commission findings, Internal Affairs changed at the NYPD. Prior to the Mollen Commission, IAB worked out of the borough commands, as well as headquarters. This meant that IAB investigators were in part monitored by borough chiefs. The NYPD changed this, and today IAB works exclusively from One

Police Plaza. To monitor each precinct, IAB places under-cover investigators who report back to the bureau.

I don't split hairs between on-duty and off-duty mis-conduct. An incident of off-duty police brutality was one of the first Internal Affairs investigations that I launched. On May 26, 1996, Constantine Chronis, a ten-year NYPD veteran, his friend, Austin Offen, and a group of others were partying at Club Marakesh in Westhampton, Long Island, when a brawl broke out in the parking lot of the club. When the dust cleared, a young African-American man, Shane Daniels, was left beaten and unconscious out-side of the club. He would remain in a coma for a week and a half.

Investigators found car keys in the lot and traced them back to Chronis and Offen, and eyewitnesses identified Chronis in photo arrays and lineups as the man who'd threatened a group of witnesses to the crime with a gun, holding them at bay. On May 28, Chronis was arrested, charged with first-degree assault, and held on $1 million bail for participating in the near-fatal beating of Daniels with an anticar-theft device.

To investigate Chronis's behavior, and to ascertain that no other off-duty cops were there that night, I assigned two-dozen IAB officers to assist the Suffolk County inves-tigators in their search for suspects. I stressed that it was of the highest priority that all those involved were brought to justice, even if we uncovered additional police miscon-duct. We interviewed suspects, ran down leads, and put to rest a rumor that Chronis was in the company of a confidential informant out of prison on a special pass.

The incident was complicated by allegations of racism—witnesses claimed that the fight was spurred by the fact that Daniels was in the company of a white woman and that Chronis and Offen, who are white, had taken offense at the interracial relationship. During the beating, racial epithets were hurled and witnesses were taunted with racial slurs.

Alcohol was another factor. Both Chronis and Offens were under the influence; and during the evening prior to Daniels's beating, they had ordered bottle after bottle of champagne. Cops and alcohol are a dangerous mix, and police misconduct—both on duty and off—is often linked to drinking. Police officers should always be prepared for that call or page to appear for duty; and although they have the right to use alcohol when they are off duty, they do not have the right to get drunk. As a police officer you are expected to be able to perform at all times.

The NYPD has had its share of alcohol-related police misconduct, including the public drunkenness of NYPD officers at a 1995 police memorial weekend in Washington, D.C., where dozens of officers from many police departments rampaged through several hotels. There was also the conviction of off-duty officer Joseph Gray for the DWI manslaughter of Maria Herrera, her son Andy, four, her unborn child, and her sister Dilcia Pena, sixteen, in 2001. Alcohol was at the heart of these problems and others and isn't just detrimental to citizens; it is also a factor in many cop suicides. To help officers understand the dangers of alcohol abuse and receive treatment, we worked with the police unions to educate them, disciplined those caught drinking on the job, as well as those who were arrested for drunken-driving charges.

But the vicious beating of Daniels by Chronis defied explanation. Nothing about Chronis indicated that he would violate his oath to serve and protect. Married and a father of two, Chronis had no disciplinary record and no known problems with alcoholism. After the beating of Daniels, Chronis retired from the NYPD. In his 1999 trial,

Chronis claimed that he had acted in self-defense after being confronted by an angry crowd and receiving a head wound, but this did not stop the Suffolk County judge from finding him guilty of assault, menacing, and official misconduct and sentencing him to a four-to-eight-year prison sentence. Austin Offen pleaded guilty and was sentenced to ten years in prison for the beating.

If you do something unbecoming a police officer off duty, as did Chronis, you should be held accountable, just as if you were on duty. Every interaction that the public has with the police should reinforce the community's sense of justice and order; and all police-initiated enforcement actions, including but not limited to arrest, stop-and-frisk, and motor vehicle stops are based on the standards required by the Fourth Amendment of the U.S. Constitution.

Officers were reminded that the use of characteristics such as religion, age, gender, gender identity, race, or sexual orientation as the only factor for taking police action is prohibited. Officers must have reasonable suspicion for a stop and question or probable cause for an arrest. However, there is nothing wrong with using descriptive information, racial or physical, as long as you don't use it as the only reason to stop. We stopped people based on descriptions given by victims, not because of race. Stopping someone on the Upper East Side in a Mercedes because they happen to be black—that's racial profiling and that should not be tolerated, but police must use descriptive information to stop people and solve crimes.

The fact is that certain precincts have populations that are 90 percent people of color; and so that the NYPD could better reflect the community it represented, in 1999 we launched a massive recruitment campaign in an effort to get more minorities on the force. Because there is a link between the criteria for hiring and job performance, we

were more discerning in our selections. When you look at
the cycle of corruption, you can almost always go back
seven to ten years and find a reduction in recruiting standards. Seven years later, when you look at the people before Internal Affairs, they are the people recruited under
lower standards.

I think the standards for recruitment should be more
stringent, and we should aspire to a higher caliber of recruit; but to do that we're going to have to pay them a
living wage. I wanted recruits who were interested in ca-
reers of service, not adventure; and the characteristics I
looked for were maturity, poise, sensitivity, tolerance, education, and initiative. There is nothing wrong with en-
joying interesting and exciting work, but you want people
who understand that the work is a calling. We screened
out potential problems by running background records
and checking the educational and employment history of
potential recruits. In the interest of getting mature and
experienced candidates, we raised the minimum age from
twenty to twenty-two and increased the college credit requirement to sixty credits or two years of military service.

All members of the department were trained in CPR
values and techniques and in-service training. The Officer
Safety and Survival Course and In-Service Tactical Training (In-Tac) are realistic training courses for uniformed
cops that stress the importance of professional, tactical
responses to resolve confrontations with minimal force.
We trained all incoming officers in the Police Academy's
Basic Plainclothes Course, which utilizes lectures, mock
scenarios, video tapes, and video-simulation firearms
training using the Firearms Training System (FATS). We
drilled officers in the appropriate use of deadly force,
courtroom testimony, and the definition of perjury; the
handling of physical evidence; standards of proof; car

stops; search and seizure; weapons and drug presumption; interrogations; and eyewitness identifications. Tactics taught at the NYPD Police Academy include interview techniques, safety tactics, weapon retention, gun disarming, control holds, pressure points, confrontation situations, speed cuffing, felony car stops, field skills, and physical skills, as well as stop, question, and frisk procedures.

The NYPD is well trained, but any department can benefit from continuing to look at training. After the shooting of Amadou Diallo, the Police Academy curriculum has expanded to include verbal judo tactics, which helps officers learn how to deflect violence with tactical conversation, and cultural diversity training.

Members of the Street Crime Unit attended a course that focused on judgment training and verbal judo, the legal issues of stopping and frisking suspects, and an explanation of cultural diversity. They got a refresher course in firearms training with FATS and the isolation and containment of suspects in close combat, and, most important, classes on how to avoid mass reflexive response or chain-reaction shooting.

We have seen that when you have more police, crime tends to go down, but it is not just more police; it's what you do with them that counts. The skill, direction, and tactics of your force make the difference, and keeping experienced officers in your force is important. To stop the most experienced cops from retiring after the minimum twenty years of service, we need to encourage people financially to stay. After twenty years, officers are eligible for their pension; and currently the system bases your yearly pension on the amount of money that you made during your last year in the force. Because of September 11, and the many hours of overtime officers worked during and after the crisis, many of those who could retire did; and in 2002, the NYPD lost 3,700 of the best, brightest, and most experienced people in the department. This could undoubtedly have an effect on crime reduction. To counter this, the NYPD and other departments should follow the federal system—"high three," which takes the average of an officer's highest three years as the base for pensions.

As with anything, policework benefits from strategy, skill, and common sense. Departments need to think outside the box and find new ways to solve old problems. Specialty squads and operations that address specific crimes—especially narcotic sales and illegal gun possession—and violent locations are effective, but they are always the first to go when there is a budgetary crisis or when crime inches up. Many citizens have the perception that if they can't see uniformed officers on every corner, there is a decreased police presence. Saturating the streets with patrol officers can have an impact on reducing street crimes; however, these tactics have very little effect on the number of reported crimes taking place indoors or in locations where officers cannot see and prevent them.

People like "feel good" cops. They like to see an officer on the corner and get to know him. That may work in small-town Mayberry, but the reality is that crime reduction is not accomplished by merely a uniformed presence. Uniformed presence is important but it is reactive not proactive. It doesn't stop people from selling drugs, committing rapes, or getting involved in organized crime. It is important to keep the streets safe from targets of opportunity; and for real crime reduction, you need a uniformed presence supplemented by a healthy dose of special units, and investigations, specifically directed toward drugs, street crimes, violence, and guns.

When the entire department focuses its attention and activity on a few simple goals, there is a corresponding steady decline in the crime rate. Goal-Oriented Neighborhood Policing gives precinct commanders more flexibility and responsibility, holds middle management accountable for identifying and addressing problems via a coordinated and strategic response to crimes specific to each precinct. By setting clear directions from the top we brought crime down in each of the city's precincts.

We must continue to be vigilant and proactive against crime. The analogy that now that crime is down, the "illness" has been cured and we no longer need assertive policing is a serious mistake. Crime is never cured—it is a never-ending war. If we do not pay attention, it flares up and becomes acute. Local law enforcement needs to strike the right balance between focused, strategy-driven law-enforcement efforts and community-oriented policing.

Senior police managers have to insist on good training, better technology, adequate resources, competive salaries, and proper conduct from their officers. They cannot cave in to buzzwords like "community policing" or to the misdirected pressures of police unions. A police executive's goal should not be popularity. Effective crime reduction, public trust, and community safety are the measures of success. One of my predecessors, Theodore Roosevelt, said:

> It is not the critic who counts, not the man who points
> out how the strong man stumbled, or where the doer of
> deeds could have done better. The credit belongs to the
> man who is actually in the arena; whose face is marred
> by the dust and sweat and blood; who strives valiantly;

who errs and comes short again and again; who knows the great enthusiasms, the great devotions and spends himself in a worthy cause; who at the best, knows in the end the triumph of high achievement, and who, at worst, if he fails, at least fails while daring greatly; so that his place shall never be with those cold and timid souls who know neither victory or defeat.

Police executives need to be in "the arena"; to do less is not acceptable.

SOURCES

Chapter 1: GOAL-ORIENTED NEIGHBORHOOD POLICING

Books, Criminal Justice Reports, and Documents
Goldstein, Herman. *Problem-Oriented Policing*. New York: McGraw Hill, 1990.
Lardner, James, and Thomas Repetto. *NYPD: A City and Its Police*. New York: Owl Books/Holt, 2000.
Maple, Jack, with Chris Mitchell. *The Crime Fighter: How You Can Make Your Community Crime-Free*. New York: Broadway Books, 1999.
New York City Police Department. *Policing New York City in the 1990s: The Strategy for Community Policing*, January 1991.
New York City Police Department: *Strategy '97: Office of Management Analysis and Planning*, 1997.
New York City Police Department. *Strategy 4: Breaking the Cycle of Domestic Violence*, 1994.
New York City Police Department. *Strategy 8: Reclaiming the Roads of New York*, 1995.

New York City Police Department. *Annual Reports,* 1996–2002.

New York City Police Department. *Spring 3100,* 1996–2000.

Silverman, Eli B. *NYPD Battles Crime: Innovative Strategies in Policing.* Boston: Northeastern University Press, 1999.

Testimony of Rudolph W. Giuliani on Fighting Crime at the Local Level to the House's Committee on Government Reform and Oversight. Capitol Hill, March 3, 1999.

U.S. Department of Justice, Research Forums. *Looking at Crime from the Street Level,* 1999.

Essays, Editorials, Articles

Anderson, David C. "Crime Stoppers." *New York Times,* February, 1998, sec. 6, p. 47.

Carpenter, John. "Chicago Has More Murders Than New York." *Chicago Sun-Times,* December 4, 1998.

Cooper, Michael. "For Greedy Fugitives, It's 'Go Directly to Jail,' " *New York Times,* February 4, 1997, sec. B, p. 3.

Fan, Maureen, and John Marzulli. "Domestic Violence Spikes Murder Rate." *Daily News,* March 11, 1999, p. 12.

Karmen, Andrew. "Murders in New York City." In *Crime and Justice in New York City,* edited by Andrew Karmen. New York: McGraw Hill, 1998.

Kelling, George L., and William H. Sousa. "Policing Does Matter." *City Journal* 12, no. 1 (Winter 2002): pp. 6–7.

Kocienewski, David. "Giuliani Is Quick to Point Another Drop in Crime Rate." *New York Times,* May 19, 1998.

Kocienewski, David. "Murders Drop 25 Percent As Violent City Crime Falls Again." *New York Times,* July 2, 1998, sec. B, p. 3.

Krauss, Clifford. "Giuliani Plans a New Effort for Arresting of Fugitives." *New York Times,* October 25, 1996, sec. B, p. 4.

Levitt, Leonard. "Bronx Sting Nets 261 Fugitive Arrests."
    Newsday, February 4, 1997, p. A23.

MacDonald, Heather. "America's Best Urban Police Force."
    City Journal Summer 2000, 10, no.3, pp. 14–31.

Marzulli, John. "City Slays Plunge to a 35-Year Low—
    Cops," *Daily News,* December 3, 1998.

Marzulli, John. "Apple's a Safer Place," *Daily News,* Decem-
    ber 4, 1998.

Weiss, Murray. "City Murder Rate Plummets Twenty Per-
    cent," *New York Post,* December 3, 1998.

Weiss, Murray. "Drunk Drivers Can Kiss Cars Goodbye."
    New York Post, January 22, 1999, p. 2.

Chapter 2: QUALITY OF LIFE

Books, Criminal Justice Reports, and Documents
Ellis, Edward Robb. *The Epic of New York City.* New York:
    Kodansha, 1966.

Gladwell, Malcolm. *The Tipping Point: How Little Things
    Can Make a Big Difference.* New York: Backbay Books/
    Little, Brown, 2002.

Kelling, George L, and Catherine M. Coles. *Fixing Broken
    Windows: Restoring Order and Reducing Crime in Our
    Communities.* New York: Martin Kessler Books, 1996.

Kelling, George L. *Broken Windows and Police Discretion.*
    Washington, D.C.: U.S. Department of Justice, Office of
    Justice Programs, National Institute of Justice, 1999.

New York City Police Department. *Summer '96: Quality of
    Life Initiative, Building on Success,* 1996.

New York City Police Department. *Strategy 2: Reclaiming
    the Public Spaces of New York,* 1994.

New York City Police Department. *Traffic Safety: Quality of
    Life Plan of Action,* 1998.

Essays, Editorials, Articles

Bertrand, Donald. "Precinct's Initiatives Help Crime Drop 17 Percent," *Daily News,* December 22, 2000, p. 5.

Bollinger, Ann V. "Rulings Clear Way for Lollipop Lady," *New York Post,* December 18, 1997, p. 32.

Breslin, Jimmy. "Unknown Face Haunted City," *Newsday,* June 14, 1995, p. A04.

Daly, Michael. "Fingered with an Easy Print. Mar. Bust Led to Crucial Match," *Daily News,* June 14, 1996, p. 41.

Dwyer, Jim. "Getting a Grip as City Glares." *Daily News,* June 16, 1996, p. 4.

Firestone, David. "For Giuliani a Day of Police Praise and Policy Vindication." *New York Times,* June 15, 1996, sec. 1, p. 25.

Foreman, Jonathan. "Toward a More Civil City," *City Journal* (Winter 1998): pp. 56–64.

Hester, Jere. "Royster's Story Haunts New York on Father's Day," *Daily News,* June 17, 1996, p. 1.

Horowitz, Craig. "What Should Cops Do Now?" *New York,* July 20, 1998, pp. 30–33, 102.

Kappstatter, Bob. "First-Quarter Stats Show Crime's Down: Double-Digit Rates," *Daily News,* April 14, 1998.

Kashbaum, William K. "Justice Was Just a Turnstile Away," *Daily News,* June 14, 1996, p. 4.

Kelling, George L. "How to Run a Police Department," *City Journal* 5 (1995).

Kocieniewski, David. "City Police Open Hot Line for Quality of Life Violations," *New York Times,* September 14, 1996, sec. 1, p. 23.

Kolker, Robert. "Quality-of-Life Control," *New York,* January 14, 2002, p. 12.

Kriegel, Mark. "Letters from the Grim Side." *Daily News,* February 25, 1998, p. 10.

Morrison, Dan. "Crime Wave of One/Confession in Park Beating, Park Avenue Slay," *Newsday,* June 14, 1996, p. A05.

Sexton, Joe. "A Trail of Violence: The Investigation. A Suspect in Custody Prays, and Then Confesses to Four Brutal Crimes Against Women." *New York Times,* June 14, 1996, sec. B, p. 5.

Ross, Barbara, and Wendell Jamieson. "Grim Details: Suspect Outlines Jun. Crime Spree." *Daily News,* July 17, 1996, p. 7.

Salstonstall, David. "Squeegees, Graffiti Seen as Signs of Bad Old Days," *Daily News,* August 13, 2000, p. 4.

Sherill, Martha. "Rudy Giuliani Is a Colossal Asshole. Which Is Precisely What Makes Him the Best Mayor in America," *Esquire* (October 1997): pp. 75–82, 146.

Sullivan, John. "Trial Focuses on Sanity of Man Held in Attacks," *New York Times,* January 22, 1998, sec. B, p. 7.

Sullivan, John. "Man Is Guilty in Three Attacks, Including a Woman's Murder." *New York Times,* March 7, 1998, sec. B, p. 1.

Chapter 3: TECHNOLOGY AND POLICING

Books, Criminal Justice Reports, and Documents

"Managing Police Operations: Implementing the NYPD Crime Control Model Using CompStat," Phyllis Partial McDonald, et al. From Goldsmith, Victor and Philip G. McGuire, John H. Mollenkopf, Timothy A. Ross, Editors. *Analyzing Crime Patterns: Frontiers of Practice,* Thousand Oaks: Sage, 2000.

Tobias, Marc Weber. *Police Communications.* Springfield: Thomas, 1974.

National Institutes of Justice. *Electronic Crime Scene Investigation*, July 2001.

National Institutes of Justice. *Mapping Crime: Principle and Practice*, December 1999.

New York City Police Department. *Office of Technology and System Development Annual Reports*, 1996–2000.

New York City Police Department. *The Compstat Process*, 1994.

Essays, Editorials, Articles

Bloomberg, David. "Cons Hit the Internet." *Law and Order* (June 2001).

Flynn, Kevin. "Fighting Crime with Ingenuity, 007 Style. Gee-Whiz Police Gadgets Get a Trial Run in New York." *New York Times*, March 7, 2000, sec. B, p. 1.

Gardiner, Sean. "NYPD Detectives Make Vegas Arrest. Busboy Allegedly Used Internet to Sell Drugs." *Newsday*, February 25, 2000, p. A34.

Greenman, Catherine. "A Well-Equipped Patrol Officer: Gun, Flashlight, Computer." *New York Times*, January 21, 1999.

Kashbaum, William K. "Police Department Takes Steps to Modernize Its Technology." *New York Times*, March 23, 2002, sec. B, p. 3.

Kocieniewski, David. "Police Effort to Speed 911 Lagging Badly." *New York Times*, June 12, 1998, sec. B, p. 1.

Kashbaum, William K. "Crime-Fighting by Computer: Scope Widens." *New York Times*, March 24, 2002, p. 43.

Marzulli, John. "Cops Go Hi-Tech to Net Stalkers." *Daily News*, October 21, 1999, p. 32.

McFee, Michele. "Drug Deals Busted on Internet." *Daily News*, August 7, 2000, p. 5.

"NYC's CompStat Continues to Win Admirers." *Law Enforcement Journal* (October 31, 1997): p. 55.

Rayman, Graham. "Dispatch System Not Ready." *Newsday,* December 11, 1998, p. A43.

Patterson, Shane. "1 Adam 12, 1 Adam 12, Go to the Wireless . . ." *Wireless NewsFactor* (September 4, 2001).

Rogers, Donna. "Trends in Crime Analysis and Crime Mapping." *Law Enforcement Technology* (May 2000): p. 36.

Walsh, William. "CompStat an Analysis of an Emerging Managerial Program." *Policing: An International Journal of Policing Strategies and Management* 24, issue 3 (2001).

Chapter 4: CRIME-SCENE EVIDENCE AND FORENSICS

Books, Criminal Justice Reports, and Documents
Baden, Michael, and Marion Roach. *Dead Reckoning: The New Science of Catching Killers.* New York: Simon and Schuster, 2001.

Crime Scene Investigation: A Guide for Law Enforcement. U.S. Department of Justice, January 2000.

Crime Scene to Court: The Essentials of Forensic Science, Peter White, ed. Cambridge: Royal Society of Chemistry, 1998.

Crime Scene Search and Physical Evidence Handbook. U.S. Department of Justice.

Forensic Science: An Introduction to Scientific and Investigative Techniques, edited by Stuart H. James, and Jon J. Nordby. Boca Raton: CRC Press, 2003.

Inman, Keith. *Principles and Practices of Criminalistics: The Profession of Forensic Science.* Boca Raton: CRC Press, 2001.

Lee, Dr. Henry. *Henry Lee's Crime Scene Handbook.* San Diego: Academic, 2001.

Lee, Dr. Henry, and Dr. Jerry Labriola. *Famous Crimes*

Revisited: From Sacco-Vanzetti to O. J. Simpson. Connecticut: Strong, 2001.

Marriner, Brian. *On Death's Bloody Trail: Murder and the Art of Forensic Science.* New York: St. Martin's Press, 1993.

Morton, James. *Catching the Killers: The Definitive History of Criminal Detection.* London: Ebury, 2001.

Essays, Editorials, Articles

Becker, Mari. "NYPD's Forensics Lab Gets Seal of Approval." *Daily News,* June 9, 2000, p. 1.

"Chemist Accused of Shoddy Work Is Fired." Associated Press, *New York Times,* September 26, 2001, sec. A, p. 16.

"Cleared of Murder, Four Men Sue Police and Prosecutors." Associated Press, January 21, 2002.

Clines, Francis X. "Work by Expert Witness Is Now on Trial." *New York Times,* September 5, 2001, sec. A, p. 12.

Fisk, Margaret Cronin. "Lawyer Frees Chicago Trio After Retesting of Lab Sample." *National Law Journal* 24, no. 16 (December 17, 2001): p. A6.

Forero, Juan. "Review of Police Lab Faults Chemists, Hindering Accreditation." *New York Times,* November 30, 1999, sec. B, p. 6.

Hodel, Martha Bryson. "Crime Lab Chemist on Trial for Fraud." Associated Press, September 3, 2001.

Hodel, Martha Bryson. "West Virginia Jury Deadlocks in Lab Case." Associated Press, September 18, 2001.

Kornblut, Anne E. "Megan Mom Relives Horror." *Daily News,* May 6, 1997, p. 7.

"Oklahoma Governor Says He Will Not Block an Execution." Associated Press, *New York Times,* May 1, 2001, sec. A, p. 19.

"Oklahoma Will Study Capital Cases." *New York Times,* July 18, 2001, sec. A, p. 14.

Osborne, Lawrence. "Crime Scene Forensics: Dean Men Talking." *New York Times,* December 3, 2000, sec. 6, p. 105.

Romano, Lois. "Police Chemist's Missteps Cause Oklahoma Scandal." *The Washington Post,* November 26, 2001.

Scarborough, Steve. "New AFIS Looks at Partial Prints." *Law Enforcement Technology* (May 2001): p. 80.

Scheck, Barry, and Peter Neufeld. "Junk Science, Junk Evidence." *New York Times,* May 11, 2001, sec. A, p. 35.

Stern, Seth. "A Finger at the Crime Scene." *The Christian Science Monitor,* June 28, 2001, p. 20.

Strandberg, Keith. "Fingerprinting Ballistic Evidence." *Law Enforcement Technology* (May 2000): p. 58.

Strandberg, Keith. "The Facts Don't Lie." *Law Enforcement Technology* (June 2001): p. 20.

Chapter 5: DNA PROFILING

Books, Criminal Justice Reports, and Documents
Convicted by Juries, Exonerated by Science: Case Studies of the Use of DNA Evidence to Establish Innocence After Trial. U.S. Department of Justice Research Report, June 1996.

DNA Profiling and DNA Fingerprinting, Jörg T. Epplen, ed. Basel/Boston: Thomas Lubjuhn, Birkhauser Verlag, c. 1999.

DNA Crime Labs: The Paul Coverdell National Forensic Sciences Improvement Act: Hearing Before the Committee on the Judiciary. United States Senate, 107th Congress, first session, May 15, 2001. Washington: U.S. G.P.O.: For sale by the Supt. of Docs., U.S. G.P.O., [Congressional Sales Office], 2002.

Genetic Secrets: Protecting Privacy and Confidentiality in the

Genetic Era. Mark A. Rothstein, ed. New Haven: Yale University Press, c. 1997.

National Commission on the Future of DNA Evidence. National Center for Rural Law Enforcement, February 28, 1999.

Innis, Michael A., David H. Gelfand, John J. Sninsky. *PCR Applications: Protocols for Functional Genomics.* San Diego: Academic Press, c. 1999.

Post-Conviction DNA Testing: When Is Justice Served? Hearing before the Committee on the Judiciary, United States Senate, 106th Congress, second session, June 13, 2000. Washington: U.S. G.P.O.

Post-Conviction DNA Testing: Recommendations for Handling Requests. Report by the National Commission on the Future of DNA Evidence, U.S. Department of Justice, September 1999.

Rudin, Norah, and Keith Inman. *An introduction to Forensic DNA Analysis.* Boca Raton: CRC Press, c. 2002.

Essays, Editorials, Articles

Amar, Akhil Reed. "A Search for Justice Is in Our Genes." *New York Times,* May 7, 2002, sec. A, p. 31.

Briggs, Jonathon. "DNA Data Shift Is Due." *The Baltimore Sun,* November 18, 2000, p. 1B.

Chivers, C. J. "In First Case from DNA Bank, Police Link Inmate to Rape." *New York Times,* Thursday, January 13, 2000, sec. B, p. 2.

Chivers, C. J. "Pataki Proposes DNA Panel to Review Overturned Convictions." *New York Times,* May 8, 2000, sec. B, p. 4.

Clines, Francis X. "Virginia May Collect DNA in Every Arrest for a Felony." *New York Times,* February 17, 2002, sec. 1, p. 22.

"The Failure of the Death Penalty in Illinois: A Five Part Series." *Chicago Tribune*, (November 1999).

Fettmann, Eric. "Isn't Crime the Worst Privacy Invasion of All?" *New York Post*, December 20, 1998, p. 81.

Garrett, Laurie. "DNA Only Hope for Closure." *Newsday*, September 20, 2001, p. A68.

Goldberg, Carey. "DNA Databanks Giving Police a Powerful Weapon, and Critics." *New York Times*, February 19, 1998, sec. A, p. 1.

Mahoney, Joe. "Solitary for Inmates Who Nix DNA Samples." *Daily News*, September 13, 2000, p. 3.

Rayman, Graham. "The Race to Identify; Concern That the DNA of September 11 Victims Will Decompose." *Newsday*, November 19, 2001, p. A07.

O'Shaughnessy, Patrice. "Pieces of Bone Hold: Labs Unravel DNA to Identify Remains." *Daily News*, March 25, 2002, p. 20.

Pollack, Andrew. "Identifying the Dead 2,000 Miles Away." *New York Times*, September 30, 2001, p. 6.

Pyle, Richard. "DNA Technology Explainer." Associated Press, December 15, 1998.

Safir, Howard, and Peter Reinharz. "DNA Testing: The Next Big Crime-Busting Breakthrough." *City Journal* (Winter 2002): pp. 49–57.

Weiss, Murray. "NYPD Taking DNA Lesson from Scotland Yard." *New York Post*, October 15, 2000, p. 11.

Weedn, Victor Walter, and John W. Hicks. "The Unrealized Potential of DNA Testing." National Institutes of Justice, June 1998.

Chapter 6: MURDER

Books, Criminal Justice Reports, and Documents

Gourevitch, Philip. *A Cold Case*. New York: Farrar, Straus and Giroux, 2001.

Havill, Adrian. *The Mother, the Son, and the Socialite: The True Story of a Mother-Son Crime Spree*. New York: St. Martin's Press, 2001.

Karmen, Andrew. *New York City Murder Mystery: The True Story Behind the Crime Crash of the 1990s*. New York: New York University Press, 2001.

Kelleher, Michael D., and David Van Nuys. *"This Is the Zodiac speaking": Into the Mind of a Serial Killer*. Westport: Praeger, 2002.

King, Jeanne. *Dead End: The Crime Story of the Decade. Murder, Incest, and High-Tech Thievery*. New York: M. Evans and Company, 2002.

Westveer, Arthur E. *Managing Death Investigations*. U.S. Dept. of Justice, Federal Bureau of Investigation, 1997.

Essays, Editorials, Articles

"A Violent Loner with a Love for Weapons," *New York Post*, June 19, 1996, p. 2.

Barnes, Julian. "Man Says Murder Suspects Discussed Dumping Body." *New York Times*, February 29, 2000, sec. B, p. 3.

Barnes, Julian. "Witness Says Socialite Worried About Tenant." *New York Times*, February 18, 2000, sec. B, p. 4.

Barnes, Julian. "Informer in Murder Case Testifies He Sold Guns to Mother and Son." *New York Times*, March 29, 2000, sec. B, p. 7.

Barnes, Julian. "Untangling a Complex Chain of Schemes." *New York Times*, February 15, 2000, sec. B, p. 3.

Barnes, Julian. "Tricky Enough to Beat a Used-Car Dealer,

the Prosecutor Says." *New York Times,* February 28, 2000, sec. B, p. 6.

Barnes, Julian. "Defense Sees Rush to Judge in Arrest of Mother and Son." *New York Times,* February 16, 2000, sec. B, p. 3.

Barstow, David, and William K. Kashbaum. "In Queens, Shock at the Methodical Massacre of Five." *New York Times,* May 26, 2000, sec. A, p. 1.

Cooper, Michael. "Homicides Decline Below 1964 Level in New York City." *New York Times,* December 24, 1998, sec. A, p. 1.

Cooper, Michael. "Some Evidence of Forgery, but No Sign of Missing Widow." *New York Times,* July 17, 1998, sec. B, p. 4.

"Cops Hear Zodiac Horror-Scope." *New York Post,* June 20, 1996, pp. 2–3.

De La Cruz, Donna. "Man Charged in Wendy's Massacre Admits Killing Three, Wounding Two." Associated Press, January 22, 2001.

Donohoe, Pete. "Death Penalty Sought for Massacre Suspect." *Daily News,* June 11, 1997, p. 22.

Fenner, Austin. "Cop Who Foiled Zodiac Killer Is Named a Star for Heroism." *Daily News,* July 15, 1998, p. 34.

Fenner, Austin. "Chilling Tale of Wendy's Slaying." *Daily News,* July 28, 2000, p. 8.

Finkelstein, Katherine E. "Mother and Son Are Given Life Sentence." *New York Times,* June 28, 2000, sec. B, p. 6.

Finkelstein, Katherine E. "Investigators Want to Check Kimeses' Story." *New York Times,* November 17, 2000, sec. B, p. 3.

Freifeld, Karen. "Detective Testifies at Zodiac Hearing." *Newsday,* December 10, 1996, p. A25.

Freifeld, Karen. "Jurors Hear of Zodiac's Bloody Trail." *Newsday,* May 15, 1998, p. A06.

Freifeld, Karen. "Zodiac Case Goes to Jury." *Newsday,* June 24, 1998, p. A31.

Freifeld, Karen. "No Doubt About It. Jury Quickly Finds Seda Guilty of Being the Zodiac Killer." *Newsday,* June 25, 1998.

Garett, Ronnie. "Time Travelers with a Purpose." *Law Enforcement Technology* (June 2001): p. 46.

Gearty, Robert, Tom Rafferty, and Pete Donohue. "Hot Collar in 'Cold' Slays." *Daily News,* October 16, 1996, p. 8.

Gearty, Robert, Blanca Quintanilla, and Corky Siemaszko. "Cops I.D. Queens Massacre Suspect." *Daily News,* July 12, 1996, p. 24.

Geller, Andy. "Reign of Terror Took Tragic Toll." *New York Post,* June 19, 1996, p. 5.

Gest, Emily, and Mike Claffey. "Victim's Battle for Life: Bound and Shot, He Saves Pal." *Daily News,* May 26, 2000, p. 5.

Gonnerman, Jennifer. "Life Without Parole." *New York Times Magazine,* May 19, 2002.

Kashbaum, William K. "Shooter Says He Was the Zodiac." *Daily News,* June 20, 1996.

Kennedy, Helen, and Wendell Jamieson. "Twisted History of a Killer." *Daily News,* June 20, 1996.

Kim, Rose. "Indictment in Zodiac Killings." *Newsday,* June 27, 1996, p. A29.

Kocienewski, David. "Mother and Son Face Questioning in Socialite's Disappearance." *New York Times,* July 8, 1998, sec. A, p. 1.

Kocieniewski, David. "Police Say Socialite Signed Papers Before She Vanished." *New York Times,* July 9, 1998, sec. B, p. 3.

Kocieniewski, David. "Police Hope Clues in Car Lead to Missing Woman." *New York Times,* July 15, 1998, sec. B, p. 3.

Lin, Wendy. "Is It the Return of the Zodiac?" *Newsday,* August 5, 1994.

Markowitz, Dan. "Albany Plan to End Parole Raises Dispute." *New York Times,* November 7, 1999, sec. 14WC, p. 21.

Marzulli, John. "Safir Orders In-Depth Study of Slays." *Daily News,* February 2, 2000, p. 12.

Marzulli, John. "Fugitive Is Returned. Queens Triple-Slay Suspect Found in Tennessee." *Daily News,* August 22, 1996, p. 33.

Marzulli, John. "Terrifying Tale of Death." *Daily News,* May 26, 2000, p. 2.

Massarella, Linda. "Devil's Den Was Helluva Scary Place." *New York Post,* June 20, 1996, p. 2.

McFadden, Robert D. "Tests Show a Suspect's Pistol Was Used to Kill Five at Wendy's." *New York Times,* May 28, 2000, sec. 1, p. 29.

McFadden, Robert D. "In Levin Killing Details Are Revealed and Denials Offered." *New York Times,* sec. B, p. 1.

McQuillan, Alice. "DNA Bust Gives Hope to Officials." *Daily News,* March 14, 2000, p. 26.

McQuillan, Alice, John Marzulli, and Corky Siemaszko. "Gunman Admits to Serial Shootings." *Daily News,* June 20, 1996.

Morrison, Dan. "Cops Find Zodiac End Bittersweet." *Newsday,* June 23, 1996, p. A0.

Murphy, William. "Zodiac's Penance." *Newsday,* July 23, 1998, p. A03.

O'Shaughnessy, Patrice. "Cop Sealed Zodiac's Fate." *Daily News,* July 12, 1998, p. 13.

Purdy, Matthew. "Manhunt Leads to Two Arrests in Levin Killing." *New York Times,* June 8, 1997, sec. 1, p. 1.

Ravo, Nick. "Case of Zodiac Gunman Sparked Panic in 1990." *New York Times,* June 19, 1996, sec. B, p. 3.

Rohde, David. "Two Now Face Murder Charge in Widow's Disappearance." *New York Times,* December 17, 1998, sec. B, p. 1.

Rohde, David, and Julian Barnes. "Without a Body, Murder Case of Widow Relies on Circumstantial Evidence." *New York Times,* May 16, 2000, sec. B, p. 1.

Rohde, David. "Mother and Son Found Guilty of Killing a Socialite Who Vanished in '98." *New York Times,* May 19, 2000, sec. A, p. 1.

Rohde, David. "Police Are Allowed to Test Evidence in Widow's Disappearance." *New York Times,* July 28, 1998, sec. B, p. 12.

"Siege Shooter's Prints Match Chilling Notes." *New York Post,* June 19, 1996, p. 3.

Rohde, David. "When a Conviction Brings No Closure." *New York Times,* November 14, 1998, sec. B, p. 3.

Rohde, David. "Jury Deliberates Levin Murder Case and Asks Questions." *New York Times,* November 10, 1998, sec. B, p. 5.

Rohde, David. "Haunting Choice for Jurors in Levin Case." *New York Times,* sec. B, p. 3.

Rohde, David. "Suspect Says Second Man Killed Teacher." *New York Times,* October 20, 1998, sec. B, p. 1.

Rohde, David. "Investigator Says Bullet Was in a Murder Suspect's Pack." *New York Times,* October 30, 1998, sec. B, p. 4.

Rohde, David. "Jurors Convict Youth in Killing of His Teacher." *New York Times,* November 11, 1998, sec. A, p. 1.

Santangelo, Michael. "Zodiac Link: Fingerprints, Magic Sign Net 1990 Terror Spree Suspect." *Newsday,* June 19, 1996, p. A03.

Spencer, Gary. "Charges Against the Zodiac Killer Upheld." *New York Law Journal* (May 12, 1999): p. 1.

Sullivan, John. "Ex-Student Denies Killing Levin and Tells of Gunmen." *New York Times,* July 8, 1997, sec. B, p. 3.

Sullivan, John. "Last Moments of Levin Are Described by Suspect." *New York Times,* June 27, 1997, sec. B, p. 3.

Toy, Vivian S. "Brooklyn Man Is Guilty in Three Zodiac Killings." *New York Times,* June 25, 1998, sec. B, p. 3.

Weiss, Murray. "Zodiac's Chilling Letter to *Post* Tells of Five New Victims." *New York Post,* August 5, 1994.

Chapter 7: SPECIAL VICTIMS

Books, Criminal Justice Reports, and Documents

Committee on the Judiciary Subcommittee on Crime. *Violent Offender DNA Identification Act of 1999, DNA Backlog Elimination Act, and Convicted Offender DNA Index System Support Act.* Hearing before the Subcommittee on Crime of the Committee on the Judiciary, House of Representatives, 106th Congress, second session, on H.R. 2810, H.R. 3087, and H.R. 3375, March 23, 2000.

Vachss, A. *Sex Crimes: Ten Years on the Front Lines Prosecuting Rapists and Confronting Their Collaborators.* New York: Holt, 1993.

Essays, Editorials, Articles

Baker, Al. "Suspect Gets Away from Police." *New York Times,* May 7, 2002, sec. B, p. 1.

Barnes, Julian. "East Side Rapist, Known Solely by DNA, Is Indicted." *New York Times,* March 16, 2000, sec. B, p. 1.

Balfour, Malcolm, and Angela C. Allen. "East Harlem Slay-Rape Suspect Nabbed." *New York Post,* February 20, 1999, p. 6.

Bollinger, Ann V., Mike Pearl, and Tracy Connor. "Jovanovic's Lawyer Vows He'll Appeal This Travesty of Justice." *New York Post,* April 16, 1998, p. 4.

Chivers, C. J. "As DNA Aids Rape Inquiries, Statutory Limits Block Cases." *New York Times,* February 9, 2000, sec. B, p. 1.

Cooper, Michael. "Suspect in a Murder and in the Rapes of Two Teenagers Vanishes with Girl, 15." *New York Times,* February 16, 1999, sec. B, p. 3.

Dunleavy, Steve. "Brainy Grad Bests Amoeba-Brained DA." *New York Post,* March 23, 2002, p. 20.

Gardiner, Sean. "Clue in the Genes: At Large Suspect Indicted in Rapes by DNA Sample." *Newsday,* March 16, 2000, p. A5.

Egbert, Bill. "Slay Suspect Dodges Cops," *Daily News,* February 16, 1999, p. 4.

Finkelstein, Katherine E. "Deal Proposed for Defendant in Net Sex Case." *New York Times,* November 22, 2002, sec. B, p. 1.

Gardiner, Sean. "Miami Manhunt Ends," *Newsday,* February 20, 1999, p. A3.

Gardiner, Sean. "A Top-Priority Manhunt." *Newsday,* August 7, 2002, p. A8.

Gregorian, Dareh. "Same Judge OK'd for Cybersex Trial." *New York Post,* October 20, 2000, p. 14.

Hamblett, Mark. "Shield Law. Consent Issues Arise in 'Cybersex' Appeal." *New York Law Journal* (February 3, 1999): p. 1.

Herbert, Bob. "Take the DNA Kits Off the Shelves." *New York Times,* April 15, 2002, sec. A, p. 23.

Italiano, Laura. "Cyberfiend Sex Conviction Tossed." *New York Post,* December 22, 1999, p. 5.

Italiano, Laura. "Ollie Beats Rap in Cybersex Case." *New York Post,* November 2, 2001, p. 21.

Italiano, Laura, and Ikimulisa Sockwell-Mason. "DA Takes a Strand on the East Side Rapist: John Doe Indicted Via DNA." *New York Post,* March 16, 2000, p. 2.

Kapstatter, Bob. "Suspected Rapist Pried His Way Out." *Daily News,* May 17, 2002, p. 32.

Kapstatter, Bob. "Intense Manhunt for Fugitive Serial Rapist." *Daily News,* May 31, 2002, p. 1.

Kocsis, Richard. "Psychological Profiling of Sexual Murders: An Empirical Model." *International Journal of Offender Therapy and Comparative Criminology,* vol. 46 issue 5 (October 2002): pp. 532–54.

Lefer, David. "East Side Rapist Alert." *Daily News,* March 7, 1999, p. 18.

Lowe, Herbert. "Law Would Aid DNA Testing." *Newsday,* September 10, 2001, p. A13.

McFee, Michele, and Bob Kapstatter. "Cops Craft Phone Trap for Fugitive." *Daily News,* November 6, 2002, p. 14.

McQuillan, Alice, William K. Kashbaum, and Wendell Jamieson. "Cybersex Suspect an Eerie Charmer." *Daily News,* December 11, 1996, p. 8.

Rohde, David. "Ex-Student to Get New Trial in Internet Sex-Assault Case." *New York Times,* December 22, 1999, sec. B, p. 3.

Rohde, David. "Call for Sex-Abuse Trial Is Said to Harm Rape Shield Law." *New York Times,* December 23, 1999, sec. B, p. 3.

Ross, Barbara. "Cyberwhiz. Other Pals Bailed Out." *Daily News,* December 10, 1996, p. 8.

Ross, Barbara, and Patrice O'Shaughnessy. "Cops Drag Net in Molest. Grad Student Suspected of Prior Attacks." *Daily News,* December 8, 1996, p. 5.

Ross, Barbara. "Trial Tests Cybersex Privacy." *Daily News,* August 17, 1997, p. 8.

Ross, Barbara, and Dave Goldiner. "Cybersex Testimony: Sure Torture Would End in Murder, Woman Says." *Daily News,* March 18, 1998, p. 7.

Ross, Barbara, and David Goldiner. "Cybersex Conviction. Grad Student Guilty of Kidnap, Sex Abuse." *Daily News,* April 16, 1998, p. 8.

Ross, Barbara, Alice McQuillan, and Dave Goldiner. "John Doe Is Indicted on DNA Evidence." *Daily News,* March 16, 2000.

Rutenberg, James. "Climate of Terror. Torture-Date Suspect Stalked Me Says His Ex." *Daily News,* December 12, 1996, p. 5.

Stout, David. "Biologist Is Charged in Sex Abuse of Student." *New York Times,* December 7, 1996, sec. 1, p. 28.

Sullivan, John. "Others Tell of On-Line Chats with Torture Suspect." *New York Times,* December 10, 1996, sec. B, p. 3.

Sullivan, John. "Attack That Began on Internet Is Described." *New York Times,* March 17, 1998, sec. B, p. 3.

Sullivan, John. "Woman in Internet Case Says Accused Beat Her." *New York Times,* March 18, 1998, sec. B, p. 5.

Sullivan, John. "An Ambiguous Email Trail in Torture Case." *New York Times,* March 23, 1998, sec. B, p. 5.

Swarns, Rachel L. "Arrest at Columbia Shows Risks in On-Line Dating." *New York Times,* December 8, 1996, sec. 1, p. 51.

Weir, Richard. "25G Bounty on Escapee." *Daily News,* May 24, 2002, p. 10.

Chapter 8: SURVEILLANCE

Books, Criminal Justice Reports, and Documents

Bouza, Anthony V. *Police Intelligence: The Operations of an Investigative Unit.* New York: AMS Press, 1976.

Uniting and Strengthening America by Providing Appropriate Tools Required to Intercept and Obstruct Terrorism (USA Patriot Act) Act of 2001. U.S. Congress, Washington, D.C., 2001.

Essays, Editorials, Articles

Carey, Jack. "ACLU Decries Super Bowl Surveillance." *USA Today,* February 2, 2001, p. 1C.

Cushman, John H. "Airlines Seek EZ Pass for Fast Security Check." *New York Times,* January 13, 2002, sec. 5, p. 3.

Dershowitz, Alan. "Why Fear National ID Cards?" *New York Times,* October 13, 2001, sec. A, p. 23.

Flynn, Kevin, and Jacob H. Fries. "Threats and Responses: Surveillance." *New York Times,* September 26, 2002, sec. A, p. 18.

Gay, Lance. "We're Increasingly Becoming Must-See TV." Scripps Howard, February 12, 2001.

Guerra, John L. "Carnivore: FBI's Packet Sniffer May Have Loose Fangs." *Billing World and OSS Today* (April 2002).

Halbfinger, David. "Protestors Assail Rising Use of Police Cameras." *New York Times,* February 2, 1998, sec. B, p. 3.

"Increased Post–Sept. 11 Enforcement of Immigration Laws." *New York Law Journal* (January 28, 2002).

Kirkpatrick, Michael D. "Solving Cold Cases with Digital Fingerprints." *Sheriff* (July–August 2001): pp. 14–17.

Kocieniewski, David. "Police to Press Property-Crime Fight and Install Cameras." *New York Times,* February 5, 1997, sec. B, p. 4.

Kopel, Dave. "Don't Press the Panic Button." *National Review* (September 21, 2001).

Landler, Mark. "Fine-Tuning for Privacy, Hong Kong Plans Digital ID." *New York Times,* February 18, 2002, sec. C, p. 1.

Lee, Denny. "Residents Say Drug Campaign Just Sweeps Dealers from View." *New York Times,* October 17, 1999, sec. 14, p. 6.

Lee, Felicia, R. "Keeping Watch in Washington Square." *New York Times,* Jan. 3, 1998, sec. B, p. 3.

Lee, Jennifer. "Welcome to the Database Lounge." *New York Times,* March 21, 2002, sec. G, p. 1.

Levitt, Leonard. "NYPD Seeks to Overturn Surveillance Rules." *Newsday,* September 26, 2002, p. 4.

Levitt, Leonard. "No Connection to Intelligence." *Newsday,* September 30, 2002, p. A12.

Marzulli, John. "Cops Are Offered Dog's-Eye View." *Daily News,* September 9, 1996, p. 7.

Mbugua, Martin. "Cops Want Spy Law Axed." *Daily News,* September 26, 2002, p. 36.

Parascandola, Rocco. "Tale of the Tapes: NYPD Must Go by the Book." *New York Post,* April 20, 2000, p. 4.

Perotta, Tom. "Police Request Broader Surveillance Rights." *New York Law Journal* 228 (September 26, 2002), p. 1.

Peterson, Molly M. "Video Surveillance Network Raises Questions on Civil Liberties." *National Journal's Technology Daily* (May 22, 2002).

"Plain View Evidence Not in Warrant Can Be Seized Even if Anticipated. *People vs. Sheldon Wasserman.*" *New York Law Journal* (November 24, 1997).

Plesser, Ronald L. "USA Patriot Act for Internet and Communications Companies." *The Computer Lawyer* 19, no. 3 (March 2002): p. 1.

Strandberg, Keith W. "Speeding Up Identifications." *Law Enforcement Technology* (May 2001): pp. 42–47.

Streitfeld, David, and Charles Piller. "Big Brother Finds an Ally in Once-Wary High Tech." *Los Angeles Times,* January 19, 2002, part A, p. 1.

Sweeney, James F. "Proliferating Cameras Spark Privacy Debate." *The Plain Dealer,* January 11, 2002.

"To Better Fight Terror." *New York Post,* September 27, 2002, p. 30.

Tyrangiel, Josh. "Terror in the State House." *Time* (January 21, 2002): p. 51.

"Uncuff the NYPD." *Daily News,* September 29, 2002, p. 48.

Chapter 9: HOMELAND SECURITY

Books, Criminal Justice Reports, and Documents

Miller, John, and Michael Stone. *The Cell: Inside the 9/11 Plot, and Why the FBI and the CIA Failed to Stop It.* New York: Hyperion, 2002.

"Bill 16:15: Federal-Local Information Sharing Partnership Act of 2001." Introduced by Congressman Charles Schumer to the 107th Congress, Washington, D.C., on November 1, 2001.

Local Law Enforcement's Role in Preventing and Responding to Terrorism, Report prepared by the Police Executive Research Forum, Washington, D.C., October 2001.

New York City Police Department. *Terrorism Awareness for Citizens: How You Can Help the NYPD Fight Terrorism,* 2002.

Essays, Editorials, Articles

Barry, Dan. "Bombs in Brooklyn." *New York Times,* August 1, 1997, sec. A, p. 1.

Barstow, David. "A Community Stunned, and On Edge." *New York Times,* December 31, 1999, sec. A, p. 17.

Brinkley, Joel. "Mayors Seek Payback of Spending on Security." *New York Times,* January 24, 2002.

Brune, Tom, Graham Rayman, and Dan Morrison. "A Link to Terror: Cops Arrest Brooklyn Man." *Newsday,* December 31, 1999, p. A03.

Campanile, Carl, and Rocco Parascandola. "N.Y. Landmarks on Terror Alert." *New York Post,* August 22, 1998, p. 8.

Capeci, Jerry, William K. Kashbaum, and Jere Hester. "Subway Was Bomb's Target." *Daily News,* August 1, 1997, p. 3.

Fried, Joseph P. "Suspects in Bomb Plot Had 'Warped' Politics, Prosecutor Says." *New York Times,* July 22, 1998, sec. B, p. 7.

Fried, Joseph P. "Palestinian Gets Life Sentence for Planning to Bomb Subway." *New York Times,* March 2, 1999, sec. B, p. 3.

Gamboa, Suzanne. "Feds Want to Fingerprint Foreigners." Associated Press, June 5, 2002.

Hersch, Seymour. "Missed Messages: Why the Government Didn't Know What It Knew." *New Yorker* (June 3, 2002).

Herszenhorn, David M. "Bombs in Brooklyn: The Security." *New York Times,* August 2, 1997, sec. 1, p. 24.

Kapstatter, Bob. "He Bagged Bomb Suspects." *Daily News,* August 10, 1997, p. 1.

Kifner, John. "Police Security for Millennial Celebration." *New York Times,* December 5, 1999, sec. 1, p. 55.

Kifner, John. "Calls Said to Link Woman to Man with Explosives." *New York Times,* January 13, 2000, sec. B, p. 1.

Kifner, John, and William K. Kashbaum. "Brooklyn Man Is Charged with Aiding in Bomb Plot." *New York Times,* December 31, 1999, sec. A, p. 1.

Lefkowitz, Melanie. "Target: City Landmarks." *Newsday,* May 22, 2002, p. A03.

MacDonald, Heather. "Use CompStat Against Terror." *Daily News,* November 4, 2001, p. 43.

Lehrer, Eli. "Teaching the FBI: From Terror to Kiddie Porn, G-Men Can Learn a Lot from Local Cops." *New York Post,* July 27, 2002, p. 15.

McFee, Michele. "Cops Shoot Two in Bomb Raid." *Daily News,* August 1, 1997, p. 3.

Millner, Judith. "Suspect in New Year's Terror Plot Is Arrested in Algeria." *New York Times,* December 7, 2000, sec. A, p. 3.

Morrison, Dan. "Subways Were a Target." *Newsday,* August 1, 1997, p. A05.

"NYPD Plans for Bio and Suicide Attacks." *New York Post,* October 10, 2001, p. 23.

O'Shaughnessy, Patrice. "NYPD's Prepping for War." *Daily News,* March 3, 2002, p. 27.

O'Shaughnessy, Patrice. "Learning Methods of Detection, Strategy." *Daily News,* May 19, 2002, p. 5.

O'Shaughnessy, Patrice. "NYPD Takes Terror Fight Overseas." *Daily News,* July 14, 2002.

Port, Bob. "Security Pros Say Deadly Bombings Are Likely in the City." *Daily News,* May 19, 2002, p. 4.

Pyes, Craig. "Canada Adds Details on Algerians Suspected Bomb Plot." *New York Times,* January 21, 2000, sec. A, p. 3.

Revkin, Andrew C., and Barnaby J. Feder. "Counting to

2000, New York Asks, 'What if?' " *New York Times,* November 27, 1999, sec. A, p. 1.

Ratish, Robert. "Hero Cops Last Order: Be Careful." *Newsday,* August 3, 1997, p. A21.

Ratish, Robert. "Kudos for Cops: Quick Action Cited in Averting Bomb Plot." *Newsday,* August 6, 1997, p. A07.

Risen, James. "The Year 2000: Keeping Watch." *New York Times,* January 2, 2000, sec. 1, p. 12.

Smith, Greg B. "Sheik Gets Life in Jail." *Daily News,* January 18, 1996, p. 7.

Smith, Greg B. "Eleven Years in Jail for Blast-Plot Terrorist." *Daily News,* October 16, 1999, p. 5.

Smith, Greg B. "Terrorist Cites Jailhouse Order in Bomb Plot." *Daily News,* July 4, 2001, p. 6.

Sullivan, John. "Algerian Arraigned in Explosives Smuggling Case." *New York Times,* August 15, 2000, sec. B, p. 3.

Weiser, Benjamin. "U.S. in Pursuit of Bomb Plot, Indicts Man Held in Canada." *New York Times,* January 19, 2000, sec. A, p. 1.

Weiser, Benjamin. "Defense Says Arrest Was Timed to Deny Terror Suspect's Rights." *New York Times,* February 1, 2000, sec. B, p. 3.

Weiser, Benjamin. "Man Held in Terrorists Plot Agreed to Talk, Agents Say." *New York Times,* September 19, 2000, sec. B, p. 6.

Weiser, Benjamin. "Terror Suspect Had Been an Informer." *New York Times,* September 21, 2000, sec. B, p. 3.

Weiser, Benjamin. "NYPD Blue Has Soft Side." *New York Times,* September 24, 2000, sec. 1, p. 46.

Weiser, Benjamin. "Brooklyn Man Charged in Terror Plot Is Held Without Bond." *New York Times,* January 1, 2000, sec. B, p. 1.

Chapter 10: GETTING GUNS OFF THE STREETS

Books, Criminal Justice Reports, and Documents

Citizens Crime Commission, *Reducing Gun Crime*, p. 44.

Di Maio, Dr. Vincent. *Gunshot Wounds: Practical Aspects of Firearms, Ballistics, and Forensic Techniques.* New York: Elsevier, 1985.

Lott, John R. *More Guns, Less Crime.* Chicago: The University of Chicago Press, 2000.

New York City Police Department. *Strategy 1: Getting Guns off the Streets of New York,* 1994.

Essays, Editorials, Articles

Aukamp, William M. "No 'Individual' Gun Right." *New York Law Journal* (June 14, 1999): p. A22.

Blair, Jayson, and Sarah Weissman. "The Biography of a Gun." *New York Times,* April 9, 2000, sec. 4, p. 18.

Butterfield, Fox. "U.S. to Develop a System for 'Fingerprinting' Guns." *New York Times,* December 20, 1999, sec. A, p. 18.

Cooper, Michael. "Steep Drop in Random Killings Signals Shift in New York Crime." *New York Times,* December 29, 1996, sec. 1, p. 25.

Cooper, Michael. "New York Police Will Start Using Deadlier Bullets." *New York Times,* July 9, 1998, sec. A, p. 1.

"Deadly Commerce." *New York Times,* April 30, 1997, sec. A, p. 20.

Donash, Shelly Feuer. "Database Program Targets Illegal Gun Traffic." *New York Times,* May 13, 2001, sec. 14LI, p. 1.

Firestone, David. "Mayor Wants Time to Assess New Bullets." *New York Times,* March 5, 1997, sec. B, p. 1.

Goldschlag, William. "Part of Brady Law Foils No Local Gun-Buyer Screening." *Daily News,* June 28, 1997, p. 5.

Graham, Jessie. "Cops Bust Bronx Gun-Run Gang." *New York Post,* August 30, 2001, p. 22.

Hurtado, Patricia. "DA: Need Law to Cap Gun Buys." *Newsday,* April 30, 1997, p. A29.

Krauss, Clifford. "Hollow Point Ammunition Saves Lives." *New York Times,* March 6, 1997, sec. B, p. 3.

Chapter 11: ORGANIZED CRIME

Books, Criminal Justice Reports, and Documents

Friedman, John. *Red Mafiya.* New York: Little, Brown, 2000.

Klein, Malcolm. *The American Street Gang.* New York: Oxford University Press, 1995.

New York City Police Department. *Anti-Street Gang Strategy,* 1997.

New York City Police Department. *Strategy 2: Curbing Youth Violence in the Schools and on the Street,* 1994.

New York City Police Department. *Strategy 6: Reducing Auto-Related Crimes in New York,* 1995.

Vona, Daniel. "Organized Crime in New York City." In *Crime and Justice in New York City,* edited by Andrew Karmen. New York: McGraw Hill, 1998.

Essays, Editorials, Articles

Celona, Larry. "NYPD Gathers Its Troops for All-Out War on Gangs." *New York Post,* May 29, 1999, p. 4.

Claffey, Mike, Nancie L. Katz, and Leo Standora. "Agnello OKs Plea Deal: Mobster Admits to Racketeering." *Daily News,* August 17, 2001, p. 17.

Claffey, Mike. "Arrest of Informant Mars Case—Agnello." *Daily News,* December 20, 2000, p. 8.

Claffey, Mike. "Agnello: FBI Lied, So Ax Bail." *Daily News,* November 10, 2000, p. 50.

Claffey, Mike. "Gotti Kin Agnello Jailed on RICO Rap." *Daily News,* March 7, 2000, p. 15.

Colangelo, Lisa L. "Bill Would Let NYPD Halt Gang Gatherings." *Daily News,* November 20, 2000, p. 8.

Conner, Tracy. "Gott'-Cha! Cops Nab Don's Kin." *New York Post,* January 26, 2000, p. 4.

Cooper, Michael. "Sixty-one Arrested in Drug Raids at South Bronx Tenements." *New York Times* December 18, 1996, sec. B, p. 1.

Crowley, Kieran. "Judge 'Parts' from Agnello Bail Case." *New York Post,* January 28, 2000, p. 7.

Fenner, Austin, and Michele McFee. "Agnello Defense: Pills and Ills." *Daily News,* October 6, 2000, p. 5.

Fenner, Austin, and Bill Hutchinson. "Badda-Sting! Gotti In-Law Taped, Busted." *Daily News,* January 26, 2000, p. 7.

Francescani, Christopher. "Carmine Gets Nine: Plea Makes Prison a Family Affair." *New York Post,* August 17, 2001, p. 17.

Holloway, Lynette. "The Fear Is Real Enough: The Gangs Are Another Story." *New York Times,* February 15, 1998, sec. A, p. 4.

Hurtado, Patricia. "Bail Denied for Agnello." *Newsday,* March 18, 2000, p. A08.

Hurtado, Patricia. "Two Indicted in Boxer's '95 Killing." *Newsday,* March 29, 2000, p. A07.

Kocieniewski, David. "Youth Gangs from West Coast Become Entrenched in New York." *New York Times,* August 28, 1997, sec. B, p. 1.

Kriegel, Mark. "Searching for the Champ: Chasing Shadows in the World of Russian Boxer." *Daily News,* March 28, 1999, p. 82.

Levitt, Leonard. "Twenty-two Arrested in Auto-Theft Sting in Queens." *Newsday,* May 17, 2000, p. A25.

MacFarquhar. "Two Charge in Killing of Russian Boxer." *New York Times,* March 29, 2000, sec. B, p. 4.

Marzulli, John. "Cops Act to Stem the Tide: Task Force Formed." *Daily News,* January 21, 1997, p. 14.

Marzulli, John. "Cops Gang Up on Blood in Sweep." *Daily News,* August 28, 1997, p. 5.

McFadden, Robert D. "Ninety-four Latin Kings Are Arrested Citywide." *New York Times.* May 15, 1998, sec. B, p. 4.

Morrison, Dan. "How'd They Know? Auto-Shop Targets Avoid Law Enforcement Sweep." *Newsday,* March 21, 1997, p. A03.

Morrison, Dan. "Feds Prosecute Gotti's Kin." *Newsday,* June 25, 2000, p. A19.

Morrison, Dan, and Patricia Hurtado. "Eighty Kings Charged." *Newsday,* May 15, 1998.

Mustain, Gene, and Jerry Capeci. "Slay Suspect Has Mob Big in His Corner." *Daily News,* April 21, 1997, p. 7.

Mustain, Gene, and Jerry Capeci. "Mob Russian in Time for Crime Time." *Daily News,* April 20, 1997, p. 6.

O'Connell, Paul, and Frank Straud. "Why the Jails Didn't Explode." *City Journal* 9, no. 2, (Spring 1999): pp. 28–37.

Onishi, Norimitsu. "Mayor Moves to Stanch Gang Violence." *New York Times,* October 9, 1997, sec. B, p. 1.

O'Shaughnessy, Patrice. "New Assault on City's Gangs: NYPD Beefs Up Units to Fight Growing Menace." *Daily News,* April 8, 2001, p. 4.

Rayman, Graham. "City's Faded Blue." *Newsday,* October 12, 1997, p. A07.

Reinharz, Peter. "The Crime War's Next Battles." *City Journal* 8, no. 1 (Winter 1998): pp. 48–55.

Roane, Kit R. "Twenty-Four Members of Crips Gang Are

Arrested in Sweep by Police." *New York Times,* October 30, 1997, sec. B, p. 3.

Roane, Kit R. "New York Gangs Mimic California Original." *New York Times,* September 14, 1997, sec. 1, p. 37.

Shifrel, Scott, and Alice McQuillan. "Cops Padlock Brooklyn HQ of 'Kings' gang." *Daily News,* September 11, 2000, p. 10.

Stone, Michael. "Killer Cowboys." *New York,* December 1993, pp. 59–64.

Chapter 12: DRUG ENFORCEMENT

Books, Criminal Justice Reports, and Documents

National Institute on Drug Abuse. *Epidemiologic Trends in Drug Abuse Advance Report,* December 2001.

New York City Police Department. *Proposal for Enhancement of NY/NJ HIDTA,* April 1996.

Office of National Drug Control Police. *New York, New York: Profile of Drug Indicators,* May 2002.

New York City Police Department. *Unified Federal/New York City Drug Strategy Proposal,* May 1996.

New York City Police Department. *Strategy 3: Driving Drug Dealers Out of New York,* 1994.

U.S. Department of Justice. *Speaking Out Against Drug Legalization,* October 1995.

U.S. Department of Justice. *ADAM 2000 Findings on Drug Use and Drug Markets: Adult Male Arrestees,* December 2001.

Essays, Editorials, Articles

Blair, Jayson. "Striking Drugs Bosses, Not Street Dealers, Pays Off, the Police Say." *New York Times,* June 17, 1999, sec. B, p. 16.

Blair, Jayson. "New Tactic Goes Citywide After It Ends Drug Bazaars." *New York Times,* October 3, 1999, sec. 1, p. 47.

Chivers, C. J. "Approval and Wariness in Poll on Police." *New York Times,* September 15, 2000, sec. B, p. 9.

Cooper, Michael. "Complaints Against Police Decline by 21 Percent Through May." *New York Times.* June 20, 1997, sec. B, p. 3.

Dewan, Shaila K. "Hopes Fading for Revision of Rockefeller Drug Laws." *New York Times,* August 22, 2002.

Donohue, Pete. "Driving Drugs off the Road: Cops Nail Dealers on Roadway Citations." *Daily News,* February 1, 1998, p. 6.

Finder, Alan. "At the Heart of Report on Police, Some Modest Proposals." *New York Times,* March 28, 1998, sec. B, p. 2.

Flynn, Kevin. "Arrests Soar In Crackdown on Marijuana." *New York Times,* November 17, 1998.

Flynn, Kevin. "Anti-Drug Units Will Lose Part of Their Funds." *New York Times,* April 8, 2000, sec. B, p. 1.

Flynn, Kevin. "Legal Claims Filed Against Officers Decline Sharply." *New York Times,* July 21, 2000, sec. A, p. 1.

Gardiner, Sean. "Drug Gangs Busted: Sold to Big Spenders." *Newsday,* October 10, 1998, p. A08.

Kapstatter, Bob. "Drug Dealing Squeezed." *Daily News,* February 5, 1999, p. 1.

Kashbaum, William K. "Eyeing Crime Rate, Police to Work Overtime on Drug Arrests." *New York Times,* January 21, 2000, sec. B, p. 3.

Kashbaum, William K. "Police Suspend Extra Patrols for Ten Days." *New York Times,* October 12, 2000, sec. B, p. 1.

Krauss, Clifford. "Police Initiate Campaign for Better Community Ties." *New York Times,* June 27, 1996, sec. B, p. 3.

Marzulli, John. "Anti-Drug Initiative Back After Brief Hiatus." *Daily News,* October 12, 2000, p. 7.

Marzulli, John. "Murder Rate in City Suddenly Slows." *Daily News,* July 3, 2000, p. 8.

Rayman, Graham. "Drug Search Warrants Up." *Newsday,* June 17, 1999, p. A53.

Rohde, David. "102 Indicted in Crack Sales to White-Collar Workers." *New York Times,* October 10, 1998

Weiss, Murray. "Central Park Added Decoy Cops to Drug Blitz." *New York Post,* January 16, 1998, p. 20.

Chapter 13: MANAGING THE POLICE

Books, Criminal Justice Reports, and Documents

Commission to Combat Police Corruption. *Commission to Combat Police Corruption: Report of the Commission,* 1996.

Commission to Investigate Allegations of Police Corruption and the City's Anti-Corruption Procedures. The Knapp Commission Report on Police Corruption. New York: George Braziller, 1972.

Giuliani, Rudolph W. *Mayoral Task Force on Police Community Relations,* 1997.

Halper, Andrew, and Richard Ku. *New York City Police Department Street Crime Unit: An Exemplary Project.* Washington: U.S. Dept. of Justice, Law Enforcement Assistance Administration, National Institute of Law Enforcement and Criminal Justice, for sale by the Superintendent of Documents, U.S. Government Printing Office, 1975.

New York City Police Department. *An Investigation into the Police Department's Conduct of the Dowd Case,* November 1992.

New York City Police Department. *Strategy 7. Rooting Out Corruption, Building Organizational Integrity in the New York Police Department,* 1996.

New York City Police Department. *Strategy 10: Courtesy, Professionalism and Respect,* 1997.

New York City Police Department. *Police Practices and Civil Rights in New York City,* 1999.

New York City Police Department. *Internal Affairs Bureau, Annual Reports,* 1996–2000.

New York City Civilian Complaint Review Board Semi-Annual Status Reports, 1996–2000.

Walker, Samuel. *A Critical History of Police Reform: The Emergence of Professionalism.* Lexington, Mass: Lexington Books, 1977.

Essays, Editorials, Articles

"A Stronger Civilian Review Board." *New York Times,* August 13, 1999, sec. A, p. 20.

Arce, Rose Marie. "Surveillance and DNA Testing Are Among the Latest Police Weapons. But How Will We Balance Fighting Crime and Preserving Civil Rights?" *Newsday,* May 30, 1999, p. A17.

Barry, Dan. "The Scandal at Midtown South." *New York Times,* July 18, 1998, sec. A, p. 1.

Barstow, David. "The Louima Case: The Strategy." *New York Times,* June 9, 1999, sec. B, p. 9.

Barstow, David. "Police Officers Charged with Taking Bribes from Brothel." *New York Times,* April 28, 1999, sec. B, p. 3.

Breen, Virginia. "City Wary of Copy Cats Call for Stepped-Up Security." *Daily News,* April 22, 1999, p. 32.

Corry, John. "Prince of the City Explores a Cop's Anguish." *New York Times,* August 9, 1981, sec. 2, p. 1.

Crowley, Kieran. "Cop on Trial in Bias Beating." *New York Post,* January 23, 1999, p. 14.

Eisenberg, Carol, Mitchell Freedman, and Steve Wick. "A

New Theory. Police: Chronis May Not Have Wielded Club." June 2, 1996, p. A7.

Flynn, Kevin. "Rebound in City Murder Rate Puzzling New York Officials." *New York Times,* November 5, 1999, sec. A, p. 1.

Gearty, Robert. "Three More Fingered. New Suspects, New Version of Beating." *Daily News,* June 4, 1996, p. 5.

Gearty, Robert. "One Cop Eyed in L.I. Beating." *Daily News,* June 6, 1996, p. 7.

Gearty, Robert. "Cop Put at Attack Scene." *Daily News,* April 11, 1997, p. 4.

Goldiner, Dave. "Ex-Cop's Guilty in Bias Beat." *Daily News,* February 24, 1999, p. 19.

Hardt, Robert. "Slow Go for Civilian Complaint Panel." *New York Post,* April 23, 1999, p. 22.

James, George. "Second Police Inquiry Begins into Drug Dealing Charge." *New York Times,* June 16, 1992, sec. B, p. 27.

James, George. "New York Expands Scrutiny of Police." *New York Times,* June 24, 1992, sec. B, p. 1.

Kashbaum, William K., and John Marzulli. "Safir Takes on Pols to Defend Crime Unit." *Daily News,* April 20, 1999, p. 8.

Kashbaum, William K. "Victim's Beaten When He's Down." *Daily News,* May 30, 1996, p. 7.

Kashbaum, William, K. "Cops in Sex Scandal." *Daily News,* July 17, 1998, p. 3.

Kempley, Rita. "Soiled 'City,' Gritty 'Prince.' " *Washington Post,* October 2, 1981, p. 17.

Kocieniewski, David. "Perjury Dividend—A Special Report. New York Pays a High Price for Police Lies." *New York Times,* January 5, 1997, sec. 1, p. 1.

Kocieniewski, David. "The Scandal at Midtown South." *New York Times,* July 18, 1998, sec. B, p. 3.

Levitt, Leonard. "Louima Assault Distressing." *Newsday,* June 15, 1999, p. A31.

MacDonald, Heather. "How to Train Cops." *City Journal* (Autumn 2000): pp. 46–61.

"Monitoring New York's Police." *New York Times,* July 15, 1999, sec. A, p. 22.

Magnet, Myron. "In Prospect." *City Journal* 9, no. 2 (Spring 1999): p. 5.

McCalary, Mike. "The Wheels of Justice Turn Slowly But Surely." *Daily News,* June 6, 1996, p. 7.

McCalary, Mike. "Witness Feared Getting 'Popped.' " *Daily News,* May 31, 1996, p. 6.

Morrison, Dan. "Second Cop Cuffed: Charge Officer Pinned Louima During Assault." *Newsday,* August 16, 1997, p. A4.

Morrison, Dan. "A Peace Offering. Safir Plan Would Allow More Pay for a Few." *Newsday,* February 14, 1999, p. A6.

Morrison, Dan. "Precinct Houses to Replace Sergeants with Lieutenants." *Newsday,* October 1, 1997, p. A61.

"No Cop-Out for NYPD." *Daily News,* September 9, 1997, p. 38.

Onishi, Normitsu. "Be Polite or Else." *New York Times,* February 26, 1998.

Parascandola, Rocco, and Larry Celona. "Elite Unit Thrives on NYPD's Dirty Work." *New York Post,* February 6, 1999, p. 4.

Polner, Robert. "Mayor Raps Cope Report." *Newsday,* Mar. 27, 1998, p. A6.

Rayman, Graham. "Waves of Louima Case Rock Cops." *Newsday,* October 4, 1997, p. A16.

Rayman, Graham. "The NYPD After Louima." *Newsday,* June 13, 1999, p. A6.

Reel, Bill. "NYPD Must Stop Tolerating Drunk Cops." *Newsday,* December 13, 1998, p. B04.

Reel, Bill. "Booze Clashes with the Color Blue." *Newsday*, June 2, 1996, p. A6.

Roane, Kit. "Prostitution Still Thrives in the Shadows." *New York Times*, July 19, 1998, sec. 1, p. 25.

Salcedo, Michele. "Abuse Net Widens." *Newsday*, August 18, 1997, p. A3.

Smith, Kati Cornell. "Schwarz Slammed." *New York Post*, June. 26, p. 15.

"Two Accused of Gun Running: Firearms Traced to Georgia." *Newsday*, April 3, 1997, p. A27.

ABOUT THE AUTHOR

Howard Safir is a former New York City police commissioner (1996–2000), and during his four-year tenure the city experienced a 38 percent reduction of major crimes and a 44 percent decline in homicides. As commissioner of an organization with over forty thousand officers and fourteen thousand civilians, almost twice the size of the FBI, Mr. Safir held perhaps the most powerful law-enforcement job in the United States. As commissioner, he instituted a variety of programs, including Model Block; Courtesy, Professionalism, and Respect; and Drug Abuse Resistance Education (DARE), and the largest antidrug initiative of its kind. Safir was appointed commissioner after a career in law enforcement that started in 1965 in the New York office of the Federal Bureau of Narcotics, now the U.S. Drug Enforcement Administration (DEA). In 1977, he was named assistant director and during the 1980s was chief of the Witness Security Division and associate director of the United States Marshals Service. He was a member of the executive committee of the International Association of Chiefs of Police and served as a delegate to Interpol and the National Drug Policy Board. Mr. Safir uses the expertise he has culled from many fields of law enforcement and his national and international contacts in the FBI, the DEA, the CIA, the NYPD, the LAPD, Interpol, and local police forces, which provide him with invaluable resources in his investigation of contemporary police tactics. He is currently the chairman and CEO of SafirRosetti, a worldwide security consulting and investigative company.

INDEX